Global Urbanisation Experiences

Published in association with
Observer Research Foundation
New Delhi

Observer Research Foundation (ORF) is a public policy think-tank that aims to influence formulation of policies for building a strong and prosperous India. The ORF pursues these goals by providing informed and productive inputs, in-depth research and stimulating discussion. The Foundation is supported in its mission by a cross-section of India's leading public figures, academics and business leaders.

Supported by
Rosa Luxemburg Stiftung
Germany

The Rosa Luxemburg Stiftung (RLS) is one of the largest political education institutions in Germany today and sees itself as part of the intellectual current of democratic socialism. The foundation evolved from a small political group, "Social Analysis and Political Education Association", founded in 1990 in Berlin into a nationwide political education organisation, a discussion forum for critical thought and political alternatives, as well as a research facility for progressive social analysis.

Global Urbanisation Experiences

Editor

Rumi Aijaz

ACADEMIC FOUNDATION
NEW DELHI

www.academicfoundation.com

First published in 2013
by

ACADEMIC FOUNDATION
4772-73 / 23 Bharat Ram Road, (23 Ansari Road),
Darya Ganj, New Delhi - 110 002 (India).
Phones : 23245001 / 02 / 03 / 04.
Fax : +91-11-23245005.
E-mail : books@academicfoundation.com
www.academicfoundation.com

in association with the
Observer Research Foundation, New Delhi

Supported by:
Rosa Luxemburg Stiftung, Germany
(Rosa Luxemburg Foundation)
www.rosalux.de

Cataloging in Publication Data--DK
Courtesy: D.K. Agencies (P) Ltd. <docinfo@dkagencies.com>

Global urbanisation experiences / editor, Rumi Aijaz.
p. cm.
Includes bibliographical references (p.).
ISBN 9789332700130

1. Urbanization--Congresses. 2. Urbanization--India--Congresses. 3. Cities and towns--Growth--Congresses. 4. Cities and towns--India--Growth--Congresses. I. Aijaz, Rumi. II. Observer Research Foundation.

DDC 307.76 23

Typeset by Italics India, New Delhi.

Printed and bound by The Book Mint, New Delhi.
www.thebookmint.in

Contents

List of Tables and Figures

Tables

Figures

About the Conference Organisers

The Observer Research Foundation (ORF) is India's premier think tank engaged in developing and discussing policy alternatives on a wide range of issues of national and international significance. The fundamental objective of ORF is to aid and influence formulation of policies for building a strong and prosperous India. ORF pursues its goal of providing productive inputs to decision-makers in the government, civil society and the business leadership of India through in-depth research and stimulating discussions. ORF firmly believes that in the next 25 years, India will be one of the world's greatest economic powers and contribute to a significant transformation in the quality of life of humanity.

The Foundation was established in the early 90s during the troubled period of India's transition from a protected economy to a new engagement with the international economic order. At that time, a need was felt for an independent forum that would examine the critical problems facing the country and help develop coherent policy responses in a rapidly changing global environment. ORF was thus founded and subsequently supported by many of India's leading intellectuals, academics, public figures, social activists, business leaders and institutions of higher learning. Headquartered in New Delhi, ORF has chapters in Chennai, Kolkata and Mumbai. The key areas of research undertaken by ORF include: international relations, security, resources management, politics, governance, economy and development.

ORF views collaboration with think tanks and research organisations across the globe as a vital part of its mandate. For international partners, ORF represents an institution that is able to generate real time and quality analysis on a diverse range of public policy issues. ORF believes that collaborative exercises must be initiated and sustained as equal partnerships in conceptualisation, funding and management. Some important partners are Rosa Luxemburg Stiftung, Germany; ZEIT Stiftung Ebelin und Gerd Bucerius, Germany; Heritage Foundation, USA; Brookings Institution, USA; Fudan University, China. More information about ORF is available from: *www.orfonline.org.*

The Rosa Luxemburg Stiftung (RLS) is one of the largest political education institutions in Germany today and sees itself as part of the intellectual current of democratic socialism. The foundation evolved from a small political group, "Social Analysis and Political Education Association", founded in 1990 in Berlin into a nationwide political education organisation, a discussion forum for critical thought and political alternatives, as well as a research facility for progressive social analysis. In 1996, RLS was officially recognised as a nationwide affiliated trust of the Party of Democratic Socialism (PDS), presently known as "DIE LINKE" (The Left). As such it works closely with DIE LINKE affiliated state foundations and associations nationwide.

RLS aims to: organise political education and disseminate knowledge about social relations in a globalised, unjust and hostile world; provide a venue for critical analysis of current capitalism; act as a hub for programmatic discussions about a modern democratic socialism; act as a socialistic think-tank for political alternatives; be a forum in Germany and internationally that supports dialogue between left-socialistic powers, socialistic movements and organisations, left-minded intellectuals and non-governmental organisations; grant funding to young scholars via undergraduate and postgraduate scholarships; give impulses to self-defining socialistic political activities and support commitment to peace and international understanding for a socially just and solitary union.

Forming the Rosa Luxemburg Stiftung are: the general and sustaining members of the association and the executive board members; academic scholars and scientists in advisory boards and as authors of RLS publications, scholarship recipients, liaison professors and hundreds of volunteers; more than 100 employees who work in the Academy for political education, the Centre for International Dialogue and Cooperation, the Institute for Critical Social Analysis, etc. More information about RLS is available from: *http://www.rosalux.de/english/foundation.html.*

About the Editor/Contributors

Editor:

Rumi Aijaz is Senior Fellow at the ORF, New Delhi, India. His educational qualifications include a Master's in Geography (JNU, 1992), Regional Planning (SPA, 1994) and PhD in Urban Governance (SPA, 2004). He has been a post-doctoral visiting fellow at the Asia Research Centre, LSE (2006). He is also an associate member of the Institute of Town Planners, India. He has worked with the NGO *Sanket* (1994-95) and the National Institute of Urban Affairs (1996-1999 and 2004-05). He has also undertaken a study on gender for the Royal Netherlands Embassy (1996-97). During his education and professional career, he has been involved in numerous studies covering a range of social science topics such as socioeconomic and human development, ecology and physical environment, small scale industries, women empowerment, public health, transportation and urbanisation. His writings and views have found place in leading world journals, and acknowledged by prominent Indian and foreign institutions and news agencies.

Contributors:

Andrej Holm is Research Fellow, Department of Urban and Regional Sociology, Humboldt University, Berlin, Germany. He was awarded his doctorate in social sciences from Humboldt University, Berlin, having worked on the topic "Restructuring Space and Societal Power in an Urban Renewal Area." From 1998 to 2001, he worked as a research assistant on the German Research Foundation project "Urban Renewal in East Berlin." From 2001 to 2003, he received a doctoral scholarship from Rosa Luxemburg Stiftung. In the years 2005-06, as a research assistant he coordinated the URBACT research project "The European Urban Experience." In 2008-09, he worked as a research assistant at the Institute for Human Geography of the Johann-Wolfgang-Goethe-University Frankfurt am Main and coordinated the research programme "New Orders of the Urban in the Age of Neoliberalism." From 2009 to 2011, he took a temporary position in the Urban Research Department at Oldenburg University before returning to Berlin. Holm's research interests include: gentrification, international and comparative housing policy and European urban policy.

Paul Kennedy is Corporate Energy Manager, City Surveyor's Department, City of London Corporation, London, United Kingdom. He is a Chartered Building Services Engineer with 30 years experience in maintenance, design and energy management in the public sector. He graduated from the University of Hertfordshire in 1992 with a degree in Building Services Engineering. In addition, he has a Masters Degree in Interdisciplinary Design for Built Environment from University of Cambridge, where his research focus was on climate change adaptation. Paul sits on the committee for the London Borough's Energy Management Group where he was Chairman between 1997 and 1999. He is currently undertaking a Professional Doctorate through Anglia Ruskin University, looking into the preparedness of local authorities to meet the expectations of significant CO_2 emission reduction targets. He is a visiting lecturer at City University, London, where he also sits on the steering committee of the Masters in Energy, Environmental Technology and Economics course.

Hermann Knoflacher is Professor Emeritus, Institute for Transport Planning and Technology, Vienna University of Technology, Vienna, Austria. He has been a professor at the Vienna University of Technology since 1975. In 1985, he became Head of the Institute for Transport Planning. His research focuses on spatial planning, urban planning and transport planning. He is one of the key contributors to the sustainable transport movement. Prof Knoflacher is well-known for his criticism of excessive automobile usage and its effects on humans and the environment. Since 2004, he is the president of the Club of Vienna. He is also a member of the Club of Budapest and the global pedestrian representative of the United Nations.

Stefan Krätke is Chair of Economic and Social Geography, European University Viadrina, Frankfurt (Oder), Germany. He studied urban planning with main emphasis on urban and regional economics in Dortmund and Berlin. Since 1994, he holds the Chair of Economic and Social Geography, European University Viadrina, Frankfurt (Oder), Germany. In 2008, he was a Visiting Professor at the Institute for European Studies, University of British Columbia, Vancouver, Canada, and in 2009, Visiting Professor at the Fordham University New York (Urban Studies Programme) and at the New York University, among others. Prof Krätke's main fields of research include: European urban and regional development, comparative metropolitan studies, globalisation and the world city network, regional clustering of the knowledge economy, knowledge networks in the regional and international context, the role of creative industries in urban development and economic and social change in the capital city region of Berlin.

Eduardo Samper is Professor (Art Faculty), Universidad Nacional de Colombia, Bogotá, Colombia. He is Bachelor of Architecture, Universidad de los Andes, Bogotá, 1974, with a specialisation in Environmental and Urban Planning at Rutgers New Jersey State University (USA), with the Hubert Humphrey Fellowship Program, 1998. He is Professor at the School of Architecture and Urban Planning at the Universidad Nacional de Colombia since 1986, and an invited professor and lecturer at universities in Europe, United States and Latin America. His architectural and landscape work has been published in Colombia and internationally. For his architectural works, he has won several awards at the Colombian Architectural Biennale (2004, 2002, 1998, 1996); the Quito (Ecuador) Biennale (2004, 1998, 1986); and one award at the Architectural Marble Awards in Carrara, Italy (1988). He is author of the book "Modern Architecture in Colombia: Golden Age" 2000.

Jayshree Sengupta is a Senior Fellow at the ORF, New Delhi, India. After graduating from Delhi School of Economics, Delhi University with MA in Economics, she studied at the London School of Economics where she completed MSc and MPhil in Economics. She worked in the National Institute of Economic and Social Research, London. She was a lecturer in Miranda House and Indraprastha College (Delhi University, 1970-1977); programme coordinator at Indian Council for International Economic Relations (ICRIER), New Delhi (1981-1985); consultant for World Bank Washington D.C. (1985-1990) and in OECD (Paris) (1991). She has worked on commodities trade—tea, jute, leather and cotton. She was a Consulting Editor at the *Observer* of Business and Politics, New Delhi (1994-1998); Senior Editor in *Hindustan Times* (1998-2004). She coauthored a book with Prof S. Sideri of ISS (Hague): *The 1992 Single European Market and the third World* (1992). At the ORF, she has written a book: *A Nation in Transition: Understanding the Indian Economy* (2008). She has recently edited the book: *Global Meltdown, EU and India Perspectives* (2012). She has been a columnist in all major newspapers in India and has a column in the *Tribune*. She has presented papers in various international conferences on India, China, Nepal, Sri Lanka and the EU on subjects of urbanisation, rural development, health care in India and among BRICS, future global economic trends, global financial architecture and empowerment of women.

Ulrich Schachtschneider, Freelance Author, Energy Advisor and Trainer, Oldenburg, Germany, is an active member of the discussion group "Sustainability", of RLS. Working as an energy consultant, social scientist and author, his research focuses on environmental policies and how they are related to structures of modern capitalistic societies, the main ideas of changing the society to achieve ecological sustainability and how social and environmental policies can be integrated. His publications include "Sustainability as another Modernity? Scope for non-technical Strategies for Sustainable Development" and "Green New Deal, Sufficiency or Ecosocialism? Conceptions for Societal Ways out of the Ecological Crisis."

Raymond J. Struyk is former Senior Fellow, International Projects Department, National Opinion Research Center (NORC) at the University of Chicago, Bethesda, Maryland (MD), USA. He joined the International Projects department of NORC in September of 2007. He previously held the position of chief-of-party for the USAID-financed Egypt Financial Services Project. He has held several other positions, including senior fellow at the Urban Institute, and Deputy Assistant Secretary for Research and Evaluation at the US Department of Housing and Urban Development. Dr Struyk, who worked in NORC's Washington, DC office as a senior fellow, is best known for his work on social assistance, policy formulation, and housing sector reform. He has led major projects fostering independent think tanks in countries undergoing economic transition, and he has over 20 years of experience working in transition and developing countries, including a six-year residency in Russia, three years in Budapest, and a year in Cairo.

Yue Wu is Director, Tongji University Center for Urban Development Studies, Shanghai, People's Republic of China. He had been working for the Building Design Institute of the Ministry of Construction of China as the Chief of Project Design Team before he went to USA to pursue his doctoral study in urban planning. He was chosen as the Chief Planner for Shanghai New Area, through a world-wide recruiting act, after he received Doctor of Design degree from Harvard University in 2002. He was appointed as Director of Tongji University Center for Urban Development Studies the same year. In 2003, he was invited to teach at Harvard Design School as Lecturer in Urban Planning and Design. After finishing his duty in government, Dr Wu founded Design Future Studio in 2005. His practice and interest covers many fields such as urban planning, urban design, architecture, landscape architecture, interior design, sculpture and painting. He published numerous design projects and research papers and actively promoted new sustainable concept of urban development by providing lectures to local leaders of Chinese cities. He was awarded "Architectural Society of China (ASC) Young Architect Award" in 1995. He received "Howard T. Fisher Prize in Geographic Information Science" at Harvard in 2002, and "Ten-Best Youth of Shanghai Pudong Award " in 2005.

1 Editorial Introduction

Rumi Aijaz

People living in rural areas in most countries of the world tend to migrate to towns and cities to improve their living conditions and gain a better quality of life. This phenomenon has been a common occurrence since long, leading to unending increase in urban population.

Data compiled and analysed by the Population Division of the Department of Economic and Social Affairs of the UN Secretariat (UN, 2012) show that the world urban population was more than one billion in 1960, two billion in 1985 and three billion in 2005. In 2011, 3.6 billion persons were found living in urban areas. It is estimated that the number will be over four billion by 2020, five billion by 2035 and six billion by 2050. It is further reported that the estimates and projections of urban population are, thankfully, dependent upon the "continuation of fertility reductions in the developing world." Otherwise, world urban population would be seeing an "increase to 7.4 billion by 2050."

In percentage terms, the proportion of world population living in urban areas rose from about 30 per cent in 1950 and 40 per cent in 1985. Since 2010, more than half of the world's population (51.6%) are living in urban areas. It is estimated that by 2050 over 67 per cent of the world's population will reside in urban areas.

Percentage wise, however, the overall average annual rate of change in urban population reveals a declining trend at the world level. There were fluctuations until 2000-2005, in which a gradual decline was witnessed after high urbanisation waves at different time periods. Europe and North America experienced the first wave during 1750-1950, and subsequently the less developed regions observed a similar transition on a higher scale and at a faster pace. In the coming years, the numbers and proportions will increase, but the percentage of annual increase or the overall rate of urban growth will come down (Figure 1.1).

Figure 1.1

Average Annual Rate of Change of Per cent World Urban Population

Source: United Nations (2012).

The share of urban population differs among various world regions. In Northern America, Latin America, Caribbean, Europe and Oceania, percentages are high (between 70% and 85%) as compared to Asia and Africa, where 40 to 45 per cent of the people live in urban areas. It is estimated that the less developed regions of the world will experience rapid urbanisation in the near future.

Over the next four decades (2011-2050), growth of urban population will be highest in Asia and Africa. Other world regions will experience growth on a lesser scale. Country wise, largest increases in urban population are expected to be in India, followed by China, Nigeria, the US and Indonesia. City level projections further show that large cities and the adjoining regions in various parts of the world will experience phenomenal growth of urban population.

Megacities, or urban agglomerations having population of 10 million or more, have increased from 2 [megacities] in 1970 to 10 in 1990 and to 23 in 2011. This number is projected to grow to 37 by 2025. Their present geographical distribution is as follows: 13 are situated in Asia, 4 in Latin America and Caribbean, and 2 each in Africa, Europe and Northern America (Figure 1.2). The data show that about 10 per cent of the world's urban population lives in mega cities, and the five largest mega cities today having population of more than 20 million are Tokyo followed by Delhi, Mexico City, New York-Newark and Shanghai.

Figure 1.2

Percentage of Urban Population and Agglomerations, 2011

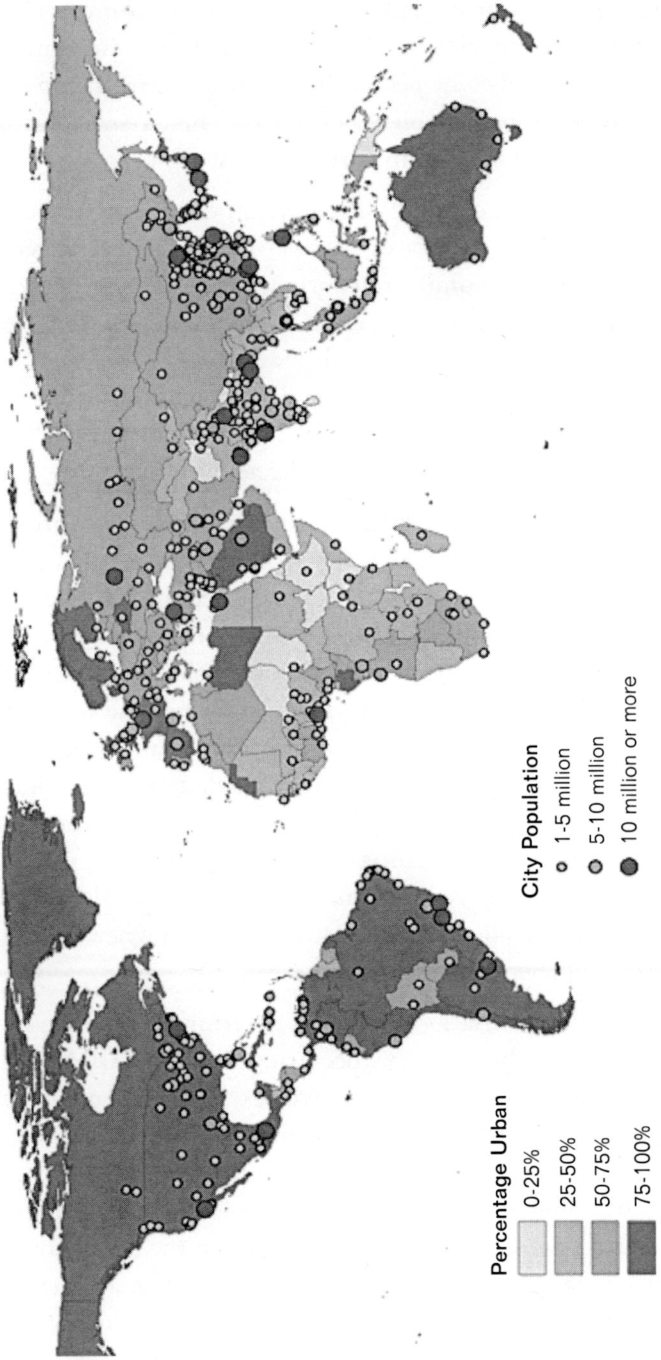

Source: United Nations (2012).

Presently, the world's 23 largest urban agglomerations have a population ranging between 10 and 37 million. In some of these settlements, the number of people living in a square kilometre of area (or population density) is as high as 25,000. This is an indication of the pressure of population on land in current times.

The cluster effect of increasing population and activities in urban settlements has many advantages, as also some negative effects. It leads to a country's socioeconomic transformation by way of contribution to economic growth, employment generation, reduction of poverty, availability of infrastructure and services (health, education, water and sanitation, energy, transport, banks) to the city and the region's population. Urban centres also function as a transportation and wholesale hub for smaller urban and rural settlements situated in the adjoining areas.

However, a high concentration of people in and around cities also creates a number of problems, particularly in some of the largest cities in developing countries. There are examples galore, such as inappropriate utilisation of urban spaces; growth of slums and unauthorised settlements; unsafe housing; traffic congestion and environmental pollution; infrastructure and service inequities; increase in rent and land values; threat to heritage and; increase in crime and violence. In many cities situated in developed countries, new challenges to sustainable urban development are being experienced. For instance in the transport sector, experts are desperately searching for ways to promote non-motorised vehicles, mitigate noise, reduce emissions to protect the environment, ensure road safety, mobilise revenue for implementing new projects, and to transport goods efficiently within urban areas.

International organisations, national governments and the civil society are concerned about the problems occurring due to growing urbanisation. The UN (2012a) has reported that while "unprecedented increase in urban population will provide new opportunities to improve education and public services in Africa and Asia, ... this will also pose new challenges of providing urban jobs, housing, energy and infrastructure to mitigate urban poverty, expansion of slums and a deterioration of the urban environment." Urban problems and challenges were also identified as a critical issue and taken up for discussion at the Earth Summit 2012 (or Rio+20). Constantly, efforts are being made in various parts of the world to address the present day urban challenges. New combinations, mechanisms, approaches and strategies are being developed, tried and tested for achieving the goals of equity and sustainability. There is an emphasis on sharing of experiences and documentation of success stories (or best practices).

The ORF-RLS Conference on Urbanisation

Considering the significance of urbanisation in current times, the Observer Research Foundation (ORF) and the Rosa Luxemburg Stiftung (RLS) organised an International Conference on "Global Urbanisation Experiences" in New Delhi on 8-9 November, 2011. Urban experts from Austria, China, Colombia, Germany, India, UK and USA participated and presented papers in the Conference. They shared valuable information and suggested ways to overcome contemporary problems. The main idea behind holding the event was that since urban problems experienced by various nations were different, much benefit would be derived by sharing research findings and practical experiences.

The conference had the following objectives:

- bring together urban experts for exchanging knowledge about urbanisation;
- deliberate upon complex urban issues and challenges to progress;
- explore options and opportunities for the creation of habitable and sustainable urban centres, and
- publish and disseminate the proceedings and research papers.

Conference Themes

The conference aimed to cover five important topics/themes, namely urban governance and participation, planning and design, transportation and networks, energy consumption and emissions, and social exclusion. The scope of each of the identified themes is described below.

Urban Governance and Participation: Creating Innovative Structures

With increasing urban population and challenges of urbanisation, conventional approaches are losing relevance. To deal with the problems, some governments have undertaken innovative reforms. For this theme, the following questions were identified for discussion:

- What are the major challenges of urbanisation, and how are governments responding to these challenges? How can we implement policies efficiently?
- With a change in the government's role from a traditional 'provider' of services to that of a 'facilitator' or 'enabler', and the adoption of democratic or good governance principles, how much has been the progress achieved?
- In what ways can we promote constructive interaction between the three important actors, namely the state, civil society and the private sector, for better governance?
- What has been the experience of community and private sector participation in urban governance (policymaking, decision-making, implementation, service delivery, operation and maintenance, budgeting, etc.)?
- Are there any successful examples of good urban governance?

Urban Planning and Design: Using City Spaces Efficiently

The efficient utilisation of land, public spaces and built structures is a prerequisite for the making of sustainable cities. Such principles when not applied often result in utter chaos and wastage of resources. As city densities grow, the significance of urban design, urban planning, landscape architecture, cannot be overlooked. For this theme, the following questions were identified for discussion:

- Can we solve the urbanisation challenges by rethinking on the design aspects? Are there any successful examples?
- In an attempt to increase urban densities, do we need to debate the merits of vertical cities as against horizontal spreads?
- How do we ensure effective coordination between multiple agencies responsible for design, construction and management of public spaces, buildings, transport systems, services and amenities?

- Can we design the proverbial 'ubiquitous city'?
- In designing new cities, how can we give greater importance to equality issues, such as meeting the needs of disabled people?

Urban Transport and Networks: Building Sustainable Systems

The availability of a good road and rail transport network along with efficient public transport facilities is a basic requirement of the urban population as it allows them to pursue various activities in a well-organised manner. Other necessities are reduced traffic congestion, travel time, emissions of carbon dioxide, etc., and socioeconomic development. Governments of large cities/megalopolises across the world are confronted with a major transport challenge—meeting the mobility needs of a very large population. For this theme, the following questions were identified for discussion:

- What are the major urban transport sector priorities and concerns of the developed and the developing nations? What are the different innovative measures undertaken to address these concerns?
- Why are some countries unable to resolve their urban transport problems?
- How can we mobilise additional funds for comprehensive development of the urban transport sector?
- In what ways can we integrate multiple transport modes? What has been the experience of existing integrated/multi-modal urban transport systems?
- How can we reduce the phenomenal growth of private vehicles in cities?
- What role can advanced technology play in improving urban transport systems?

Energy Consumption and Urban Emissions: Developing Alternate Scenarios

A high concentration of population and the associated development in urban areas has led to an increased demand for energy. The quantum of energy required to run cities today goes well beyond the available amount. Moreover, energy consumption levels at some places have risen phenomenally, thereby leading to greater emissions and the subsequent degradation of the environment. For this theme, the following questions were identified for discussion:

- As urban concentrations increase, can we rely on traditional energy supply chains or do we need to rethink the model? How can we develop a new socioecological framework? What is the experience of new urban energy models?
- Would it be more useful to define the energy chain on the basis of consumption rather than on the traditional generation driven models? How does the climate and sustainability debate impact on this discussion?
- What are the emerging drivers of emissions, and what are the local responses that may be further examined and developed?
- How can we create local supply chains and response mechanisms?
- How can we reduce vehicular pollution/green house gas emissions? What are the energy conservation measures that can be undertaken?
- Can we facilitate access to modern energy services for the urban poor? How can we control the rise in energy prices?
- How can we achieve the goal of energy efficient cities?

Urban Social Exclusions: Questioning the Right to the City

All too visible is the degeneration of city areas caused by urbanisation—the salient ills being poverty, the persistent inequality in wealth, ever expanding slums and the spread of informal sector activities, besides violence and criminality. Many studies indicate that such problems occur because the voices and needs of some sections of the society are ignored at the time of policymaking. Thus, social exclusion poses a major challenge for urban policymakers and governance experts in their quest for cities with balanced economies. For this theme, the following questions were identified for discussion:

- In what ways can we overcome the problem of rising urban exclusion?
- How can we achieve the goal of creating equitable cities?
- What are the problems being experienced in the formulation and implementation of inclusive urban policies? What are the ways in which we can offer inclusive and sustainable support to the urban poor?
- What has been the experience of 'gentrification' in cities?
- How valid is the concept of 'gated community'?

About the Publication

This publication documents modern experiences of urbanisation in developing and developed countries. The information is presented under three main sections. An Editorial Introduction at the beginning describes world urban population patterns and trends, and the consequences of urbanisation. Against this backdrop, the necessity of organising an International Conference on urbanisation is explained. This is followed by a description of the conference objectives and themes. A summary of the main ideas presented by distinguished experts who participated in the conference is provided below in the following sub-sections. The next section of the publication comprises 10 papers contributed by these experts on important urban topics. The arguments put forward by the authors are supported by numerous tables, figures, photographs and references. A comprehensive bibliography of urban studies is provided towards the end of the publication.

It is expected that the information provided in this publication would draw the attention of readers towards complicated urban issues, innovative practices in use and challenges to progress. The publication will be useful for national, regional, and urban policymakers and planners in India and abroad, Indian state and local government functionaries engaged in implementation of projects and programmes, national and international research organisations, non-government organisations engaged in urban studies and action-oriented programmes, professionals in the private sector, as also faculty and students of urban studies in various academic institutions.

Bogotá: Recent Urban Transformations and Visions for its Future

The reflections on the development of Bogotá city, Colombia's capital, have been carried out through case studies on different projects and urban settings by Eduardo Samper in his paper. The author points out that architecture, landscape architecture and urban design are closely linked to the city's quality of life. However, in recent decades, the impressive fact that Bogotá had been designed and built by architects of world renown, Karl Brunner, or a visionary like Le Corbusier, got eclipsed under the shadow of the rampant growth in the population of the poor. The final section describes challenges of the 21st century Bogotá including the city and its region, within the framework for growth, i.e., mobility, densification and the ecological network.

Challenges and Strategies for China's Next Stage of Urban Development: Researches and Practices in Shanghai and Huangyuan

For the past 30 years of China's herculean task of urbanisation, the dominating criteria have been the sheer size of its scale and the rapidity with which cities have been developed or constructed. While those efficient giant urban constructions successfully sustained the nation's economic development and provided sufficient living space for the explosive growth of the urban population, challenges emerged regarding giving the cities a more humane face while retaining efficiency in a modern manner: at the same time, the need was felt for creating the country's own unique cultural identity for cities, big or small, rather than repeatedly adopting or copying the developed nations' urban pattern. Having been working on both the most developed coastal city, Shanghai Pudong New Area, as also on one of the poorest but culturally celebrated small city in the west plateau, Huangyuan, for the past eight years, Yue Wu shares his reflections on these challenges through his research and practice as an urban designer as well as an architect.

Sustainable Cities and the Transport System

Cheap and abundantly available external energy from coal, oil and gas for steamships, railways, car traffic and airplanes brought about a fundamental change in urban development. Because of the new means of transport, the cities could grow much bigger than was earlier possible. However, this was and is only possible as long as the whole globe could be used as the life supporting system for cities, and cheap fossil fuel for the transport system continued to be available. But the flipside is becoming more and more visible: increasing urbanisation means increasing energy demand. Hermann Knoflacher emphasises that this vital fact has not been realised by the planners who dream of a larger urban population in the future. For years, available resources have been used well beyond the bearing capacity of the fertile ground, the atmosphere and the ecosystem, as the analysis report to the Club of Rome in 1972 and 30 years after have shown. The author sees a future where there will be a big shift from individual motorisation to more intelligent transport solutions based on solar energy, and suggests that this is only possible by maximising the ratio of pedestrians and cyclists in the urban transport system.

Expanding Transport Networks for Urban and Regional Development in India

The National Capital Region (NCR) of India displays severe regional disparities in literacy rates, wages, employment and living conditions. In his paper, Rumi Aijaz examines the relationship between development and mobility in the NCR and makes the point that the prevailing inequities in development can be greatly mitigated by improving and expanding transport systems and networks. The author's impressions are based on an appraisal of the existing regional road and rail networks, completed and on-going projects, policies and strategies for development of regional transport sector, as also the future development challenges. It is concluded that the objective of balanced regional development can be achieved by the implementation of regional transport projects on a priority basis, attending to difficulties experienced in arranging funds and their efficient utilisation, capacity building of implementing agencies, land acquisition, and improving coordination among participating state governments.

The Contemporary Structure of the World City Network: How Industries Connect Cities across the World

The paper by Stefan Krätke concentrates on a macro-level analysis of the global urban system by investigating inter-urban linkages in a 'world city network' that comprises a multitude of cities both in the global North and South, highlighting the geographically uneven spread of globalisation as well as the rise of new urban nodes of globally connected business activity, such as, for example, Shanghai and Mumbai. Empirical research on the formation of a world city network that functions as a backbone for channelling worldwide capital flows has mostly concentrated on global service providers' organisational networks. However, this line of research has tended to neglect the role of global networks of the manufacturing sectors. Globally operating manufacturing firms are as well choosing distinct urban regions all across the world as locational anchoring points. The contribution presents selected findings of recent research on the manufacturing industries' global organisational networks. Interestingly, the 'ranking' of globally connected urban centres of manufacturing activity differs considerably from the well-known rankings of global service centres.

Meeting UK Government's 80 per cent CO_2 Reduction Target in Local Authority Corporate Estate

The paper by Paul Kennedy evaluates the ability of UK local authorities to meet UK Government expectations for significant CO_2 emission reductions targets within their corporate estate. The principle hypothesis is that UK local authorities have set far-reaching and ambitious targets for CO_2 reductions for their buildings, but the implications of achieving major energy saving measures are not fully evaluated. Properly evaluated whole-building or organisation related carbon reductions have not been undertaken. The hypothesis is supported by research suggesting that energy management by local authorities was patchy and the focus was on energy spent rather than on carbon management. The paper explores the paradigms within which the influential elements of technology, management and 'green' ethics compete. It deals with issues of concern for the management of energy in UK public sector local authorities and their operational buildings, as also the reductionist approaches to minimising carbon emissions. The research suggests a conceptual framework, identifying the six key components that influence changes relating to building performance, organisational reform, legal conformity, people, procedures and technology.

Energy Transition Policies in Europe and their Social Impact

Urban life has led to an increasing demand for energy, particularly for heating, cooling and lighting (electricity). As people in cities do not produce their own energy but obtain it from energy suppliers; they are often not aware of the negative effects of their energy consumption. In the past, cheap energy was produced by centralised systems based on fossil fuels, promoting waste of energy. The increase in energy prices ("energy crisis") and the effects of energy generation on the climate created awareness among new social movements and politicians of the need to save energy. Ulrich Schachtschneider differentiates between 'green market', 'green state', and 'green community', and suggests that the commercial energy supply system should be converted to a publicly owned non-profit system that deals with energy in a responsible way.

Addressing the Ultimate Urban Exclusion: Slums

Urban social exclusion takes many forms. A common form in developed nations is overt and covert discrimination against an economically or educationally unequal group in housing and employment. Less pernicious are gated communities and other practices resulting in the isolation of a well-to-do group from wider society, which can easily create mistrust and misunderstanding between different economic strata. Probably the most deleterious social exclusion in the developing world is manifest in slums that result from a combination of poor public policy and very limited consumer purchasing power. The paper by Raymond J. Struyk, focuses on the attributes of today's slums, the costs they impose and realistic ways to check their growth and enhance the opportunities of their residents. A slum-oriented policy perspective is too narrow. And even city-level policies are unlikely to work because of the misallocation of authority and resources between national governments, and municipal governments. Importantly, enough is known about how to improve a particular slum, but the issue is how to do so on a larger scale.

India's Rapid Urbanisation and Exclusion of the Poor

India's urbanisation has gathered momentum in recent years and concomitantly, the poor in big cities have been experiencing economic and social exclusion. In many cases their settlements have been physically removed and transplanted on the outskirts of big cities. In this paper, Jayshree Sengupta describes the plight of the urban poor and observes that they have had to bear the burden of rising transport costs and high rents due to the ongoing inflation; their children lack good schools and access to reliable medical treatment. The slums also lack basic services and are largely neglected by the municipal authorities in ensuring access to clean water, sanitation and affordable housing. Women are unable to work regularly due to lack of crèche facilities. It is concluded that unless slum development becomes an integral part of the development of the city, there will be increase in social tension.

Excluded Berlin: Housing at the Margins of Urban Citizenship

Berlin was internationally known as a tenants' city with a low 14 per cent of housing classified under self-use ownership. The overall situation was for a long time defined by a relaxed housing market. Since around 2005, however, the situation has changed, with rent prices rising in most of Berlin's neighbourhoods alongside a strong market driven allocation for housing. This rising competition affecting access to housing highlights structures of disadvantage that go beyond the economy. Pointing to the limited housing access to Roma and Turkish families, Andrej Holm, describes various kinds of discrimination. Lack of residence authorisation, racial discrimination and administrative restriction on housing reveals various shortfalls affecting urban citizenship.

References

United Nations (2012). *World Urbanisation Prospects: The 2011 Revision*. New York: Department of Economic and Social Affairs, Population Division.

———. (2012a). "Africa and Asia to Lead Urban Population Growth in the Next Four Decades". Press Release. April 5, New York.

2 Bogotá: Recent Urban Transformations and Visions for its Future

Eduardo Samper

The city is man's creation and we are proud of it, but only if we have a profound respect for nature will we be able to give a certain future to the next generations.

— Eduardo Samper

Introduction

Landscape architecture and urban design are closely linked to a city's quality of life. In recent decades, the grandeur of Bogotá city, Colombia's capital, designed by architects of global stature such as Karl Brunner and a visionary like Le Corbusier has been put into shade by the ever burgeoning dwellings of the city's poor population.

Nevertheless, at the turn of the century, Bogotá's Mayor Enrique Peñalosa[1] arrived with a new sense of the direction, the city needed to take in order to improve its living conditions. His proposal was based on the creation and the regeneration of public space—a democratic space par excellence—and the offering of a new, efficient and economic transport system with efficient buses capable of meeting the demands of a Bus Rapid Transit (BRT) System. Fortunately, Mayor Peñalosa's successors not only carried on his work but also reinforced and broadened it. In the words of Mayor Antanas Mokus, "the public budget was sacredly administrated."

Mobility, education, public space and green space were the top issues and, financed with public bonds, the architects got busy working on the projects. Their work proved that the high quality development of public space, urban and natural landscape were not just the task of professional

---

1. Enrique Peñalosa, politician, economist with urban studies, was elected mayor of the city for the period 1999-2001.

urban planners and engineers, as had been the case in the city until then. Several generations of well-known architects as also young, eager ones took on the responsibility of improving several city areas. It was a positive breakthrough for Bogotá, but it was not good enough. In the recent past years, the mobility problem has increased and the inequity between the city´s residents hasn´t been studied nor solved properly. These problems are rooted in deeper issues that influence Colombia´s cities. As is the case in large parts of the world, the root cause of the ills is poverty and violence. There cannot be an iota of doubt that, to confront the huge challenge, top priority needs to be given to improving the quality of life, widening the range of education and opening up public space for the citizens.

This paper does not try to come up with magic solutions, but to show that cities, even a low budget city like Bogotá, can overcome its problems. A lesson learnt in recent times is that it requires the democratic election of honest managers to create the political will to bring about the kind of change necessary to formulate a sound, long-term development plan for the city. It also requires committed local politicians, otherwise the opportunists among them will put hurdles in the way of the plans with their eyes on their short term political interests. The recent experience also shows that the support of architects is invaluable, as they have far more passion for their profession than others who are found sorely lacking when it comes to task of building a city. It is the architects who help structure the utopian dream of a people's city.

Background to Position Bogotá in its Urban History

Colombia is located in the tropical belt (2° N–16° N of the Equator). It is a country rich in climate and geographic variety as diverse as the hot and humid Amazon rainforest to the cold mountains of the Andes. The thermal levels change as the land rises from the sea level to ascend up the three mountain ranges that cross from north to south, where the majority of the population of the country live. Hence the tropical climate varies in temperature from hot to cold depending on the height, but the weather remains the same throughout the four seasons.

Bogotá, at 2,600 metres above sea level, has the largest urban population in Colombia that shapes politics of the nation. It's a cold city with an average temperature of 17°C, which drops to 0°C at night and has sunlight from 5:30 AM to 6:30 PM. The city is situated at the foothills of the impressive chain of East Mountains, extending from north to south. Currently, Bogotá covers an important section of the fertile savannah that extends in the north and west of the foothill (Figure 2.1).

During the pre-Columbian settlement, Bogotá comprised a gathering of small towns of which there remains no trace, as the building material used was the perishable deciduous wood. The Spanish Conquest and the Colonisation brought to all Latin American territories a new architectural concept—the courtyard, an open-air space that isolates the private world of buildings from the urban and collective spaces. But above all, the designs of all foundations in Latin America were drawn-up by the Laws of the Indies, following a grid pattern of streets and main squares. This Renaissance-based layout of the ideal city was applied in most Latin American settlements. Bogotá stands as a clear example of a layout meant for foothills that looks over the savannah to the west.

During the 18th and 19th centuries, the prevailing universal concepts of architecture and urbanism were ushered into Bogotá: French and English influence came to dominate the customs and architecture of the New Republic. Bogotá, in the mountainous centre of the country, was a geographically isolated city so that any news about the happenings in the country reached it late. Its residents were conservative, self-absorbed and provincial. With the arrival of the train in 1889 and the airplane in the early 20th century, the city gradually began to communicate with and open up to the country and the world. Bogotá, although peripheral to world events, walked slowly into modernity. The "English Garden City" was perfectly suited to the abundance of tropical vegetation. Insulated buildings replaced the urban corridors. The development of wooded boulevards and green front yards brought in the idea of a "Belle cité" or "City Beautiful", enabled by the work of the experiences of F.L. Olmstead and others who followed the principle of "architecture and landscape in the urban context". This was a new concept that, regardless of the variety of building styles, became the model applied to Bogotá and other Colombian cities. At this point, one needs to mention the contribution of the Austrian Karl Brunner (1887-1960) who, for several years, taught urban-design at the first school of architecture established in the country (National University) and, between 1933 and 1938, spearheaded two urban management plans

Figure 2.1

Section through the Central Mountains, Bogotá and the Savannah

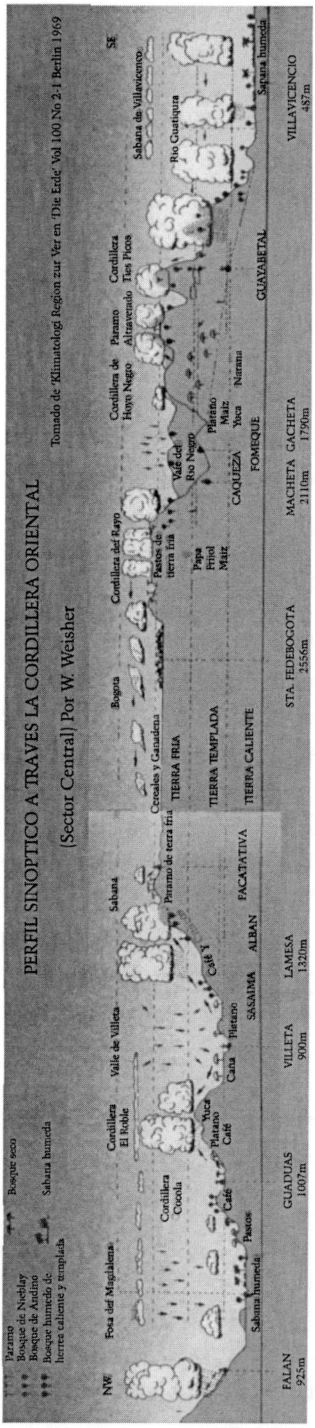

for Bogotá. The capital city at that time had 270,000 residents. Brunner applied a model that, while keeping intact the old, traditional build-up of the area, drew an architectural design that played a central role in the creation of public spaces (Figure 2.2). His proposals were highly significant legacy of Bogotá. There is no doubt that his ideas brought about the integration of the existing city with its new sectors that were subtly woven into the urban fabric.

On a parallel level, the influence of modernism began to influence the entire continent of Latin America. With theoretical foundations based on the findings of the CIAM (Congrès Internationaux d'Architecture Moderne), the city began to be designed according to the dictates of its functions—to live, to work, to entertain and to move around. This matched with the Second World War fallout—Europeans' exodus to South America. European architects who fled to Colombia worked with their Colombian counterparts educated in Europe and the United States; together they introduced the new Brazilian architecture exemplified by the Bauhaus, the work of Le Corbusier and the Colombian architects.

In the late 40s, two historic events revolutionised the City's architectural concept. The first was the landmark uprising, the *Bogotázo*, triggered by the murder of the Liberal leader Jorge Gaitan on 9th April, 1948. It erupted into the biggest riot since Independence: a big section of the city was razed to the ground, paradoxically, opening up "never before imagined" possibilities of urban intervention in the capital. The second trigger was the visit of Le Corbusier to Bogotá, who was invited in 1947 to develop the *Plan Piloto of Bogotá* (Figure 2.3). Le Corbusier finished his pilot plan in 1951 and the Town Planning consulting firm of Wiener and Sert Associates was commissioned to prepare a design based on the master plan. Although it was never implemented, Le Corbusier strongly influenced the younger generation of Colombian architects and many of his principles were incorporated into the plan for the next decade. Le Corbusier was at that time designing the plan for Chandigarh, the capital of Punjab. However, while Chandigarh's design was drawn for a virgin "green field", for Bogotá, the design was meant for "a new network of sectors" that was to "overlay an existing city fabric." This plan never materialised. It was 50 long years later that, with only the main lines of the road plan remaining,

Figure 2.2

Bogotá around 1938 with the Karl Brunner Urban Designs in Grey

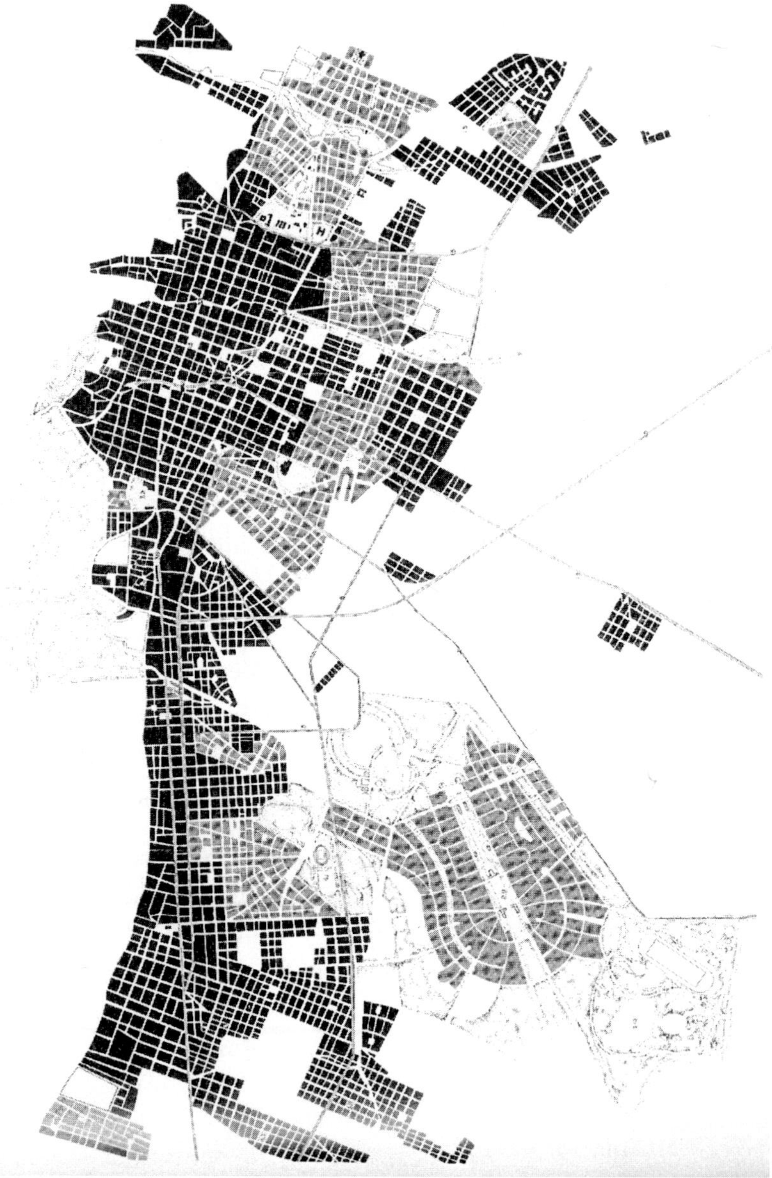

Figure 2.3

Plan Piloto of Bogotá (Le Corbusier, 1951)

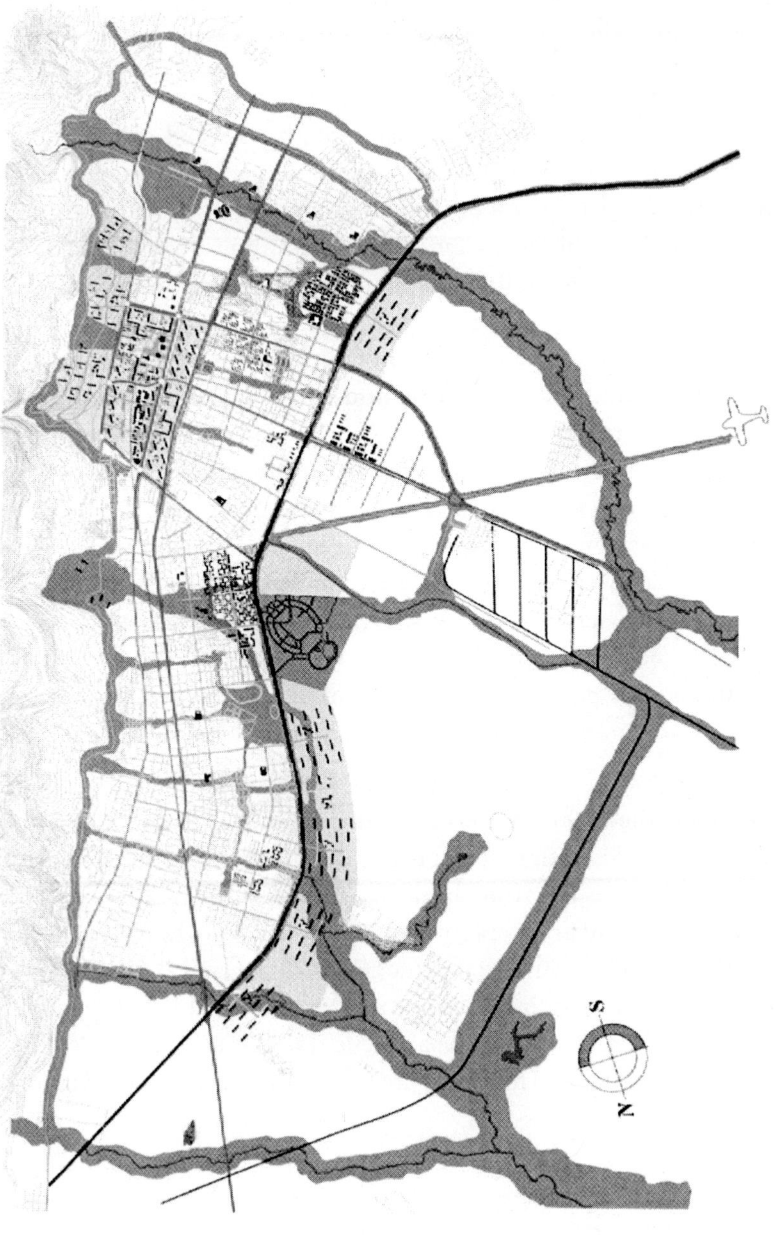

one finally came to recognise the significance of his geographic and landscape approach—a vision that inspired the design of the city.

Growth of Bogotá and City Characteristics

Bogotá had 600,000 inhabitants in 1950, and the projection in the master plan was 2,500,000 inhabitants by the end of the century. In the next two decades, the population grew far beyond this projection. Bogotá became host to an uncontrolled migration from the countryside. The city of 2011 is home to more than 7 million people and has outgrown the geographical boundaries mapped by the mountains and the river. The informal city which since 1940 had been labelled as an area born of "clandestine development", now encompassed more than half of the Capital region. The growth of mid-century low income housing design with low-density development, besides being illegal (euphemistically termed informal) was insufficient and it proliferated. This growth resulted in a nightmare of a vast dwelling area without even the basic water and sanitation systems that surrounded green, institutionalised neighbourhood. The task during the last decades has been to legalise these areas and provide basic services, but at a much higher cost. The city was polarised from the beginning into two contrasting areas: the wealthy suburbs in the north and the poor habitants in the south. Today, in the 21st century, the city lies fractured by a poverty belt of segregation.

Faced with the hard reality of low income housing shortage in the mid 60's, the architect Germán Samper Gnecco[2] began successive projects that proposed solutions to housing densification in the low altitude areas, recognising the fact that building houses on a progressive basis would ultimately result in economic wellbeing, though the degree would depend on the growth of financial strength of the owners. In a study on public housing called "Minimum Standards",[3] conducted in 1970 for the District Planning Administrative Department (DPAD) of Bogotá, the fundamental principles of urban planning approaches were summarised (Figure 2.4). This

2. Architect graduated at Universidad Nacional de Colombia in 1947, made a professional practice for 5 years with Le Corbusier, practicing in Colombia since 1953.

3. Study made by Consultécnicos. Germán Samper led the urban theoretical model.

Figure 2.4

Theoretical Schemes of Minimum Standards

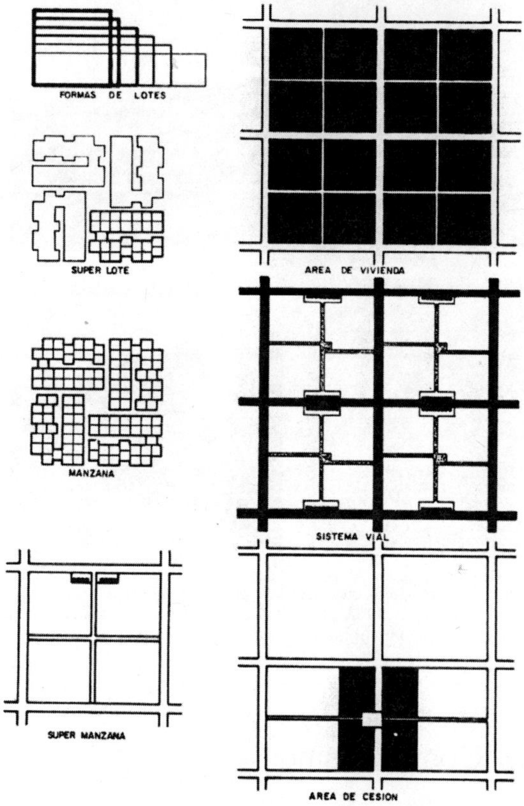

Figure 2.5

Urban Enclosure Concept

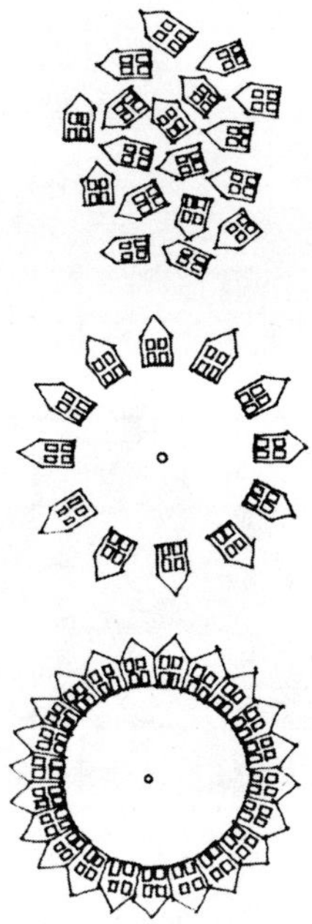

study was mooted as the practical alternative within the ambit of law—spontaneous solutions that would make it possible to avoid unacceptable conditions for neighbourhood development in the future. Nevertheless, the fact is that today, conditions have worsened because of the lack of housing policies and the shortage of urban land (Figure 2.6).

Figure 2.6

Types of Houses in the Bogotá's Stratification

Note: Classification of population by type of house: Total city population: 7,363,000 (100%); photo 1: 743,000 people (10%); photo 2: 2,886,000 people (39%); photo 3: 2,661,000 people (36%); photo 4: 693,000 people (10%); photo 5: 198,000 people (3%); photo 6: 130,000 people (2%).

Source: Percentages from Secretaria de Planeacion Distrital (SDP) Statistics, 2009.

Two Case Studies of Low Cost Housing

Ciudadela Colsubsidio (1985-2000): A 12,000 Low Cost Housing Apartments Project[4]

Ciudadela Colsubsidio, a small "city within a city," was designed mostly with the concept of five-story buildings on a 150-hectare plot of land. It was developed under the Constitution of the *Caja Colombiana de Subsidio* (Colsubsidio) that lays down a percentage of their resources on housing for union members. This regulation gave the clout to the planners (architects, among others) to control the project's architectural design and the pattern of urbanisation.

4. Designed by architect Germán Samper.

Reflected in the project were the decades of theoretical and practical experiences of Samper's research work—the salient points being: the separation of vehicular streets from the pedestrian walks, a minimum density of 100 houses per hectare for single families homes and a higher density for multifamily housing and; the use of the concept of "urban enclosure" (Figure 2.5), in which the architecture shapes the urban space. The public space became the basis for the design, and a critical look at the precepts of his teacher, Le Corbusier, explains the return to the concept of streets and the Main Square. This piece of city (though not the only one) was an exemplification of the fact that the task of architecture was to make contributions, however small, to the growth of the city—the main aim being to improve the residents' quality of life (Figures 2.7 and 2.8).

Figure 2.7

Colsubsidio, Bogotá from West and Juan Amarillo Wet Land at the Left

Figure 2.8

Images/Sketch of Different Parts of Colsubsidio

El Recreo, Metrovivienda (2000-2010): A 8,000 Low Cost Income Houses Project[5]

During the governance of Mayor Enrique Peñalosa (1999-2001) a public company, Metrovivienda, was set up with the aim of creating a land bank for the development of housing projects for low-income people. "Underground" developments are much more efficient in the economic sense. The supply of lots or land to be built by its owners generates a good commercial value and increase the sale value for the large land owners. The pirate developers bought up acres and acres of land, did not construct roads or provide related services and made a fast buck by hustling up a "fast city" and selling the plots dirt cheap. The challenge for Metrovivienda was to work out a relatively competitive price (according to the funding available) for developed urban land that would then be sold to private developers, who would otherwise be dealing with housing for people with higher incomes.

The objective of this urban planning was to establish realistic rules that would allow different architectural solutions through a progressive

5. Designed by architects Konrad Brunner, Guillermo Perry and Eduardo Samper, with the consultancy of Germán Samper and Ioannis Alexiou.

single housing development and to build the public space from the beginning. This would eliminate instant solutions under unacceptable conditions. The urban structure has its origins in the alternate networks studies developed by Samper. The road networks, based on their function, class and character, aims to build: routes for fast vehicular traffic; routes leading into sectors; distribution channels within the sectors for pedestrian or mixed use and; a system for subdividing the land into superblocks. These small pieces of land drew private developers to build affordable housing.

Unlike *Colsubsidio*, *El Recreo* was developed by private investors and developers who did not correlate the urban design with the architectural fabric of its already existing parts. Only the planned public spaces were controlled, and the architecture of its blocks was ignored. In the design of low-income housing projects, the ongoing transformation of the urban landscape is the rule (Figure 2.9 and 2.10). The houses are economically productive; the new users convert the lower floor of the two story houses into stores or put it to other commercial uses.

Figure 2.9

Images of Different Parts of El Recreo

Figure 2.10

El Recreo from the West

Urban Transformations in Bogotá in the Late 20th Century: The Recovery of the Public Space

The several areas of Bogotá that were transformed in the last decade acquired the basics of modern living—recovery of public space, mobility, education, recreation, and green areas.

Since 1980, there have been concerns over the lack of public space. Until then, the mayors focused on expanding roads and building bridges to facilitate private vehicular traffic. The vehicle became the motivator of city building. In Bogotá, the space for people was disappearing, the sidewalks were becoming car parks and public transportation became private. The town heard few voices of complaint, and only in few instances were small-scale projects carried out. Architectural works based on geography and landscape created by Salmona and his students had ensured that there were

Figure 2.11

Carrera 15

plenty of public spaces; the ones by the Germán Samper, who created the neighbourhood design, gave greater importance to pedestrian space than to vehicular traffic. Another contribution was closing the vehicular traffic on Sundays so that arterial roads would be open for bikes and recreational outings. However, these efforts were isolated and did not reach the entire population. There was chaos on the roads. It was at the end of the Mayor Paul Bromberg's term in office (1997) that the first steps were taken to open up space for the public citywide. Three designs came up under Bromberg:

- *Carrera 15*, a high-intensity pathway aimed at commercial recovery by reducing the expanse of platforms on a vehicular traffic lane (Figure 2.11).[6]

6. Designed by architect Fernando Cortes Larreamendy.

- *Environmental Axis*, which proposed turning the Jiménez Avenue into a semi-pedestrian street that runs parallel to the route of the old San Francisco River in the historic city centre (Figure 2.12).[7]
- *Calle 80*, a new arterial road in the city, a major entry and exit route to the west rising into the mountains, making it an extension of the bus route operating in the *Avenida Caracas* (Figure 2.13). The *Calle 80* would thus be the first Transmilenio road.[8]

They were accepted by Peñalosa administration, and the three designs with some modifications were immediately taken up for execution. Such swift action by an administration, that has duration of only three years, is rare, but it was possible because it fit perfectly into the Mayor's vision of the city.

Figure 2.12

Environmental Axis

7. Designed by architects Rogelio Salmona and Luis Kopec.
8. Designed by architects Germán Samper, Eduardo Samper and Restrepo & Uribe engineers.

Figure 2.13

Calle 80

Calle 80, Bogotá, 1996

The Calle 80 was the first main axis of the city built with an integrated bus transportation system. During the studies of this 10 km road (conducted around 1996, two years before the implementation of the Transmilenio system—the BRT), the professional team concluded that the central area of the section was the correct route for buses and Transmilenio stations. Although the administration didn't want to go in for new buses (since left doors were needed), the road was designed to keep the space free for future options. Two years later, the buses arrived and the Transmilenio system had the Calle 80 as the first line—ready to be built. Stations every 500 metres, wide pedestrian space, service roads to avoid congestion on the car ways to the main street and other such considerations were kept in mind. The final design included new station architecture and pedestrian bridges. The Calle 80 was the first corridor redevelopment work in Bogotá that integrated mass bus transit, cycling mobility and private vehicles. This corridor connects the suburban residential areas with the financial centres and has become an important area for re-densification and economic betterment.

Integrated Bus Transportation System, Transmilenio, as Urban Corridors for Redevelopment

By far the most important project of the Peñalosa administration was the Bus Rapid Transit (BRT), named Transmilenio[9] (Figure 2.14). This transport system was inspired by Curitiba, Brazil, and was applied to a city almost four times larger with surprising results. The BRT is what structures and controls all the city's business and density to the great benefit of the citizens. The subway system may well be a bold facilitator of mobility in large cities, but it is too expensive and would take years to build. The bus system required a tenth of the budget and could cover the entire city in a decade. It required great political will to put it into action, as bus transportation was a monopoly of completely private business. Chaos spawned by the competing individual interests was unsustainable. Public transport had to be controlled by the state. Taking on the private carriers was a task that no politician had ever dared to do in Bogotá. The way out was to involve them in the business. The bus companies became the owners, but under strict state regulation and control. The state invested in building the infrastructure necessary for its proper operation.

Public Schools for Neighbourhood Transformation

The Peñalosa administration was the first to propose far reaching improvement in the education field. The 800 public schools in the city not only lacked the capacity to expand, but also functioned in partially built buildings with poor physical infrastructure. The initial approach was to build schools with the facilities that could compete with the best private schools. This initiative was taken up by successive mayors and finally became the priority programme under Mayor Lucho Garzón (2004-2007). The result was the provision of high quality public facilities in the slums that are becoming a positive point of reference for public property, appreciated by all residents and promoting the recovery of neighbourhoods.

This silent revolution and small but effective improvements in the poor neighbourhoods were accompanied by a policy to combat hunger

---

9. The design for the stations and the public space design of the first axis of Transmilenio was won in public competition by architects Gabriel Jaime Giraldo and Javier Vera.

Figure 2.14

Images of Transmilenio

among the most affected populations. It led to the state funded dining halls for students. These projects now are looking not only for the modernisation and automation of school education, but for technical and pre-college programmes. This is also a realistic employment policy in a society that would find too many college graduates unsustainable, but is in dire need of technical professionals primed for the industry and other fields in the globalised world.

The city has also addressed the task of conservation and recovery of old school buildings, all located in the historic centre of the city and in worn out neighbourhoods with the potential for urban renewal. With the expansion and improvement of these facilities, the state's aim is not just to improve the central neighbourhoods, but is sending the message that the architecture is part of the collective memory, and the extension of its useful life is an achievement that should be extended to privately owned buildings (Figure 2.15). The design of the new buildings should harmonise with heritage buildings, as it is the only way to keep alive the historical identity of a city.

Within this framework of ideas, public libraries were established during the Peñalosa administration. The success of these educational and cultural establishments was immediate. Not only did people come out to read in the parks where the libraries were located, it also started off a new and highly welcome trend: people of all ages came and gathered around the new public facilities. Three libraries were set up between 1999 and 2001, and another one recently in 2011 (Figure 2.16).

Creating Parks, Spaces for Peace and Democracy, Bike Mobility, Recreation, Education and Culture

Simon Bolivar Park was designed in 1968, but built two decades later. Being the largest land area meant for entertainment in the middle of the city, it has 300 acres of trees, public buildings, lakes, botanical gardens and space for recreation and sports. However, the effort to keep this 'great green lung' of Bogotá healthy is just not enough for a city where the large spread of poor neighbourhoods are bereft of trees, greens and sports fields, in stark contrast, to the abundance of green areas in the rich neighbourhoods of the city. With the aim of bringing about some balance to this unequal

Figure 2.15

Images of Bogotá's Public Schools (Designed by Architect E. Samper)

Figure 2.16

Images of El Tintal Library (Designed by Architect D. Bermudez) and Virgilio Barco Library (Designed by Architect R. Salmona)

situation, the Peñalosa administration decided to create the park system we have today. An unprecedented tree planting operation was carried out in the existing avenues and parks, and with great difficulty space was acquired to open new parks. Many of the plots were bought during Peñalosa's administration and the parks were built by the administrations that followed. These parks became a welcome addition to the runoffs and green corridors that descend from the mountains to the Bogotá River. In the past centuries, these areas were wetlands that had been filled up; but the water problem is so serious in the city that every time it rains, several neighbourhoods and streets are flooded by the water that flowed back to its former space. Le Corbusier, during his visit to Bogotá had envisioned the creation of linear parks along the rivers that descend from the mountains. Now 50 years later, his ecological dream has been realised.

Bicycles and paths in the park have long had an intimate relationship. In Bogotá, 200 kms of bicycle paths run along parks and roads. It has also led to the creation of pedestrian–cum-bicycle avenues along the river Bogotá (Figure 2.17).

Two Case Studies of Parks Connected to Principal Hydria System of the City

Timiza Park, 1999-2002[10]

The Timiza Park is an example of Bogotá's administration's genuine efforts to satisfy the need for sport and leisure time for its citizens. The whole purpose is to increase the green areas of the city and to develop spaces of peace and tranquillity that would quietly but surely strengthen the bonds that unite a community. Timiza Park was not designed ignoring the existing urban discontinuities. This 64 hectares park connects two communities (that were separated by a river for decades) via pedestrian "alameda" and a bridge. It is also surrounded by bicycle paths and sidewalks. The main section of the park is protected by a transparent fence. Thanks to a well thought out design, an existing football field was kept intact and a cluster of restaurants and meeting places on a terrace balcony overlooking the lake were set up (earlier the area was once nothing more

10. Designed by architects Eduardo Samper, Konrad Brunner and Gustavo Perry.

Figure 2.17

Images of Bike Paths in Bosa, South West Bogotá

Figure 2.18

Images of Timiza Park

than a wet land). The park also has separate areas for sports and relaxation (Figure 2.18).

Juan Amarillo Wet Land, 1999-2002[11]

The most ambitious cycling network was laid out in this project. The Timiza Park was also made during the Peñalosa administration. A 30-km long green corridor runs from the foothills to the Rio Bogotá along the streams, canals and wetlands, connecting many neighbourhoods of varied income classes. The long cycling pathway runs side by side with the pedestrian route, both to the east and west, connecting all the main roads on either direction.

For the 300-hectare Juan Amarillo wetland, the largest wetland area, a metropolitan park with a pacific character was designed (Figure 2.19). Due attention was paid to the ecological, urban and water aspects of this linear park. A large lake atop the wetland (50 acres) acted as both a buffer against floods and as water reservoir for the dry season. Besides, this lake attracts a plethora of migratory birds. The park's importance lies in the fact that it creates a green, contemplative ambience in an urban area which is otherwise bereft of any greenery. On one side of the lake, near the new highway, resting places were arranged and on the other side, protected by the river, a green border island gives shelter and protection to the local flora and fauna. Intersecting the urban areas and the park, is a walkway and bicycle path—but strictly no vehicles are allowed to run. The underground sewage canal along the river flows into the treatment plant. In future it is expected that this treated water could feed the water reservoir when necessary. Unfortunately, the recent administrations (2004-2011) abandoned the idea of spaces for people and nature and closed the green areas with fences to protect the wet land and flora and fauna. They meant well, but they forgot that humans are a part of the fauna and must learn how to cohabitate with the rest of nature's creations.

---

11. Designed by architect Eduardo Samper. The two other lineal parks related to the Juan Amarillo were designed by Germán Samper and Gomez & Cajio engineers.

Figure 2.19

Images of Juan Amarillo Wet Land

Challenges for the 21st Century Bogotá: The City and its Region, Mobility, Densification and the Ecological Network as the Framework for Future Growth

Bogotá and the surrounding savannah share the same future—a metropolis whose population can reach 24 million people by 2038, that is, in its fifth century since its foundation. Bogotá must therefore plan for the future taking into account its large surrounding region.

Politically, the so called rapprochement reached between the big city and the neighbouring municipalities has been a confrontationist one, born of apprehensions over losing power and a perceived fear of invasion into the backyard of the city. Municipalities have refused to play a role in the major regional plans and each one of them has formulated their own development plans ignoring the needs of Bogotá. On the other hand, migration of Bogotá's habitants to the surrounding areas, with the promise of a pleasant life in residential neighbourhoods with avenues full of trees, has resulted in an urban sprawl. The urgent need now is the involvement of all stakeholders in the formulation of the metropolitan plan.

There are two important considerations for the city region—the ecological network of the savannah and, the mobility needs of the people. First of all, the ecological parameters must be thrashed out, the most important factor being the protection of the farm lands and the hills that surround the savannah. Equally important is to find the way to mitigate the effects of the Bogotá River being flooded every winter, the rainy season. These flood prone areas, specially the western side of the river outside the city (Figure 2.20), need to be declared as an area with unacceptable level of dampening.

The second consideration is the mobility and the development of connecting roads between the towns and the city. These are potential urban corridors and their normal tendency is conurbation. The current municipal plans, keeping this tendency to grow in mind, have encouraged the establishment of industries (with tax regulations) on the outskirts of Bogotá. Potential labourers living on the periphery have generated a rapid development of these corridors (Figure 2.21).

Figure 2.20

Flooding of the Savannah, 2011

Looming over the city is a scenario of being enclosed by slums and, outside their doors, industrial corridors and savannah invaded by low-density developments. The only way to check this trend is to execute a plan that articulates metropolitan mass transit routes and protects the city's ecological health. In any case, the most realistic option, given the limited urban land, is the densification of the existing city. That includes the northern area of the city over which there were bitter discussions between the administration of Peñalosa, who wanted as high a density of 1,500,000 inhabitants along with large parks and avenues, and a group of environmentalists, led by the Ministry of Environment. The ministry froze nearly 4,300 developable acres of land to be left as green reserve. Nevertheless, there is nothing very 'frozen' about the land: it is now almost completely occupied by low density housing, private schools, social clubs and industrial farming of flowers under plastic greenhouses. The result during the last 10 years was an uncontrolled growth of low density areas just outside the city.

Figure 2.21

The West Savannah, Industrial Agriculture and New Urbanisation, 2007

With an annual growth of 120,000 residents, Bogotá's future is uncertain. Bogotá is a cosmopolitan city that welcomes people of all regions, offering the best health services, education and employment opportunities. The demand for affordable housing is huge; progressive-development housing solutions need much more area than high density apartments in high rise buildings. The high-income population has entrenched themselves in apartment buildings and countryside condominiums (5%), the narrow strip of middle class people also zero in on high-density buildings (10%), while most low-income population prefers individual housing both for the financial advantage of progressive-development and the opportunity of in-house employment (home production rate is 85%).

With the city growing inevitably towards the savannah lands, a balance is required between urban growth and ecological conservation. It is not a reasonable option to lock in the city and separately maintain the countryside and, it would be impractical to conserve large plots of land currently used for agriculture. On the other hand, the urban sprawl isn't a desirable situation either, be it condominiums for the rich residents or sub-normal neighbourhoods for low-income residents. What is required is a strong protection of flood plains and the forested mountains. Hence, the builders of the city and the protectors of nature must work together to create a dense but friendly city for its inhabitants, with parks, rivers, wet lands, social and sports facilities and well laid out roads and streets for mobility. Equally important is the protection of areas with ecological value and reservoir type areas for periodic flooding (which has become more intense today due to climate change). The bitter debate marked by intransigence and lack of communication between the actors is self defeating and comes in the way of formulating a balanced plan. Meanwhile, the city grows and grows and grows—without guidance, without direction—just as it has done for the past 50 years.

3 Challenges and Strategies for China's Next Stage of Urban Development

Researches and Practices in Shanghai and Huangyuan

Yue Wu

Introduction

The speed and the massive scale of China's urban construction over the past 30 years have led to an equally rapid economic growth, greatly improving the city dweller's living conditions. It has truly been a great achievement, but this pattern of development has led to new challenges. Today, questions are being raised as to: Why do all the new cities look the same? Why do we no longer have the intimate urban charm that we enjoyed in the past and the unique cultural identity that each of us would be otherwise proud of?

Thus, should there be a shift from the current focus on mass-production for the next phase of China's urban development, caring more about the unique conditions and demands of each city, as also a focus on "small projects" in poor areas?

Two cases, Shanghai and Huangyuan, from the country's most developed coast area and the least developed inner land are presented here to illustrate our thinking on this alternative way, achieved through research and activities we've carried out in the past eight years.

Bigness and Rapidity: The Prevailing Approach for China's Urban Development

The primary strategy during the last phase of urban development was to prioritise the physical side of development with less emphasis on cultural identity and other finer aspects. This was a reasonable move at the time because of the pressure for rapid economic development and the explosive nation-wide urbanisation. The following statistics demonstrate the effect and the extent of this approach.

In the 30 years of reform and opening up of China, with rapid economic growth, China has also experienced the fastest and greatest urbanisation movement ever seen in human history. The urban population rose from 19 per cent of the total population in 1980 to 50 per cent in 2010 (Figure 3.2), with numbers rising from 191 million people to 670 million people—a figure 3.5 times greater than that of 30 years ago. This is a net increase of 479 million people (Figure 3.1), more than 1.5 times the total population of the United States.

Figure 3.1

Growth of Urban Population in China

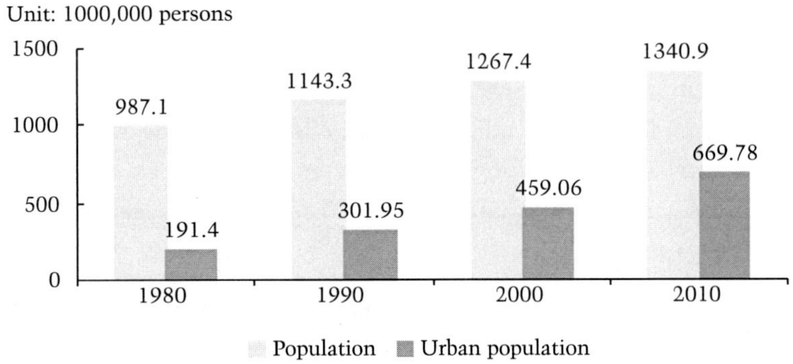

Source: *China Statistical Yearbook 2011.*

Figure 3.2

Proportion of Urban Population, 1980-2010

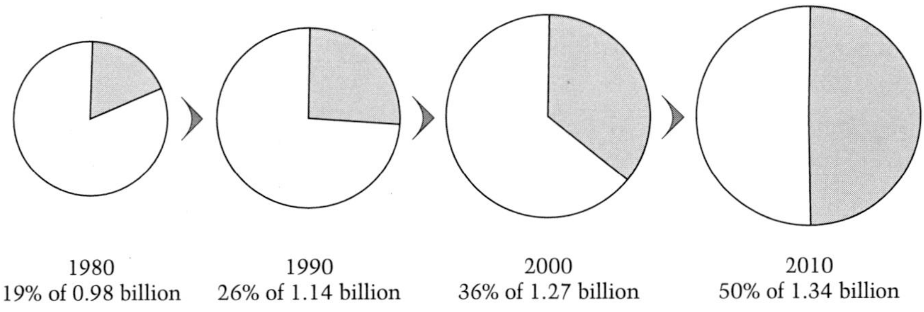

The massive scale of the construction work that came with it, included the renovation of old cities and the construction of new urban areas—particularly the construction of many industrial and technological facilities which was a necessary part of economic growth. As a result, the built urban area expanded rapidly nationwide and reached 40,058 km^2 by 2010, a number 5 times greater than the 8,842 km^2 area in 1984 (Figure 3.6). However, this has not happened evenly across the country, and coastal regions have experienced a concentrated growth of cities (Figure 3.3).

As the key part of this mega urban construction movement, residential development was certainly the most significant achievement providing urbanites with rapid improvements of living conditions. Per capita living area of China in 1980 was merely 7.2 m^2; it increased by four times to become 31.6 m^2 by 2010 (Figure 3.4).

Figure 3.3

Geographic Distribution of Cities in China

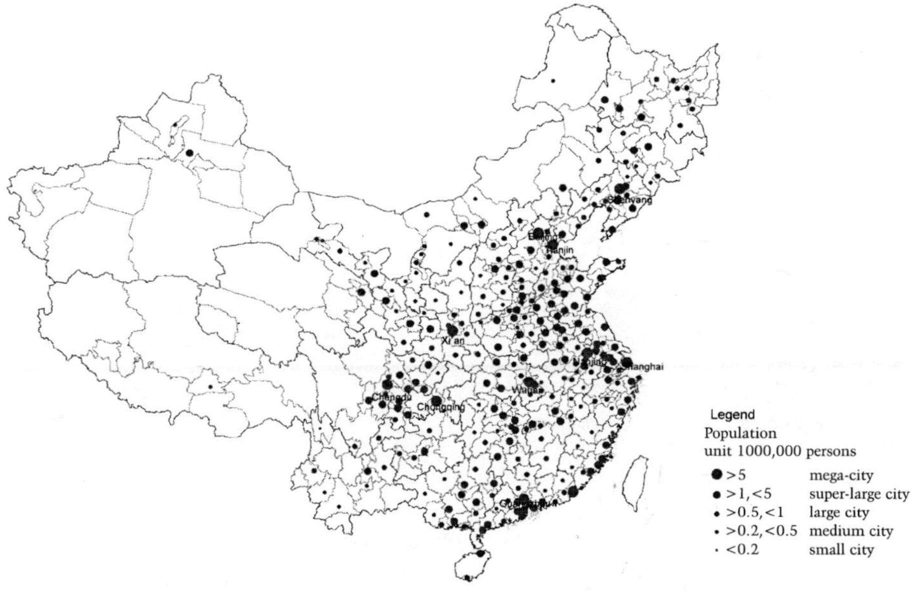

China City Population Top 10 unit: 1000,000 persons

Chongqing	Shanghai	Beijing	Tianjin	Guangzhou	Xi'an	Nanjing	Chengdu	Wuhan	Shenyang
15.43	13.32	11.75	8.03	6.55	5.62	5.46	5.21	5.15	5.12

Source: Yue Wu, Design Future Studio (Shanghai).

Figure 3.4

Per Capita Housing Area of Urban Residents of China

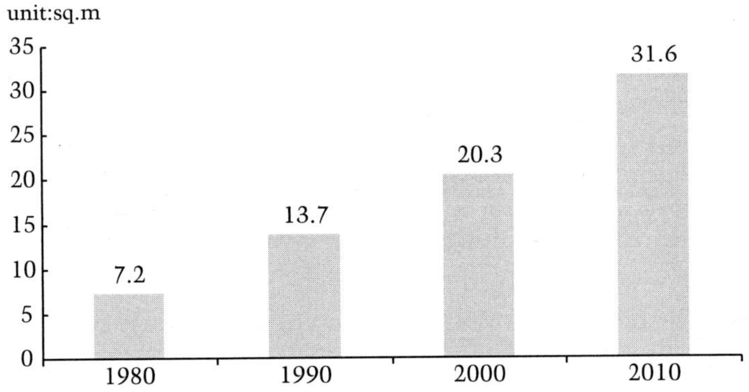

Source: *China Statistical Yearbook 2011.*

Figure 3.5

Motor Vehicle Production of China

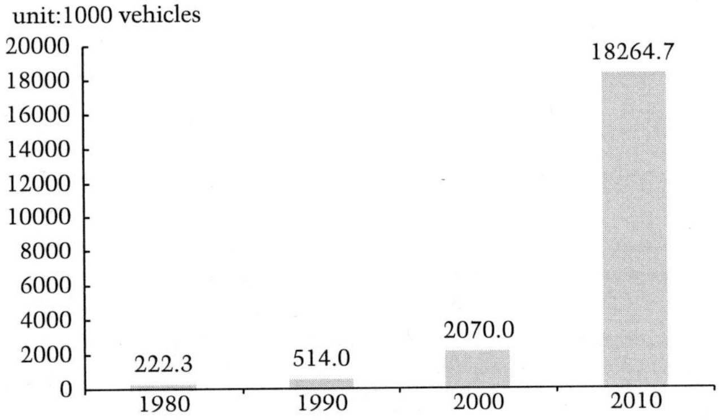

Source: *China Statistical Yearbook 2011.*

Admittedly, world events such as the Beijing Olympics and the Shanghai World Expo further stimulated the rapid development of cities across China. In host cities, opportunities were seized to boost infrastructure and meet the long-term needs of the city. For instance, Shanghai had its first subway line in 1995 and by 2010, the city had added 10 additional subways and light rail lines with 290 subway stations. With

Figure 3.6

Built Urban Area of China

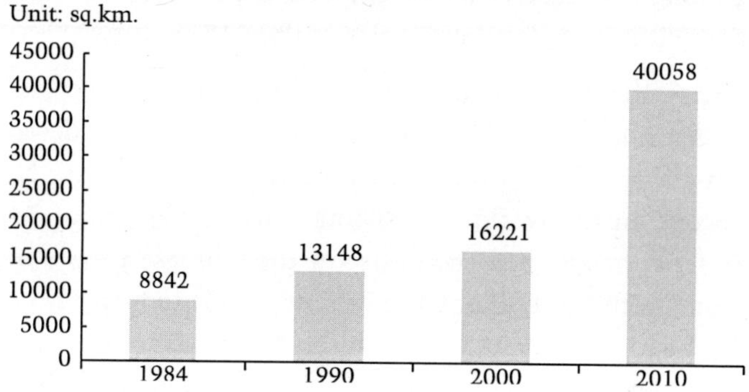

Source: *China Statistical Yearbook 2011.*

Figure 3.7

Length of Expressway (Total Route) of China

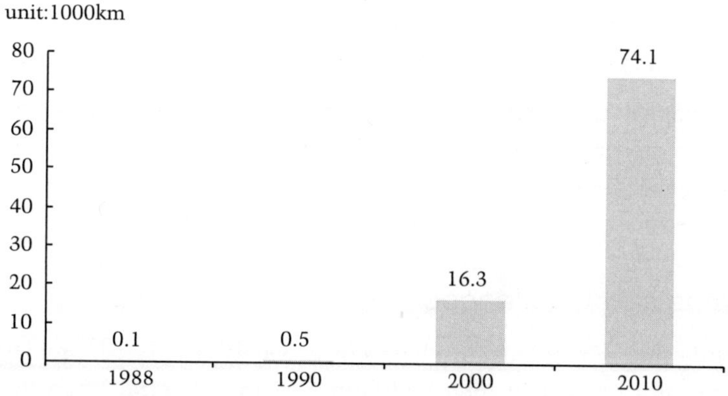

Source: *China Statistical Yearbook 2011.*

an operating mileage of 420 km, Shanghai is now ranked as the world number one in this respect.

Meanwhile, the physical image of Chinese cities underwent a fundamental change, and the world's most iconic buildings began to pop up in the major cities of China. As an example of the scale and speed of these changes, Shanghai saw its first post-concession-era high-rise building built in 1980, and it has now moved ahead of New York as home to the greatest number of high-rise buildings in the world. The Lujiazui financial district in Pudong along the East coast of the Huangpu River has undoubtedly made Chinese cities the global exemplar of the 21st century.

Along with the rapid urban growth, China has also been focusing its attention on national level infrastructure upgrades for over a decade now. In 1988, the total length of highways in China was mere 100 km. Now China is ranked second in the world with a total highway length of 74,100 km. (Figure 3.7). This has fuelled the desire of the Chinese people to buy cars and has promoted the growth of China's automobile industry from virtually nothing to what it is today. The increase of manufactured automobiles from 220,000 vehicles in 1980 to 18.27 million vehicles (Figure 3.5) in 2010 has made China the world's top car producing nation. In turn, this has impacted unexpectedly on the infrastructure of cities and pattern of development by ushering in an "age of automobiles". City traffic bore the brunt of this new development, with Shanghai being affected less than the notoriously congested Beijing. In turn, this gave rise to a corresponding form of urban sprawl and sub-urbanisation.

Indeed, all those efforts mentioned above have effectively provided support for the rapid economic growth and massive scale of urbanisation, and also gave birth to the popular image of China's pattern of urban development.

Problems and Challenges

While this miraculous development is widely celebrated, problems and challenges arose to which mere mathematics and material images couldn't provide solutions. Although this rapid pattern of development has greatly benefited China, it has also brought about increasingly visible problems and side effects. Among these problems, the following cultural observations are of particular concern.

Homogenisation of New Cities

The rapid mode of development has led to the construction of many "average cities" with no cultural identity or special characteristics. All of them have been built identically, making it difficult to distinguish one from the other. This problem also exists within a city. All residential districts are identical because majority of them being built en masse by the government or developers. Moreover the uniform and mandatory planning regulations of China, such as the requirement that every home must have equally adequate sunlight, has given rise to the typical residential pattern: all buildings run parallel facing south and all of them are equidistant from each other. A decent modernism ideology has been turned into a cultural nightmare.

Erasing Memories of the City

What happened to the cities that many of us remember as our sweet hometown? Admittedly, many were severely damaged during the initial stages of the rapid development. Old cities unfortunately were regarded as a symbol of the old times—unclean, narrow roads and certainly not modern. And so, not only were the buildings demolished but also the fine grain of street fabric was replaced by large street blocks. Today, people are beginning to wake-up and trying to stop or at least reduce this destruction of the world full of old charm and nostalgia—the soul of any country's cultural heritage. In many of the cases I faced in different cities, the challenge was no longer the issue of preservation, but rather re-building of our home as we remembered them.

The Loss of Cultural Identities

Probably due to the hunger for the cultural identity many cities today are in search of a "cultural signature" of its own. For example, a "Tang Dynasty" reconstruction movement is taking place in the famous historic city of Xi'an. The basic nature of this movement involves replacing the real traces of history with uniform fake antiques of Tang Dynasty style through mass production—a vain attempt to rebuild the past glory of the city.

In a rather different move, Shanghai launched a "One City Nine Towns" programme 10 years ago, which involved the construction of European towns on the outskirts of Shanghai, more as an expression of its open attitude. Among these towns, 'Thames Town' went to the extreme. Not only are the old British style houses faithfully replicated, but also the factories from the industrial revolution. These buildings are obviously different to those built during the concession era, because the latter are true parts of history while the former, a "theme park" built with real money have become a favourite haunt for wedding photography studios. Life gave this kind of approach the best footnote.

It is due to the lack of cultural confidence and the awareness of history's consistency that compels new cities to copy such themes blindly. An example of this is the once widely popular use of Western European architecture terminology in Chinese cities. Similarly, other motifs, such as circular shapes, because they were once considered to be modern and beautiful, are more likely selected by the visualisers. As a result, a large number of circular plazas have been produced indiscriminately across the country. All these cities are competing with each other, trying to be the best, but all they manage to do is to create another average, boring scenario.

Sub-urbanisation and Overly Large Scale

Urban sprawl phenomenon occurred in the West decades ago. Now, almost parallel to its urbanisation movement, China also experienced similar process of sub-urbanisation. The sudden coming of the urban sprawl and the age of automobiles pushed the sub-urban pattern into the heart of urban areas. As indicated by the studies on the newly developed urban areas of Shanghai, Super-block, Gated communities, lack of quality street life, etc. are among the most notable problems. The city is now more like a super sized cold machine rather than a warm space for human beings.

The problems China faces in urban development are actually no different from those faced by the rest of the urbanising world. Nevertheless, they do reflect the special circumstances of China as an emerging, developing country. In this regard, China has become particularly typical because of the speed and intensity with which the changes have occurred.

How can we pursue a "humane" policy for the development of a modern city, without losing out on the advantages of functional efficiency and technological advancements? And how can we create culturally distinctive cities that would be cherished as the collective cultural wealth of all humankind in the era of globalisation?

Figure 3.8

Comparative Locations of Shanghai and Huangyuan in the Context of China's Urbanisation

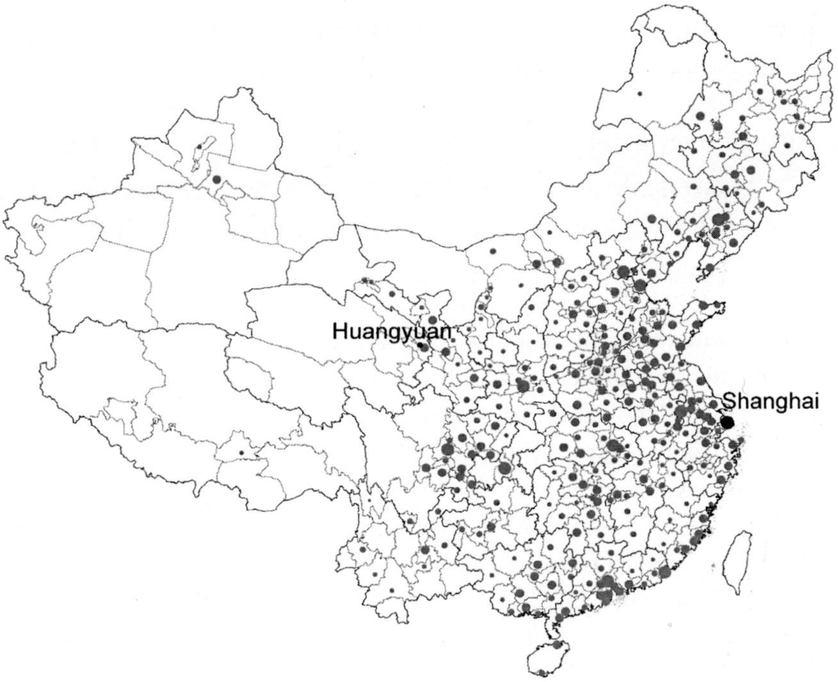

Source: Yue Wu; Design Future Studio (Shanghai).

Research and Practice

Shanghai Case: Repairing and Revitalisation of the Newly Built Urban Area

As an icon for nation's reform, Shanghai Pudong has taken the lead in the urbanisation movement in China (Figure 3.8).

After receiving my Doctor of Design degree from Harvard University in 2002, I was chosen, in a world-wide recruitment process, as the Chief Planner for Shanghai New Area for a three-year term. This was the first time that China set up a senior independent position parallel to the regular planning system to provide professional advice to the governmental decision-maker. The cases presented here are among those works I did in this position and in the Design Future Studio afterwards.

My observations indicated that, although high-end, the large-scale new buildings that had been constructed—the Huamu Cultural and Administrative Centre as a whole—still lacked key capacity to be a true urban magnetic pole. Therefore, the objective of the research set up was to repair and revitalise the newly-built district.

A surprising fact was revealed in a follow-up comparative research. At the People's Square in down town old Shanghai (which may seem 'imperfect' due to the constraints of the surrounding urban texture), all types of service and leisure facilities were accessible and that too within five minutes walking distance. But if you went to the seemingly 'perfect,' completely-new Century Plaza in Pudong, you wouldn't be able to find any basic services such as coffee shops or restaurants even if you walked for half an hour, however beautiful it may look from the sky. On the other hand, high-end community like Lianyang residential district shows off a 300-400 metre super block, but it is all fenced in with no shops or restaurants permitted along the gated wall. This kind of scale was not only far larger than that of New York (4 times the area) or Boston City Centre (9 times the area), but was also bigger than that of old Shanghai (8.4 times the area). Therefore, it was neither a Chinese nor a Western urban model: it was in fact a sub-urban model that had been wrongly applied in the heart of an urban area. In summing up our urban diagnosis, the following conclusions were made: (a) lack of urban services; (b) lack of quality 'street life'; (c) too large a block and; (d) a gated community.

A repairing and a design re-vitalisation programme was conducted, which mainly focused on increasing the mixed use of a variety of urban services. Furthermore, in terms of the physical space, city blocks were divided up to a finer grain urban fabric to make them suitable for pedestrians. Community fence walls were replaced with shopping strips, certainly a more inviting walking space for pedestrians. The specific aim of the design was to form an integrated, attractive urban centre, where it was possible to 'sight-see, stroll, sit, eat, and live.'

Following up the above overarching strategy, the renovation of Haitong Street of the same area was an in-depth effort to concretise the general idea into a real world spatial language and physical form.

Haitong Road area is a newly-urbanised locality with its residential buildings only about 15 years old and situated at the south-end of the central district of Huamu. While the area typifies the kind of residential model now found in every Chinese city, with all identical buildings set up in parallel rows, the street itself, formed by the shoulders of residential buildings and walls, apparently lack the necessary services, as also a pedestrian friendly accessible edge definition, such as shops.

Keeping in mind that the street would not see much traffic, it was built to serve as a pedestrian street on an intimate scale that not only provides all the urban services for local residents, but also serves as a draw for tourists. Contrary to the norm, there were no attempts at relocation of local residents nor a demolition of any existing building.

Function wise, taking into consideration the tradition of extremely lively living style of the local community, an electricity substation was resculpted into two dancing stages and activity plazas. Furthermore, a highly varied pedestrian shopping strip was created which included special restaurants, tourist shops, cinemas, and flower markets to cater for the large number of tourists visiting the Century Park.

In terms of physical space pattern, an in-depth research was carried out on the scale of Shanghai's traditional street, which later served as the key reference for the space design. First, the monotony of the original straight-line layout was broken up with slanting, broken lines, with several squares added in. The width of the pathways was reduced, and low-rise commercial buildings were built to create a space that was on a scale suitable to pedestrians. Here, the local culture and street life tradition were carefully integrated into up-to-date city service on a modern format (Figures 3.9-3.10).

The general proposal on the Huamu Cultural and Administrative Centre was largely accepted by the government, and significant advances have been made for reshaping relevant zones since then. However, due to complexity of the planning procedure, the renovation of Haitong Road was set aside after being revised many times. Several years later, however, similar but more evolved ideas finally were brought to fruition and tested in a tiny city, thousands of kilometres away in the west plateau of China.

Figure 3.9

Haitong Road, Bird's Eye View

Before

After

Figure 3.10

Haitong Road, The Entrance

Before

After

The Huangyuan Case: Re-formation of Local Culture Identity of a City Located in a Poverty-stricken Region

This project, which stretched over five years and encompassed architectural design, landscape design, urban design, old town renovation, and master plan, originated from a lecture that I gave to the leaders of Qinghai, a province in the north-west plateau of China. After the speech, the head of Huangyuan county, one of the poorest county in the nation, told me that he really liked my ideas, but the county was too poor to go in for any big projects; he then asked me whether I would be willing to design public lavatories for a passing highway. What concerned me was what I had already seen in the provincial capital of Xining, where the trends of coastal cities such as Shanghai, for example, rounded shape, brightly-coloured tops of buildings, etc., had been indiscriminately replicated—despite the fact that this was a region with an entirely different climate and culture. As a result, the leader's offer captured my imagination, and I accepted the invitation.

First, what impressed me was the history of the city, which lies at the confluence of Han and Tibetan cultures. Situated 2,600 metres above sea level, this ancient city with a population of just 40,000, tiny by Chinese standards, was established 2,000 years ago during the Han Dynasty, and at the time was a key stop along the well-known South Silk Road. The city walls were demolished during the 1950s, but the ancient town's architectural past can still be seen in the typical local materials that had been used, such as raw soil, pebbles, and grey bricks during the Qing Dynasty. Outside the city are also the remains of beacon towers of ancient conflicts, which imbue the area with a tranquil and contemplative atmosphere.

Secondly, I was also concerned over the current condition of the place. As one of the country's most poverty-stricken counties, Huangyuan could in no way come up with the funds needed to improve its basic public services and give the place an appearance of a modern city, in stark contrast to the booming construction business in the coastal regions. Here, the main pillar of the economy was the polluting ferrosilicon smelting industry.

Today, most areas of the Huangyuan town display a monotonous identical six storey buildings running in a parallel row, as in other such cities. Therefore, the task here was to recreate rather than preserve a unique city with cultural characteristics. The challenge lay in working out how, despite the financial straits, make urban construction play a substantive role in helping the local population pursue sustainable development, in terms of economics, environmental concerns, social equity and cultural identity, rather than just build another 'average' city.

Thus, the public lavatories project was expanded to the 'Huangyuan Yi-Zhan', an ancient Chinese name for 'Courier station' used by merchants during old times. Subsequently, a youth hostel was incorporated into the plan, as well as a restaurant showcasing the peculiarities of the local cuisine and a museum telling the story of the area's long history. The initial idea was to attract even a small segment of the 2 million tourists that travel every year on the expressway that linked the provincial capital and the famous scenic spot, Qinghai Lake, the largest salt lake in China. There would then be an opportunity for Huangyuan to develop its tourist potential which would in the long-term, guide the region away from its highly-polluting secondary industry towards a tertiary industry. Serving both as a cultural complex and a 'living advertisement', this small project could ultimately play an important role in re-orientating the city's direction of development.

In addition to reasonable functionality, what was required was that its new form must display the city's unique local characteristics. After long deliberation, however, designs with shallow eye-catching features like tall buildings or bright colours were finally abandoned in favour of using low-rise building and common local materials, such as raw earth and pebbles etc., which would blend into the traditional local context (Figures 3.11 and 3.12). How to use the language of modern design to express the characteristics of the local culture was a major challenge. A greater problem was the fact that following completion of the design, the project was suspended for more than two years due to the lack of funds. During this process, I was truly impressed by the determination of local leaders. Despite the difficulties involved, they staunchly supported the proposal. At last, after two long years of waiting, they were finally able to convince the last investor of the advantages of the design. Touched by their dedication, we continued to get more and more involved with the project and worked out the construction documents, interior design, landscape design, and sculpture design. Now, five years later, this project is finally nearing

Figure 3.11

Huangyuan Yi-zhan Architecture

Figure 3.12

Huangyuan Yi-zhan Landscape

Figure 3.13

Huangyuan Yi-zhan at the Gate of the City

completion (Figure 3.13). In China, for a project under 6,000 square metres to proceed at such a slow pace, lasting for 5 years, is unimaginable—but I believe it has been worth it. Quality takes time.

During the time when the 'Huangyuan Yi-zhan' was suspended, the local government invited me to modify the facade of three of their office buildings, which finally gave birth to the Huangyuan Public Square and Ecological Park.

After reviewing the original proposals, I boldly proposed that we, instead of just modifying the facade, should go in for totally re-designing the buildings and even revise the plans.

Again, I had taken into consideration the persistently difficult financial situation of local government in regard of urban improvement. I believed that the construction of the three governmental projects—the Forestry Bureau, the Administrative School, and the Tobacco Company (which had acquired funds from higher government organs)—could provide an important opportunity to improve the public amenities in Huangyuan and, hence exhibit its unique cultural qualities.

These three projects are located on the scenic bank of the Huangshui River, which lies outside the south of the city.[1] The original design was made up of three closed courtyards, in which there was the typical symmetrical layout of government buildings.

The strategies for the new design were, firstly, at planning and urban design level, to open up compound walls and lay out a water front area to create an integrated public open space, with a civic plaza and an open-style ecological park. The aim was to create one body with its northern sides housing all the administrative functions of the building and, on the southern side, setting up shops selling cultural goods, coffee shops, etc. on the first floor just next to the square. The Administrative School's lecture hall would open directly onto the square, becoming the 'Huangyuan Lecture Hall'. At the architectural level, the original modern form would be carefully carried out with unique local cultural characteristics, without copying the old Chinese nor the western styles. This was, indeed, the most difficult part of the task. It was expected that with the difference in design,

1. Huangyuan means 'the origin of the Huangshui River'.

an inviting 'urban lounge' together with a scenic 'city garden' would come into being as a kind of "by-product" of these three buildings. Together, the whole integrated project would become a unique cultural landmark that the city could be proud of, and radically transform the mediocre appearance of the city.

Therefore, the focus was on the following urban design imperatives: (1) making it compatible to the local texture by carefully controlling the height of the buildings and using of local materials (Figure 3.14); (2) creating a more human environment in which one could stroll around; (3) creating a sense of spontaneity and diversity to make it a more genuinely natural city, rather than simply a group of buildings built overnight and; (4) modern architectural language.

The landscape design that followed continued the same approach. The site was partially covered with natural woods and bushes, although it is very difficult for trees to grow in a harsh, cold and arid environment. During the architectural design, steps had been taken to leave the forest untouched and avoid cutting down trees. Landscape design, furthermore, was planned to display the beauty of this ecology whilst also protecting it: paths were raised above the ground, and all original plant species were retained. In addition, cheap used local stone materials were used for the paving, giving the roads a local ambience. Where Huangshui's riverbed was steep, two buffer dams were built with rubble, in order to create a level surface which people could touch, besides giving the place a natural sound effect of running water (Figure 3.15).

As a finishing touch, a sculpture with the words 'Origin of Huangshui River' was installed on a platform above the water (Figure 3.17).

What surprised me was that this bold proposal was not only accepted by the county leaders, but was also supported by all three units. An engineer was specially dispatched to Shanghai by the local Construction Bureau to train as a designer and within three years he became the main controller of construction quality.

Today, following completion of the project, this design, which people first thought of as unrealistic, has changed the people's impression that government buildings were by its very nature stern and foreboding. It received all round praise, with local residents all thronging the square, and

Figure 3.14

The Bell Tower

Figure 3.15

The Square along the Huangshui River

the park on the waterfront (Figure 3.16). It also received acclaim from the governor of the province, with the result that the Administrative School became an external base for the Central Administrative School.

Figure 3.16

Morning Exercise at the Newly-built Square

Together with the 'Huangyuan Yi-zhan' project, the construction of the 'administrative group, public centre, and ecological park' became an exemplar of master plan strategy, the aim being to promote tertiary industries through the historical and cultural tourism. As a matter of fact, back in 2007 this county had asked me chalk out the master plan, which was originally required to be completed in three months. After extensive discussion, they finally accepted my idea that three steps—macro level master plan, mid-scale urban design, and micro level architectural design—be carried out simultaneously under the guidance of the same overarching theory. By this process, the more urgent development pressure would be eased, giving enough time to think over the long term plan, so that there would be no need for any wasteful rush. Several months ago, after 4 years of research, we were able to deliver the master plan proposal. Thanks to the

Figure 3.17

Sculpture Marking the Origin of the Huangshui River

leading examples of Huangyuan Yi-zhan and the administrative centre, a new urban centre is proposed on the south of the city in order to relieve the pressure of development caused by the growing economy on an old town. The task we undertook for preserving and renovating the old town has been made possible (Figure 3.18).

Figure 3.18

Dream of the Old Home-town

Conclusion

Designing can make a big difference if the different needs and potentials of the various cities are given due importance. Cultural identity and urban memories needs to be cherished and nourished within the context of globalisation. The City, the habitat for mankind for thousands of years deserves genuine respect. Therefore, urban development should by no means be limited by the criteria of physical quantities and technology. Retaining and re-creating the richness and uniqueness of culture for each city is indeed a more challenging and far more meaningful mission for China's next stage of urban development.

4 Sustainable Cities and the Transport System

Hermann Knoflacher

The Solar Age of Urban Tradition

The precondition for urban structures and urban life has always been a surplus of production in agriculture. Cities were and are dependent on this fact. In 7,000 years of urban history, only few cities have enjoyed a long lasting life. Many cities, even capitals, have disappeared. Some were destroyed in wars with the population wiped out and the buildings razed to the ground. But environmental changes also forced people to desert their cities. Till the 19th century, cities could not grow beyond the limits of the environmental capacity available to the society. If this "ecological footprint" of the city was exceeded by overexploitation of natural and/or human resources, urban development collapsed. This ecological footprint had to be within the limits of the energy available to the society. The energy to operate the city was solar energy and the transport system during this period was also solar-based. Human beings used the energy of their bodies for walking and the energy of domesticated animals for other physical activities. Along the rivers and the coasts, wind energy was put to use.

The ancient Greeks and the Chinese learnt to balance the development of cities with the bearing capacity (ecological footprint) of its natural environment by controlling the population. If the number of people rose beyond this limit, a new settlement was established elsewhere. In Greece, the colonies were established along Mediterranean coast. China developed a hierarchy of district cities in accordance with the capacity of the agricultural environment—a system that was the result of a long tradition of wisdom and shrewd governments that worked within the natural borders of the local situation in a responsible manner. This was the situation till the 19th century.

The "Fossil Fuel" Period of Urban Development

Cheap and abundantly available external energy from coal, oil and gas for steamships, railways, car traffic and airplanes brought about a fundamental change in the process of urban development. New transport means allowed cities to grow much bigger, far beyond the environmental limits maintained earlier. Cities have always been dependent on the amount of primary products, resources and energy in their accessible environment, with only some precious and expensive products obtained from distant places. With the new transport modes, the resources of the whole globe became easily accessible. The cities began to absorb more and more people from the countryside and manpower was replaced by fossil fuel powered machines and use of fossil fuel based fertiliser became the norm in agriculture. The share of urban population passed 50 per cent of the global population in 2008 (United Nations, 2008). This is only possible as long as the whole globe can be used as the life supporting system for cities and cheap fossil fuel is available for all kinds of transport.

But the flipside is becoming visible more and more: increasing urbanisation means increasing energy demand. This fact has not been recognised by all the urban planners who dream of a further increase in the urban population. But this future is not only uncertain, but will also be very different when compared to the past 200 years. For years, available resources have been used well beyond the bearing capacity of the fertile ground, the atmosphere and the ecosystem, as the analysis report to the Club of Rome in 1972 and 30 years after have shown (Meadows *et al.*, 1972; 2004).

What will be the Future of Cities?

The only certainty about the future is that it is uncertain. Industrial output, life expectancy and available resources will decline when cheap and easy accessible fossil fuel will not be replaced by an equal amount by other energy sources. If urbanisation remains dependent on additional energy, as was the case in the past, de-urbanisation is inevitable. If this happens, the scenarios will change radically. Different ways of de-urbanisation are imaginable. By developing local energy sources (mainly solar or from underground) the cities' identity will change from 'Petropolis' to 'Ecopolis', producing not only their own energy, but also converting the existing city into a place of urban agriculture within the city borders. Does this mean "fertile ground" instead of dirty asphalt and concrete? Will this be enough to reduce the input of exergy, resources and decrease the waste-cum-pollution output to the required level? The other scenario would be a kind of "villagisation" or "ruralisation" of the society; this would not mean going back to the same old village structures, but into a future of energy efficient, sustainable local societies. Whether the dream of the technology driven "Technopolis" will become a reality under scarce commodity conditions, is a doubtful proposition.

In any case, the future will bring us a change of lifestyle away from individual motorisation to more intelligent transport solutions based on solar energy. This is only possible if the share of pedestrians and cyclists in the urban transport system is maximised.

Existing Structures will Determine Future Opportunities

Since more than half the world's population already lives in variously structured cities, their scenarios will also be very varied.

Cities with historical centres in the pre-fossil area can easily be adapted to future needs. If they slash down automobile traffic, the restructuring process will start immediately bringing people, business, culture and life back to these centres, as has been illustrated in many European cities during the last 40 years. It would also be a big advantage if the cities have not removed their rail-based public transport built in the 19th and the first quarter of the 20th century. These urban structures have a much brighter future than the big American or Australian agglomerations. If the cars are also removed from these parts of the urban regions, the population density will also increase and a variety of opportunities will be re-opened within a few years. Pedestrians and cyclists will become the mainstay in this kind of urban structures, along with a public transport system which would not be in conflict with these basic solar driven modes.

Some of India's wonderful historical centres like the Walled City in Delhi, the old parts of Ahmedabad, Mumbai, Chennai have a bright future if all motorised vehicles are removed from these precious urban structures and public money is used to upgrade the wonderful historical buildings, sanitation improved, information technology provided and public spaces are cleared of all kinds of individual motor vehicles.

Even large slum areas can become acceptable human habitations if they are not motor car dependent, like Nesa in Mexico City. If the public space is not extended for car use, the buildings renewed with the best sanitation standards, and one story huts are replaced by solid four to five storey buildings, the slums can soon be converted into urban structures fit for the future. This does not mean replicating the Hong Kong's deplorable urban structure, where the high-rise buildings are nothing more than suffocating mass-storage containers for people. Nevertheless, Hong Kong has in most of its districts a variety of opportunities like the Indian city centres.

The influence of the colonial urban style can be seen in roads that are so wide that it cuts across the urban structural entities separating functions and societies, which should be connected across the street. Filling this wide paved space with new houses and shops, will help convert these endangered structures into value added entities, especially when these structures are connected with far less disturbing public transport systems like buses or trams.

If city planning continues to be oriented to broad motorable roads, it will add up to a lot of problems in the future. A huge amount of energy for car mobility is needed to serve these cancerous urban structures developed during the second half of the 20th century. Integration into a sustainable urban body will not be possible without fundamental structural change. These settlement structures will be given up by their residents or will have to be reshaped to form new, much denser urban sub-centres, which would have to be, as far as possible, self sufficient in energy production as well as food supply, business, etc.

To start and support this healing process of the car addicted society of the 20th century, the right measures have to be implemented.

Reshaping Parking Organisation: Reshaping the City

The individual optimisation of housing and parking was the cause of the urban problems of today, creating congestion and urban sprawl on the one hand, and on the other, concentration of shopping opportunities in shopping centres was not related anymore to the urban area, as also concentration of work opportunities, etc. These individually optimised structures are based on heavy public support and will be a burden in the future. Car ownership went hand in hand with loss of local workshops, disintegration of the human society, loss of security in the public space and the loss of life space for children. In an unwanted collateral effect, congestion increased, public transport became scarce and the municipalities came to face unsolvable financial problems. Traffic flow treatment deals only with the symptom and not the disease the cities are suffering from. If we ask where the cars are coming from, we get the right answer: all cars are coming from parking lots and their destination is also in parking lots! It is the dominant parking regulation which causes these problems. The treatment will be successful only if the causes are treated.

> To develop a sustainable city it is necessary to reorganise parking from the individual garage to common garages surrounded by a car-free pedestrianised urban environment.
>
> — Hermann Knoflacher

In any case, be it in historical, colonial or the agglomeration centres where the urban density is above 150 inhabitants per hectare, this turn around measure will bring back all the shops for daily needs and majority of working opportunities, besides reviving cultural and leisure activities. A car free environment is an imperative for revitalising the social network of urban life.

Cars have to be stored in common garages. If the distance of these common garages is about 1,000 metres, the average walking distance toward these garages is not more than 250 metres. A public transport system with stops at every 500 metres can substitute car trips in a much more convenient way for distances that are too long for pedestrians or cyclists. Once these conditions are met, the demand for car traffic will be reduced to about three per cent of today's volume.

A Tender Measure, an Overwhelming Effect

Walking in a car-free, healthy and beautiful environment for over two or three hundred metres is fun compared to trudging along on a narrow, polluted, noisy and dangerous sidewalk. This happy scenario can be created only when the entire society agrees to enforce a common parking regulation to get rid of the existing cancerous individual parking system. It will also mean cheaper parking and greater security as in the past. These measures will also help re-knit the close social network of shops and jobs, instead of cutting it up into pieces with wide carriageways. It will also mean decentralisation of economy by bringing in a variety of small local shops and bring employment back to the locality where people live. The social and environmental effects will be tremendous and a great amount of energy will be saved. The energy demand for mobility is decreased by over 90%, including the energy demand for public transport. The employment effect for reshaping the agglomeration built for cars into a human scale city will be enormous, as will be the effects on the quality of life, stimulating cultural and social life, arousing hope of a far better future for the society.

References

Knoflacher, H. (1996). "Zur Harmonie von Stadt und Verkehr", *Freiheit vom Zwang zum Autofahren* 2. verbesserte und erweiterte Auflage. Böhlau Verlag Wien – Köln - Weimar.

———. (2005). *Freedom from Car Dependency: The Precondition for Liveable Cities.* Vortrag beim Auto-Free New York Meeting, New York.

———. (2007). *Grundlagen der Verkehrs-und Siedlungsplanung: Verkehrsplanung.* Böhlau Verlag Wien – Köln - Weimar.

———. (2009). *Virus Auto.* Die Geschichte einer Zerstörung. Verlag Carl Ueberreuter, Wien.

Knoflacher, H., J.M. Schopf, M. Mailer und P. Pfaffenbichler (1998). EMRECU (Effects of Realised Measures on the Reduction of Energy Consumption in Urban Transport) Auswirkungen realisierter Verkehrsmaßnahmen auf die Reduktion des Energieverbrauchs im städtischen Verkehr. Forschungsprojekt der Europäischen Kommission, Generaldirektion XVII. Energie, durchgeführt vom Institut für Verkehrsplanung und Verkehrstechnik der Technischen Universität Wien.

Meadows, Donella, J. Randers and D. Meadows (1972). *Limits to Growth.* New York: Universe Books.

Meadows, Donella, J. Randers and D. Meadows (2004). *Limits to Growth: The Thirty Year Update.* White River Junction, VT: Chelsea Green Publishing Co.

United Nations (2008). "Executive Summary", *World Urbanisation Prospects—The 2007 Revision.*

5 Expanding Transport Networks for Urban and Regional Development

A Study of the National Capital Region in India

Rumi Aijaz

Introduction: The Regional Development Context

Governments of many countries in the world are exploring ways to address the growing imbalances in development. The phenomenon is noteworthy in both developed and developing countries, where the level of development varies significantly from place to place within a country. Thus, some places (such as large cities and adjoining areas) experience progressive growth, while remotely located smaller urban and rural settlements portray a dismal picture, often characterised by poor living conditions, acute poverty, infrastructure and service deficiencies, and out-migration.

Quite often, inequalities among settlements are overcome by adopting a regional planning and development approach. This is basically spatial development planning oriented to future for a large area (i.e., a region[1]) to ensure optimal utilisation of space and optimal distribution pattern of human activities. The approach provides for controlled location of facilities and activities (markets, infrastructure, industries, transport networks, residential and work places, etc.) in a coordinated style. It is widely agreed

1. There are many definitions of a region. Geographers speak of a geographical region, agricultural specialists of an agricultural region, and urban planners of an urban region. A planning region is an area of the country composed of parts which, owing to their spatial proximity, interact and influence each other in the process of economic and social development. A region may be classified as: (i) formal region, which is an area having uniform or homogenous characteristics, e.g., natural resource region, agricultural region, etc.; and (ii) functional region, which is composed of heterogeneous units such as cities, towns and villages that are functionally related.

that in this manner, the natural, human and financial resources are optimally utilised, regional economy develops faster, and benefits of socio-economic development are equitably distributed among people within the region.

The improvement of transport links between places, as also the development and modernisation of transport infrastructure are important policy recommendations included in a regional plan document. The purpose is to facilitate flow of goods, people and information so that the population living in the region benefits from the measures. Following this approach, people can be brought into functional economic areas that offer more choices in terms of lifestyle, employment and investment opportunities, thereby leading to overall socio-economic progress. Besides, as demonstrated in this paper, the developed cities/urban places situated within the region benefit by way of reduced traffic congestion, travel time, emissions of carbon dioxide, etc.

The priority areas considered in a regional planning process vary depending on the regional characteristics. Table 5.1 provides information on regional development strategies in respect to select world regions. With regard to the transport sector, it is noted that the Sydney-Canberra Corridor Regional Strategy (Australia) recognises the need to further improve transport connections between the two cities, and to maintain strong internal connections between centres and towns (Figure 5.1; New South Wales Government, 2008). The Greater Tokyo Area Plan (Japan) lays emphasis on enhanced circular links within the Greater Tokyo Area through development of loop and arterial roads (Figure 5.2; Tokyo Metropolitan Government, 2006). The Regional Communications Plan for the Beijing, Tianjin and Hebei cluster (China) supports the implementation of inter-city railway based transportation, reconstruction of capital airport, and building of expressways (Eleventh Five Year Programme, 2006-2010). Similarly, the Spatial Development Framework for the Cape Town Metropolitan Area (South Africa) provides for strengthening of metropolitan nodes and activity corridors by developing an integrated transport system (Cape Metropolitan Council, 2001). The above-mentioned four examples are not unique and have been included in the paper for demonstration purpose. Similar regional planning practices are in use in many countries of the world.

Table 5.1

Regional Development Strategies

Country	*Region and Characteristics*	*Regional/Metropolitan Plan Components/Priority Areas*	*Transport Sector Strategy*
Australia	Sydney-Canberra Corridor Region Area: 25,000 sq. km. People: 137,000	Rural lands, primary industry, economic development & growth, regional transport, housing & settlement, natural environment, water & energy resources, cultural heritage	• Improve transport connections between Sydney & Canberra (upgrade rail line to remove slow sections) • Limit inappropriate development adjoining highways & rail lines • Development of passenger interchanges in all major regional centres & towns • Improve capacity of road, rail & bus services • Maintain & improve capacity of rail line for increased freight • Maintain strong internal conn-ections between centres & towns • Ensure appropriate access to centres
Japan	Greater Tokyo Area / Region (also called Tokyo Megalopolis Region) Area: 13,500 sq. km. People: 35 million +	Water & greenery, road network (3 loop roads), energy, disaster management, health and welfare, culture, tourism, industry, education, sports	• Strengthen airport functions • Strengthen port & harbour functions • Develop road networks (three loop roads) • Continuous grade-separated railway crossings for removal of 42 level crossings • Introduce & promote intelligent transport systems technology
China	Beijing, Tianjin and Hebei Metro-cluster Region Area: 185,000 sq. km. People: 74 million	Industry, communi-cation, energy exploration, inter-valley water diversion, commercialisation of sea water freshening, water resources & environment conservation	• Inter-city rail • Reconstruction of capital airport • Building of expressways • Oceanic shipping system
South Africa	Cape Town Metropolitan Area Area: 2,461 sq. km. People: 3.4 million	Land use, environment, transport & service infrastructure, economic development	• Expansion of existing facilities & development of new harbour/ airport facilities • New roads & railway lines to be routed so as not to cause damage to the environment • Metropolitan nodes, activity corridors to be made accessible by public transport

Source: Relevant plans (see reference section at the end of the article).

Figure 5.1

Sydney-Canberra Corridor showing Regional Transport Network Strategy

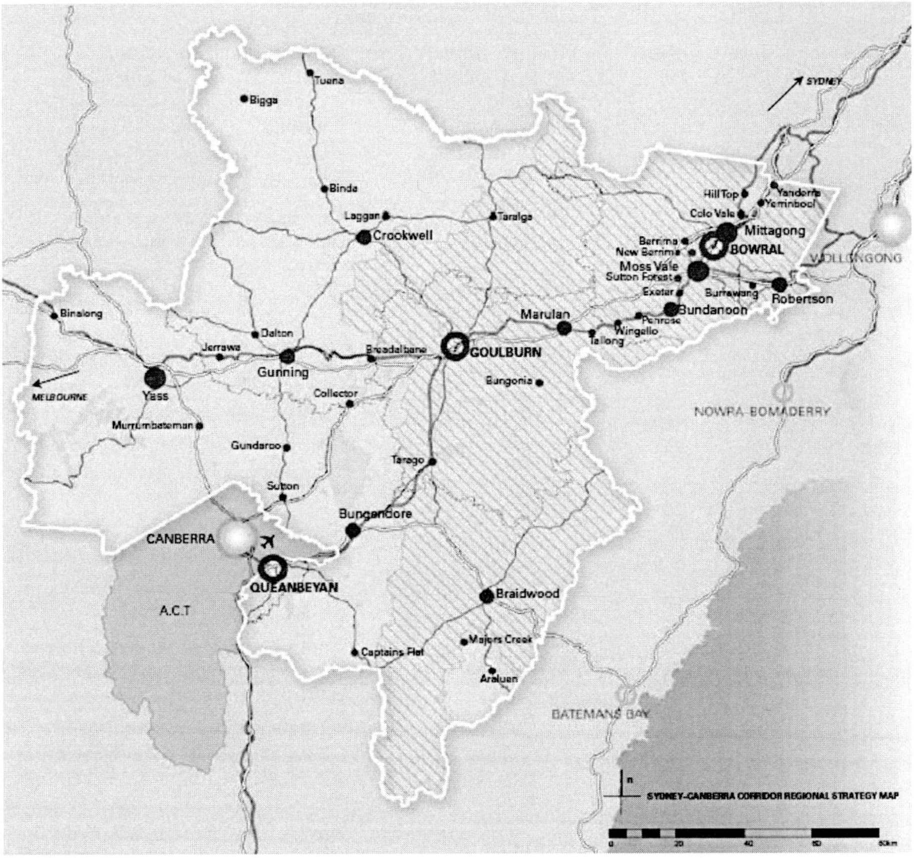

Ensuring equity in regional development, however, depends upon a number of factors, such as nature of governance policies and initiatives, regional and urban planning practices, ability of stakeholders at the national and lower levels, development priorities, quantum of funds available, financial allocations, manner in which funds are utilised, and the use of local natural and human resources. Thus, regional (including transport) planning measures implemented in different parts of the world have met with varying levels of success.

Figure 5.2

Development of Road Networks in the Greater Tokyo Area

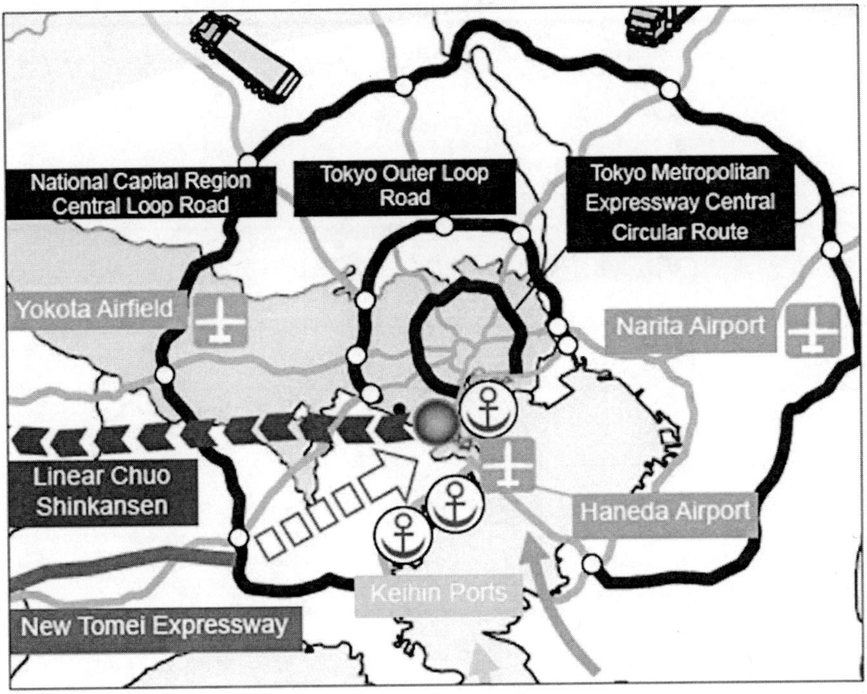

The Case Study: National Capital Region of India

In over-populated countries such as India having a predominantly rural base, there exist poor linkages between settlements. Generally, growth centres (i.e., cities and important towns) are well connected with each other by various transport modes and networks, but their connectivity with the adjoining rural hinterland as well as with small and medium towns is fairly weak or completely missing.

This problem is noticeable in the National Capital Region (NCR) of India. The region covers about 33,578 sq. km area and comprises the National Capital Territory (NCT) of Delhi[2] located in the centre of the

2. Demographic indicators for National Capital Territory of Delhi: population (16.75 million/36 % of NCR); area (1,483 sq. km./5% of NCR); decadal growth rate for 2001-2011 (20.96 %); literacy rate (86.34 %) [Census of India, 2011].

Figure 5.3

National Capital Region Constituent Areas

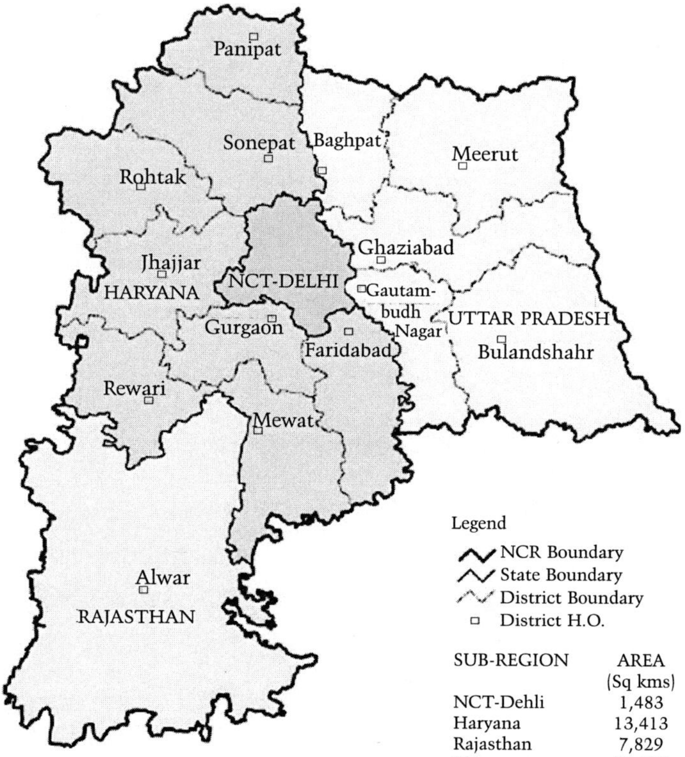

SUB-REGION	AREA (Sq kms)
NCT-Dehli	1,483
Haryana	13,413
Rajasthan	7,829
UP	10,853
Total	33,578

region, as well as some areas falling in the neighbouring States of Haryana,[3] Uttar Pradesh[4] and Rajasthan[5] (Figure 5.3). The total population of NCR was about 46.04 million in 2011, and is expected to reach 64 million by 2021. At the time of 2001 Census count, there were: 3 metropolitan/

3. Demographic indicators for Haryana sub-region of NCR: population (11.04 million/24 % of NCR); area (13,413 sq. km./40% of NCR); decadal growth rate for 2001-2011 (27.50%); literacy rate (72.28%) [Census of India, 2011].

4. Demographic indicators for Uttar Pradesh sub-region of NCR: population (14.58 million/32% of NCR); area (10,853 sq. km./32% of NCR); decadal growth rate for 2001-2011 (27.24%); literacy rate (77.14%) [Census of India, 2011].

5. Demographic indicators for Rajasthan sub-region of NCR: population (3.67 million/8% of NCR); area (7,829 sq. km./23% of NCR); decadal growth rate for 2001-2011 (22.75%); literacy rate (71.68%) [Census of India, 2011].

million plus cities, 17 class-one cities (population of 100,000+), 91 towns, and 7,528 rural settlements in NCR.[6] The maximum distance between settlements situated in the region is about 200 to 250 kms.

NCR is a functional region. Owing to spatial proximity to Delhi, there is enormous flow of people, goods, information and investment. The places are interdependent on each other. The region is delineated for promoting balanced and harmonised development. An appraisal of select socio-economic characteristics and development indicators reveals significant regional as well as rural-urban disparities in population distribution and decadal growth rates, literacy rates, wages, employment, living conditions, access to basic infrastructure and services, etc. Furthermore, due to a high number of daily/permanent migrants[7] and the subsequent increase in population size,[8] Delhi is experiencing a number of problems, such as traffic congestion because of high motor vehicle growth,[9] slow travel speed, road accidents, fuel wastage and the resultant economic loss to commuters due to traffic congestion, environmental pollution, pressure on infrastructure and services, growth of slums and illegal construction, etc.

Policies and Strategies for Development of Regional Transport Sector in NCR

The Regional Development Plan 2021[10] proposes policy measures for attaining the objectives of economic growth and balanced development, such

6. Data on number of rural and urban settlements in NCR for the year 2011 were not published at the time of writing the paper.
7. The total number of in-migrants in Delhi (from other states) increased from 1.54 million in 1991 to 2.17 million in 2001. The proportion of in-migrants has, however, declined over the years. Major influx of population was from Uttar Pradesh, Bihar, Haryana, Rajasthan and Punjab (Census of India, 2001).
8. While Delhi has observed a decline in population growth rates during 2001-2011 from 47% to 21%, the numbers are quite high: 13.85 million in 2001 and 16.75 million in 2011.
9. Number of motor vehicles in Delhi increased from about 3.03 million in 1997-98 to 5.63 million in 2007-08, registering a decennial growth rate of 85.53% (Economic Survey of Delhi, 2008-09). According to recent data (maintained by Transport Department of Delhi Government), the total number of registered vehicles as on 28th February 2011 was 6.84 million, of which 94% were private (car, jeep, motorcycle, scooter) and the remaining were commercial (auto rickshaw, taxi, bus, goods vehicle). The data further show that in Delhi there are more than 2 million cars and 4 million two-wheelers. It is estimated that more than 1,000 vehicles are registered in Delhi everyday.
10. Prepared by National Capital Region Planning Board.

as creation of employment opportunities, development of transportation networks and other basic infrastructure facilities, environment protection, etc. Financial assistance to state governments/implementing agencies is provided from a revolving fund.[11]

In order to improve accessibility and movement of goods and passengers within the region, the following objectives are identified:

- decongest Delhi roads, rail and rail terminals, by diverting the by-passable traffic from Delhi;
- construct road and rail linkages along the high-density routes, in and around Delhi and also in NCR;
- provide linkages amongst metro/regional urban settlements in the outlying areas of NCR;
- connect metro/regional centres with the capital city by an efficient and effective transport network for facilitating faster movement of traffic among such centres and Delhi;
- link the sub-regional centres with effective and efficient transport network for facilitating the faster movement of traffic among such centres and higher order settlements;
- directly link other urban nodes having maximum attracting and generating characteristics;
- improve connectivity and accessibility in the region through development of peripheral expressways and mass/regional rapid transit system;
- permit unrestricted movement of public transport (i.e., buses, taxis and auto-rickshaws) in NCR; and
- create a unified Metropolitan Transport Authority for NCR.

11. Funding sources are: Ministry of Urban Development; Government of National Capital Territory of Delhi; repayment of earlier loans; interest income on loans and other internal accruals; market borrowings; loan from multilateral/bilateral agencies such as ADB, DFID, KfW [a German government-owned development bank], UNDP, USAID, World Bank.

Regional Transport Network

Delhi occupies a central location in north India (Figure 5.4). For numerous reasons (including trade and commerce, employment, education, etc.), and for many years, it has been a destination point, as well as a major intersection for people who live in the nearby and far off Indian States of Jammu and Kashmir, Himachal Pradesh, Punjab, Haryana, Rajasthan, Uttarakhand, Uttar Pradesh, Bihar and Madhya Pradesh. The location of Delhi has, therefore, played a role in the evolution of the regional transport network.

Figure 5.4

North India

Roads display a radial pattern. The five National Highways (No. 1, 2, 8, 10 and 24) branch out in all directions from a common centre, i.e., Delhi. Carriageway varies between two and six lanes. This pattern results in heavy traffic congestion in various parts of Delhi. In the absence of alternative/by-pass routes, many vehicles enter/cut across Delhi from different directions/states to reach other destinations. At other places in the region, single/double lane State Highways and local roads connect settlements situated in the region.[12]

The road network profile in the NCR is gradually changing.[13] The Regional Transport Plan for 2021, formulated on the basis of studies on traffic and travel characteristics (such as volume of traffic, directional flow, pattern of vehicle movement) and travel and transport demand projections, provides for the implementation of following projects,[14] some of which are underway:

- upgradation/widening of National/State Highways and construction of new roads: development of a hierarchical network of primary, secondary and tertiary roads. Major towns around Delhi will be connected with each other by an Expressway. Primary roads will connect regional towns with Delhi. Secondary roads will connect small towns to larger towns and primary roads. Tertiary roads will connect rural/remote areas to sub-regional towns and secondary roads;

---

12. Ministry of Road Transport and Highways (MoRT&H) formulates and administers policies for road transport, national highways and transport research. It aims at increasing mobility and efficiency of road transport system in the country. National Highways Authority of India (NHAI) under MoRT&H is responsible for development, maintenance and management of national highways entrusted to it.

13. A major rural infrastructure development business plan formulated by the Indian government is Bharat Nirman [Building India]. The thrust is on upgradation of water supply, housing, telecommunication, information technology, roads, electrification and irrigation in villages. Under the program, a number of rural road projects (on new connectivity and up-gradation) have been implemented in different Indian States. The Indian governments' Ministry of Rural Development has also launched the Pradhan Mantri Gram Sadak Yojana [Prime Minister Rural Road Plan], a 100% centrally sponsored scheme to provide all-weather access to unconnected habitations.

14. The total investment requirement for plan implementation (including projects and related activities) is estimated to be Indian Rupees (INR) 191.41 billion at 2001 prices. As on May 20, 2011: 1 USD = 44.9 INR; 1 Euro = 64 INR; 1 GBP = 72.9 INR.

- conversion of Delhi-Gurgaon-Jaipur National Highway to eight lane toll Expressway on build-own-transfer (BOT) basis (work completed); and
- construction of orbital and other Expressways on BOT basis that would take traffic around Delhi rather than through it (work in progress).[15]

Like roads, rail network in the region is also radial comprising mostly broad gauge (5′6″) lines converging in Delhi.[16] At some places in Delhi, Goods Avoiding Lines (GAL) and Delhi Avoiding Lines (DAL) exist for bypassing congested railway stations and for providing a direct passage to other routes. In addition to long-distance trains connecting Delhi with major metropolitan cities of India, several sub-urban/regional shuttle trains (locally known as EMU/DMU trains)[17] also connect Delhi with many NCR towns. These trains move on the same rail network and are mainly used by persons coming to Delhi everyday for work.

For the development of rail network in the region, the Regional Transport Plan for 2021 provides for the following:

- regional rapid transit system to connect regional towns with each other and with Delhi;
- rail network to be extended to sub-regional centres;
- orbital rail corridor (parallel to the proposed peripheral road expressway) to connect radial rail corridor of Indian Railways at

15. Length of orbital expressway is about 240 kms and total project cost is ₹ 36.57 billion. The cost would be shared between Government of Delhi (50%), Haryana (25%) and Uttar Pradesh (25%). The construction work is awarded to a concessionaire. It is estimated that 78 per cent of vegetables and fruits, 49 per cent of fuel, 44 per cent of iron and steel, and 47 per cent of food grains traded in Delhi are destined for other Indian States. The five National Highways also bring inter-State goods vehicles into the city. Such traffic movements lead to major congestion in many areas. The orbital expressway is being developed to address such problems (*Economic Survey of Delhi*, 2008-09).

16. Indian Railways is the premier organisation for the development and management of rail network and infrastructure.

17. EMU/DMU—Electric/Diesel Multiple Unit Trains. Some indicators: moving speed of various trains: 26 to 56 kms/hr.; distance of various railway stations from Delhi: 28 to 175 kms; number of stations/halts on different routes: 6 to 26; one-way travel time on different routes: 1 to 4 hrs; travel fare for different destinations: ₹ 4 to ₹ 26.

important towns in the region to bypass the regional rail traffic around Delhi;

- mass rapid transit system for Delhi and important regional towns; and
- regional rapid transit system and mass rapid transit system to have feeder rail/road services.

The proposed rail network plan is under implementation. Projects on laying of lines for connecting important settlements, electrification and construction of freight terminal are in progress. A project that has shown good progress is the Mass Rapid Transit System (MRTS)—a non-polluting[18] and efficient rail-based transport system.[19] The network was made operational in phases beginning of December 2002 and is expanding within the city of Delhi.[20] With a total length of about 190 kms, the Metro services have also reached three adjacent urban centres outside the Delhi territory, namely NOIDA[21] and Ghaziabad (in Uttar Pradesh) and Gurgaon (in Haryana). One more centre, namely Faridabad (in Haryana) would be connected by the year 2013. The project costs are shared between the Government of India, Delhi Government, Delhi Metro Rail Corporation, Japan International Cooperation Agency, and the participating State Government.

18. It is reported that the Delhi Metro Rail Corporation (DMRC) has earned ₹ 24 million from the sale of 82,000 certified emission reductions under the Carbon Credit Scheme by the Japan Finance Carbon Ltd. in 2008 and 2009.The agency plans to channel the funds generated by the sale back into its carbon credits programme, and in research and development of technology for reducing greenhouse emissions (The Times of India, 2011a).

19. A survey conducted upon completion of 100 months (December 2002 to March 2011) of operation of Delhi Metro reveals the following improvements: Number of trains: 6 to 160; Frequency: 15 min. to 2.5 min.; Number of trips: 70 to 2,400; Length of line: 8.5 kms. to 190 kms.; Number of employees: 1,000 to 8,000; Number of women drivers: 3 to 25; Total number of drivers: 20 to 800; Average rider ship: 82,179 to 1,416,420; Number of passengers on working days: 1.5 million (The Times of India, 2011b).

20. The Delhi Metro Rail Corporation (DMRC) is responsible for implementation and subsequent operation of Delhi MRTS. The DMRC was registered in 1995 and has equal equity participation from Government of India and Government of National Capital Territory of Delhi.

21. NOIDA stands for New Okhla Industrial Development Authority.

Regional Transport Problems

In the National Capital Region of India, a number of transport-related problems exist. These are briefly described below separately for the road and rail sector.

Road Sector

Most villages situated in the region are connected to State Highways by roads. However, the roads are of inferior quality, broken, dusty and are lanes without dividers. Their condition deteriorates during the rainy season, and travel speed reduces further. The mode of transport used by the rural population is mainly non-motorised, such as bullock cart, cycle. Some affluent rural people also use tractors, cars, jeeps and two-wheelers.

The urban centres display better road connectivity. However, most State/National Highways are of single lane and without dividers. There is considerable movement of vehicles on the highways and accidents are quite common. Some highways pass through small settlements due to absence of by-pass roads, and this leads to traffic congestion that last for hours. At some places, rail over-bridges do not exist and the vehicles sometimes halt for several hours until the train passes.

The volume of traffic is enormous especially on major (radial) corridors (i.e., National Highways) leading to Delhi from all directions. Due to high traffic volume, its management becomes difficult for the local regulatory authorities once the vehicles reach Delhi. The problem is aggravated by poor road infrastructure, especially non-functional traffic lights at a large number of intersections, lack of advanced information systems and neglect by the authorities in efficient traffic monitoring. Such conditions create congestion resulting in loss of time and resources.

Some national highways have been upgraded to expressways. Examples are Delhi-Gurgaon and Delhi-Noida expressways. The toll collection points on the highway experience frequent traffic jams during peak hours.[22] This

22. Data maintained at the Delhi-Gurgaon toll collection point reveals that about 200,000 passenger car units/vehicles cross every day. Between January 2008 and August 2010, DSC Ltd. (the project concessionaire) earned ₹ 3.81 billion from toll collection, while the National Highway of India has earned ₹ 0.20 billion as its share of toll revenue from the project.

is due to rapid increase in the volume of traffic and non-adherence of rules by road users. Many-a-times, cash payers enter into the lanes designated for tag users. Problems also occur due to lack of traffic segregation based on speed and size of the vehicle, poor enforcement of rules and penalty, insufficient use of available technology, and shortage of staff to monitor traffic as it approaches the toll collection point.

In the implementation of regional road projects, such as expansion of National Highway No. 8, acquisition of land has been a major issue. The land acquisition procedures and the process of transferring it to the development agencies are quite cumbersome. Some land is owned by private individuals/rural population and they are not satisfied with the compensation they get for their land. There have been some cases of violence and conflict and many issues are in the Judiciary.

In the implementation of the Eastern and Western Peripheral Expressway (an orbital road corridor being developed around Delhi), a number of problems are being experienced, such as payment issues between concessionaire and labour contractor, late approval of designs of railway over-bridges and grade separators, land acquisition, involvement of several project clearing agencies, pending litigations, etc. The decision to impose tolls has also caused a delay in the timely completion of the project. While Planning Commission is in favour of imposing a nominal toll, the Ministry of Road Transport and Highways holds the view that if toll is collected, people will not use such roads and the issue of traffic diversion will not be addressed.

An independent project, namely the Yamuna Expressway Project, conceived to reduce travel time between Delhi and Agra and to open up avenues for industrial and urban development in the region, is beset with obstacles. The farmers are agitating against acquisition of their lands since January 2011, and there have been numerous clashes with the police. Some are demanding higher compensation for sale of their lands. They have alleged that government buys at a low price and makes profit by selling their land at high price to private developers. Analysts say that the basic problem lies in the provisions of the Land Acquisition Act which do not provide for a clear-cut method of fair valuation of land values as per prevailing market rates. A related problem is the weak follow up on relocation and rehabilitation measures for the displaced land owners.

The alignment of corridors is mostly done through actual ground reconnaissance and surveys, instead of using satellite images and digital terrain models. In some instances, lands owned by farmers are acquired by altering the road alignment to protect properties of the rich and influential persons. This is an example of a deliberate deviation from the actual transport network plan. The use of advanced technology would bring about greater transparency and could help in dealing with the problem of favouritism and corruption.

Bus is used by a large number of common people to travel between places in the National Capital Region. Due to poor maintenance and out-dated buses, breakdowns commonly occur resulting in considerable wastage of time.

Rail Sector

The existing broad gauge rail lines are laid out in a radial manner with Delhi in the centre. Sub-urban and long-distance trains bring people from the neighbouring region to Delhi everyday for work. The moving speed of most trains is fairly slow and varies between 26 and 56 kms per hour. Trains often come to a halt several times on a particular route because rail tracks are occupied by other trains that are moving ahead slowly on the same route.

Many of the sub-urban trains are extremely over-crowded with a large number of people sitting on the roof top. This is due to the dearth of trains on the congested routes. Furthermore, some routes are not electrified and there is enormous environmental and noise pollution.

Rapid rail services are not available to the regional population. The Delhi Metro, a modern rapid rail service, is a recent entry that connects only three adjoining towns of NOIDA, Gurgaon and Ghaziabad, and its expansion in the region is occurring at a slow pace.

Conclusion

Daily movement of people within a region is a normal activity witnessed all over the world. People are engaged in various professions for which they travel from one place to another within the rural/urban settlement limits or in the adjoining region. Besides work, there are numerous other reasons for which people travel every day. Thus, availability of a good road and rail (transport) network along with efficient public transport facilities and services is a basic requirement of the local population that would allow them to pursue various activities in a well-organised manner.

The study on transport networks in the National Capital Region of India presented in this paper shows that a substantial amount of work remains to be done for improving mobility in the region. There exists a good network of roads but the quality of roads, road infrastructure and services, and public transport vehicles are in a miserable condition. Similarly, sub-urban rail services are below the required standards, and rapid rail service is not available to a large proportion of the population living in the region. Some rail and road projects implemented in the recent past, such as the Delhi Metro, Delhi-Gurgaon and Delhi-Noida Expressways are playing an important role in meeting the mobility needs of the regional population. Steps have also been taken by the Haryana government to set up a Mass Rapid Transport Corporation for providing a wide range of transport services in the coming years. However, the implementation of many other regional-level transport projects, such as the upgradation of existing roads, construction of new roads, orbital expressways and rail corridors, efficient public transport vehicles, is progressing at a very slow pace due to a number of problems faced in project implementation.

The availability of efficient and economical transport networks and services at a regional level has a direct relationship with the development of places—rural and urban. The examples of regional transport network initiatives in Australia, Japan, China and South Africa described in the first section of this paper demonstrate the fact that such measures have the ability to:

- address problems of congestion experienced in large urban centres/cities by way of diverting traffic around cities, through the development of orbital networks;
- provide greater access of the young population living away from cities in the rural hinterland to numerous opportunities available in large towns and cities;

- improve living conditions and quality of life in under-developed areas. Many workers may like to work near their place of residence, instead of large towns/cities. Using fast public transport services, they can easily collect their day to day requirements from the cities on a frequent/daily basis and offer various services to the local/rural population; and
- attend to the problem of permanent migration to cities. If fast and economical transport services are available to the regional population, workers need not stay in large towns/cities, and can commute every day. This has major social and economic implications, since living costs are quite high in large towns/cities as compared to the adjoining hinterland. Thus, migrants who are mainly engaged in informal sector activities end up living in inhabitable areas/slums.

The study concludes that implementation of transport projects in the National Capital Region of India should be undertaken on a priority basis. Policymakers, transport planners and implementing agencies face difficulties in the areas of arranging funds, their efficient utilisation, corruption, availability of environment friendly technologies, capability of implementing agencies, timely project implementation, land acquisition, inter-state coordination, agreement between government and private developers, etc. An early resolution of regional transportation issues is necessary for the social and economic development of the region.

References

Cape Metropolitan Council (2001). *Metropolitan Spatial Development Framework (MSDF) Redraft 2001 for Spatial Planning and Development of Cape Town Metropolitan Area*. Available from: *http://www.capetown.gov.za/en/sdf/Documents/MSDF%20REDRAFT%202001%20v2.pdf; http://www.capetown.gov.za/en/Pages/default.aspx*

Census of India (2011). *Provisional Population Totals*. New Delhi: Office of the Registrar General and Census Commissioner.

———. (2001). *Migration Tables: D1, D2 and D3*. New Delhi: Office of the Registrar General and Census Commissioner.

eBeijing (n.d.) *Eleventh Five Year Programme for 2006-10*. Part Three (4), Section X - Regional Cooperation and Opening Up. Available from: eBeijing – The Official Website of the Beijing Government: *http://www.ebeijing.gov.cn/Government/reports/t923643.htm*

Government of National Capital Territory of Delhi (2009). *Economic Survey of Delhi 2008-09*. Chapter 12: Transport. New Delhi: Planning Department.

National Capital Region Planning Board (2005). *Regional Plan-2021*. New Delhi: Government of India.

New South Wales Government (2008). *Sydney-Canberra Corridor Regional Strategy for 2006-31*. Department of Planning. Available from: *http://www.planning.nsw.gov.au/StrategicPlanning/Regionalplanning/SydneyCanberraCorridor/tabid/213/language/en-AU/Default.aspx* ; map of Australia obtained from Google maps website.

The Times of India (2011a). "DMRC Sells Carbon Credits Worth Rs. 24 million", 13 April.

———. (2011b). "100 Months and Ready to Zip Through City", 25 April.

Tokyo Metropolitan Government (2006). "Tokyo's Big Change: The 10 year Plan for 2006-16". Available from: *http://www.metro.tokyo.jp/ENGLISH/PLAN/index.htm*

6 The Contemporary Structure of the World City Network

How Industries Connect Cities across the World

Stefan Krätke

Introduction

One of the major challenges of contemporary urbanisation is the urban areas' economic development in the context of globalisation. The economic development and internal structure of cities is increasingly affected by global influences, particularly by the cities' external relations. Hence it is increasingly difficult to analyse the 'inner workings' of the city endogenously, from what is happening inside its conventionally defined administrative boundaries. We are facing the formation of new transnational urban spaces in cities across the world. With regard to the worldwide urban system, globalisation doesn't simply lead to the formation of a small group of outstanding 'global cities' that are functioning as command and control centres of the world economy—such as London, New York and Tokyo. Rather, we are facing a continued extension of transnational economic networks that include more and more cities both in the global North and South in the complex fabric of a 'world city network'. Thus, I prefer to speak of 'globalising cities', whose economic development prospects are shaped by their specific positioning within global economic network relations and capital flows. As John Friedmann (1986) has emphasised, in the contemporary era of globalisation "the form and extent of a city's integration with the world economy and the functions assigned to the city in the global spatial division of labour will be decisive for the structural changes occurring within the city." These structural changes include the selective formation of transnational urban spaces within the city, a changing sectoral composition of urban economies that is combined with new functions and industrial upgrading processes, and the often two-sided impact of economic restructuring in globalising cities on the cities' social and spatial fabric.

My contribution takes an economically oriented geographic approach to the role of cities in globalisation. It will start from a short outline of the basic approaches and the main findings of the research on global cities. Subsequently, I will concentrate on a macro-level analysis of the global urban system by investigating inter-urban linkages in a 'world city network' that comprises a multitude of cities both in the global North and South, highlighting the geographically uneven spread of globalisation as well as the rise of new urban nodes of globally connected business activity, such as Shanghai and Mumbai. Empirical research on the formation of a world city network that functions as a backbone for channelling worldwide capital flows has mostly concentrated on global 'service providers.' In order to advance our knowledge of the contemporary world city network, my contribution will present selected findings of recent research on the manufacturing industries' global organisational networks that link cities across the world. Interestingly, the 'ranking' of globally connected urban centres of manufacturing activity differs considerably from the well-known rankings of global service centres. Thus, we have to be aware of 'multiple globalisations' in the world city network.

Basic Approaches to Research on the Role of Cities in Globalisation

With 'globalisation' having become a key term in the debate on the economic and social changes taking place in modern society, the connection between globalisation and urban development has become a central theme of urban research. As a result, 'new' rankings, hierarchies and networks of cities on a global scale have been established. Many urban researchers consider that globalisation proceeds primarily from urban centres of activity and that more and more cities are actively or passively integrated into processes of globalisation. We are facing today an increasing globality of major cities all over the world that leads to an unbounding of the metropolis (Soja, 2000) in terms of an extraordinary expansion in the scale and scope of the modern metropolis (see also Scott, 2001).

In general, two approaches to global city research can be distinguished: First, investigating particular cities' global functions and their impact on urban space and the city's economic and socio-spatial restructuring. The work of Saskia Sassen on the 'global city' might be representative for this line of research. Sassen (1991) identified New York, London and Tokyo as the prime centres of a global urban hierarchy. These global cities are functioning as major command and control centres in a transnationally organised economy on the basis of their strong local concentration of global firms of the 'advanced producer services' and the so-called FIRE (finance, insurance, and real estate) sector.

The second line of global city research is more concerned with the development of a global urban system which includes a vast number of cities beyond the group of 'leading' global cities (mentioned above). This research concentrates on investigating inter-urban linkages in order to identify the primary, secondary and tertiary nodes of a 'world city network'. Representative for this line of research is the work of Peter Taylor (2004) and the GaWC (Globalisation and World Cities Study Group). The starting point is the thesis that connectivity in the world city network is being created through the multi-local office networks of global service providers. A city where a large number of global service firms' head offices and branch offices are located becomes a central node in the world city network. This centrality is based on inter-city connectivity and can be empirically measured. The GaWC approach to global urban research resulted in the identification and classification of corporate service centres of the global economy.

The first GaWC analysis used 100 office networks of global service firms across 315 cities worldwide (Beaverstock, Smith and Taylor, 1999). In 2008, the data collection was revised and improved, leading to a renewed analysis that covers the office networks of 175 global service firms across 526 cities worldwide (Taylor *et al.*, 2010). The results of this new analysis (see Figure 6.1) indicate that the globalisation process of advanced producer services has further continued, with the expansion of offices in many cities and the extension of office networks into new ones. This might be interpreted as an expansion and increasing integration of the world city network. More specifically, the analysis confirms the premier position of London and New York at the top level of global service centres, the rapid advance of Shanghai, Beijing and Sydney, and the rise of cities in emerging markets such as Mumbai and Kuala Lumpur. However, the analysis also reveals many cities with a relatively stable position in the world city network (such as Paris, Singapore and Toronto). Overall, the world city network analysis demonstrates the inclusion of many cities within contemporary globalisation processes. It highlights the geographically uneven spread of globalisation as well as the rise of new urban nodes of globally connected business activity particularly in countries of the global South, such as China and India.

From a critical point of view, however, we might say that in both approaches mentioned before, global city research has tended to concentrate on the respective cities' function as financial centres and centres for the provision of specialised corporate services. Nonetheless, we should be aware that the prominent examples of global finance and service centres such as London and New York represent quite an unique type of urban economic structure. They represent the world centres of today's financial business that dominates the so-called 'advanced' service sector. The current failure of neoliberal finance-dominated capitalism, which has led to a global economic crisis that not only affect the countries of the disaster's origin but also economic and social development in the global South, demonstrates that there is urgent need to cut back and re-regulate the 'dealer economy' of the financial sector and to redirect economic development trajectories on real sector manufacturing activity, industrial upgrading, and technological as well as social innovation (particularly with regard to employment standards and urban living environments). Taking into account the structural diversity of the worldwide urban system, we can empirically detect that many cities in the global North and South are linked to transnationally extended production networks and continue to play an important role in industrial development. Transnationally networked cities are functioning as major locations in the global value chains of manufacturing industries (Derudder and Witlox, 2010; Krätke *et al.*, 2012). The transnational connections between urban industrial manufacturing centres might be considered as a major element in globalising cities.

Figure 6.1

Globalising Cities: Cities in Global Networks of Finance and Service Sector Firms

Urban Region's degree of connectivity according to the GaWC method (Taylor 2004, Taylor *et al.*, 2010)
Sectors: Financial Services, Management Consultancy, Accountancy, Law, Advertising

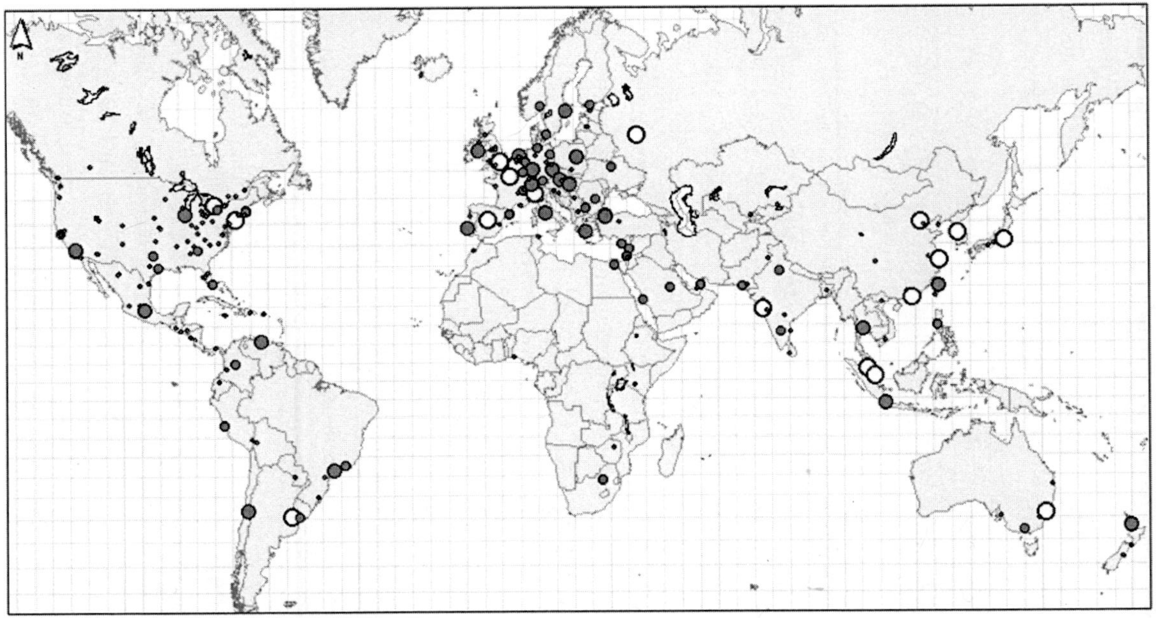

Urban Regions' Degree of Connectivity
(according to Taylor *et al.* 2010)
London=1.00

- 0.01 - 0.30
- 0.30 - 0.45
- 0.45 - 0.60
- 0.60 - 1.00

All cities included in the world city network are characterised by 'specific profiles' of globally connected economic functions. Thus the world city network includes global cities focusing on advanced producer services and the financial sector in particular, as well as many other cities with 'differing profiles' of their globally connected activities (Krätke, 2003; Krätke and Taylor, 2004). In the second part of this contribution, new findings of empirical research on the cities' role in global networks of the manufacturing industries shall be presented.

Inter-urban Linkages of Manufacturing Firms in the Contemporary World City Network

The second part of my contribution deals with the role of global networks of the manufacturing sectors that are connecting cities across the world. Not only global service firms, but also globally operating manufacturing firms choose distinct urban regions all across the world as locational anchoring points. Through their globally extended organisational networks, the manufacturing industries are contributing to a large extent to the world city network formation. The expansion and diffusion of industrial urbanism on a global scale which is led by the formation of global production networks with local anchoring points in urban regions all over the world is a most distinctive feature of the current phase of globalisation (cf. Soja, 2000). However, my empirical research demonstrates that the 'ranking' of globally connected urban centres of manufacturing activity differs considerably from the well-known rankings of global service centres.

My research started on the assumption that globalising city regions are exerting distinct functions in global value chains (for example, distinct manufacturing functions located in the urban region's industrial areas, and the supply of specific producer services for the management of these global value chains), and that many relevant nodes or chain links of global value chains are located in 'globalising' cities of the global South (Krätke *et al.*, 2012). The urban regions of Munich and Bangkok, for example, are interconnected by their functioning as spatial anchoring points of the BMW firm's transnational production network. In similar ways, the global production network of the car manufacturer VW includes the global city regions of Sao Paulo, Mexico City, Shanghai, etc.

In order to present an empirically based account of the worldwide connectivity of cities in the sphere of manufacturing industries, a network analysis was performed. The world city network can be characterised as an 'interlocking network' that allows relations between cities to be measured through data collected on firms (Taylor, 2004). An interlocking network denotes a specific type of network (cf. Knoke and Kuklinski, 1982) that consists of a nodal level—the cities—and the sub-nodal level of firms. The cities are connected through the organisational networks of global firms. They are embedded in networks of corporate relationships that enclose transnational intra-firm transactions such as knowledge flows and capital flows.

Methodical Approach

The network analysis contains three subsectors of manufacturing industries: the automotive industry, information technology industry, and the pharmaceutical and biotechnology industry. Due to time and space restrictions, my presentation will concentrate on the automotive industry. For each subsector, the 40 largest global firms were identified according to the *'Forbes 2000'* listing, which contains in total the world's 2,000 largest firms (of all sectors) in 2010. In the next step, the prominent firm data base 'corporate affiliations' (which contains more than 1 million corporations) was utilised in order to detect the selected firms' national and international organisational network and its linkages within the global urban system. The firm data base offers information on the multi-level corporate hierarchy of the firms included—such as the parent company, divisions and regional headquarters, subsidiaries, affiliates and joint ventures—and on the location of these firm units. The multi-level hierarchy means that a parent company located in city A can have a division in city B, which directs a subsidiary firm in city C. In this way, my analysis of the automotive industry's 40 largest firms contains in total more than 1,000 enterprise units, thereof 881 subsidiaries. In the procedure of registering individual firm units, the financial subsidiaries of manufacturing firms were *not* included in the analysis, since the focus of this research is geared towards capital-based interconnections in the realm of manufacturing industries' value chains. The locations of the registered enterprise units of the automotive industry sector are distributed across the world in a total of 339 cities in 65 different countries. The locational addresses of included firm units were assigned to the respective urban region. The urban region of large cities and metropolises was delimited to cover a radius of 50 kms around the city core (in the cases of Tokyo, London and New York, the radius has been enlarged to 70 kms).

The network analysis detects the geographic destination and strength of the organisational links within the global urban system. As a result, the analysis reveals the positioning of particular cities within the global production network of the automotive industry. This globally extended production network might be interpreted as an organised system of channels for capital flows between cities.

In detail, the analysis differentiates between 'incoming links' (what has been termed the 'in degree' of a city), which demonstrate an urban region's role as a destination of capital flows, and the urban region's 'outgoing links' (the 'out degree' of a city) that reveal an urban region's role as the source and control centre of capital flows. Similarly, the 'in degree' can be interpreted as a measure of an urban region's attraction power or 'relational prestige' in terms of its platform function, for example, for the penetration of foreign markets, the utilisation of local production capacities, or the access to specific knowledge resources and innovation capabilities. The out degree of a city can be interpreted as a measure of an urban region's control capacities or 'relational power'. Thus, the identification and the comparative ranking of outstanding network nodes in the global urban system is based on several different measures of centrality (such as the out degree-based and the in degree-based centrality, and, additionally, the urban region's 'betweenness-centrality' which indicates its role as an intersection in the channel system of worldwide capital flows). The methodical approach of a network analysis of the global urban system, which takes into account the direction of inter-city links (distinction between outgoing and incoming links), has been applied by Alderson and Beckfield (2004) and by Wall and v.d. Knaap (2011). These analyses, however, are based on a selection of global firms from both the service and manufacturing sectors, and thus do not reveal the role of particular manufacturing industries in the formation of the global urban network.

Presentation of Research Findings

The network analysis of the automotive industry's globally operating firms is based on more than 1,000 enterprise units with a total number of 1,668 inter-organisational links that are distributed across 339 cities in 65 different countries. Those urban regions that show a particularly large number of incoming or outgoing network links can be characterised as the outstanding centres of the respective industry on a global scale. The presentation of research findings starts with an exemplary presentation of the 'ego-net' of one selected global firm of the automotive industry, the Volkswagen AG (VW), since such ego-nets form the basis of the aggregate network structure that results from overlapping 40 parent companies' ego-nets. Subsequently, I will show a cartographic presentation of the locational centres of the automotive industry on the macro-level of the global urban system in order to demonstrate these centres' distribution over different world regions (such as North America, Asia, Europe, etc.). Finally, the comparative ranking of urban regions according to their 'relational power' and 'relational prestige' will be presented as the centrepiece of the research findings (utilising tabular as well as graphical network representations).

The organisational network of the VW Corporation (see Figure 6.2) extends over many different world regions so that VW clearly represents a globally networked corporate structure. The distinction of several hierarchy-levels within this corporate structure demonstrates that a prominent position in the locational network is not only occupied by the top level headquarter, but also by cities that are situated at the intersection of different hierarchy-levels (such as Ingolstadt or Stockholm in the VW case): these cities take on a significant role in the direction of capital flows, since they are hosting subsidiaries which themselves control further subsidiaries that are located in other urban regions.

Centres of the Automotive Industry in the Global Urban System

The cartographic presentation of the locational centres of the automotive industry's corporate establishments on the macro-level of the global urban system (see Figure 6.3) detects a distinct geographical distribution according to world regions: The locational centres are concentrated in the regions of the so-called 'global triade'—North America,

Figure 6.2

Cities in Global Networks of Manufacturing Firms: The Case of VW AG, Wolfsburg, 2010

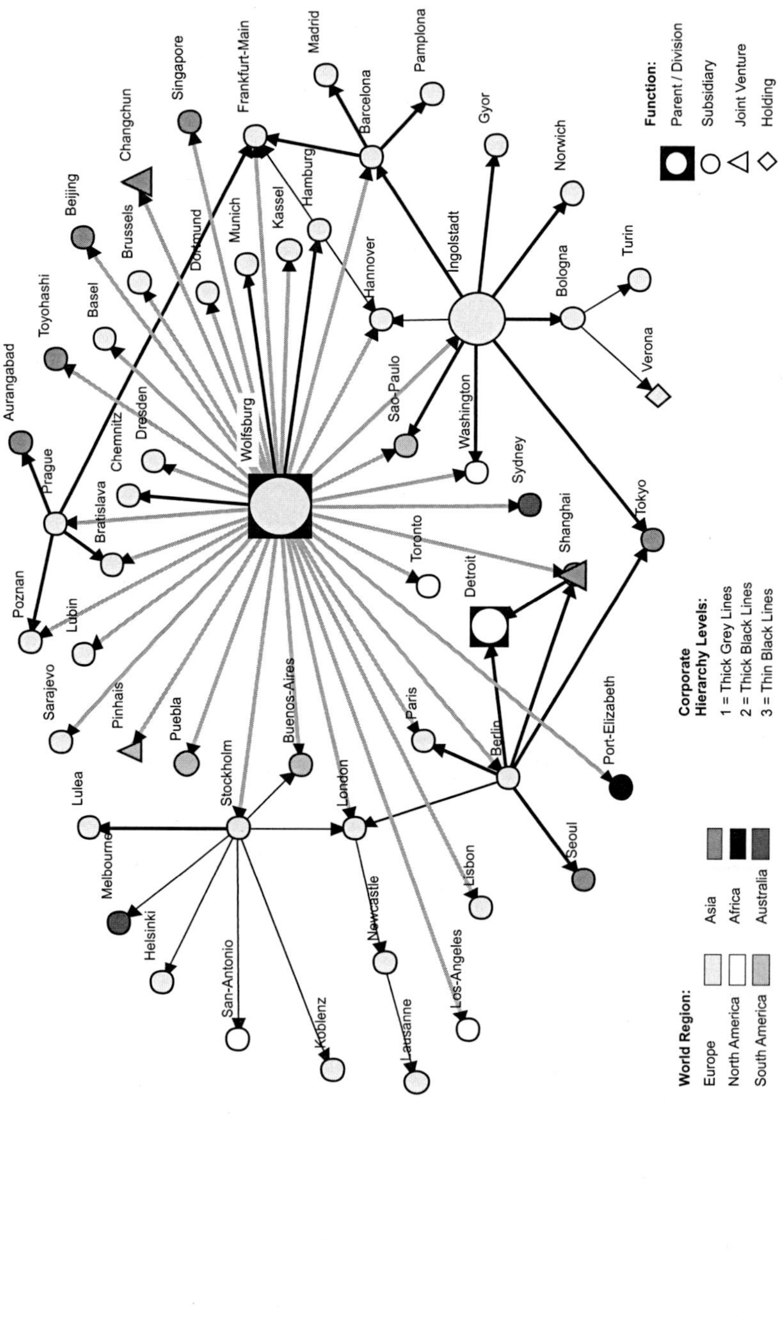

Europe, Asia (particularly East and South Asia)—where the included 40 large parent companies have their command centres and where they find their most important market spaces. In North America, particularly urban regions in the eastern part of the USA contain a large number of the automotive industry's corporate units. In Europe, we find—as seen from a global-scale perspective—a concentration of locational centres of the automotive industry in the central core area of the EU that is circumscribed by the pentagon, London-Paris-Milan-Munich-Hamburg. In Asia, the industry's locational centres of global firms' establishments are distributed over a comparatively larger geographic area which particularly includes Japan, the eastern part of China, South Korea, Thailand, Malaysia, Singapore, and India (with Mumbai and Bangalore).

Moreover, due to the distinction between 'relational power' as measured by outgoing links (out degrees) and 'relational prestige' as measured by incoming links (in degrees), the cartographic representation reveals that a comparatively large number of cities in the respective world regions are functioning as target destinations of capital-based interconnections, whereas a significantly smaller number of cities has the potential to command and control capital flows in the automotive industry. Urban regions that contain a strong command and control capacity in the automotive industry's global production network show a quite uneven geographic distribution on the world-scale. In North America, we find two prominent urban regions in the eastern part of the USA. In Europe, several cities in Germany and one city in Sweden stand out, and in Asia, the cities that have a particularly strong 'relational power' are concentrated in Japan.

In the comprehensive graphic representation of this complex network structure (see Figure 6.4), those urban regions are emphasised which function as central nodes of transnational capital flows in the automotive industry according to their outgoing links (out degree): these outstanding centres include particularly the cities of Tokyo, Detroit, Gothenburg and Stuttgart, as well as Hanover, Wolfsburg, Nagoya, Paris, Milwaukee, Frankfurt and Munich. However, the graphic representation of the network nodes doesn't enable us to come to a more accurate interpretation of individual city's positioning in the network of globally operating manufacturing firms.

Figure 6.3

Globalising Cities: Cities in Global Networks of Manufacturing Firms

Urban Region's Relational, "Power" in terms of their Outdegree and Relational "Prestige" in terms of their Indegree
Sector: Automotive Industry

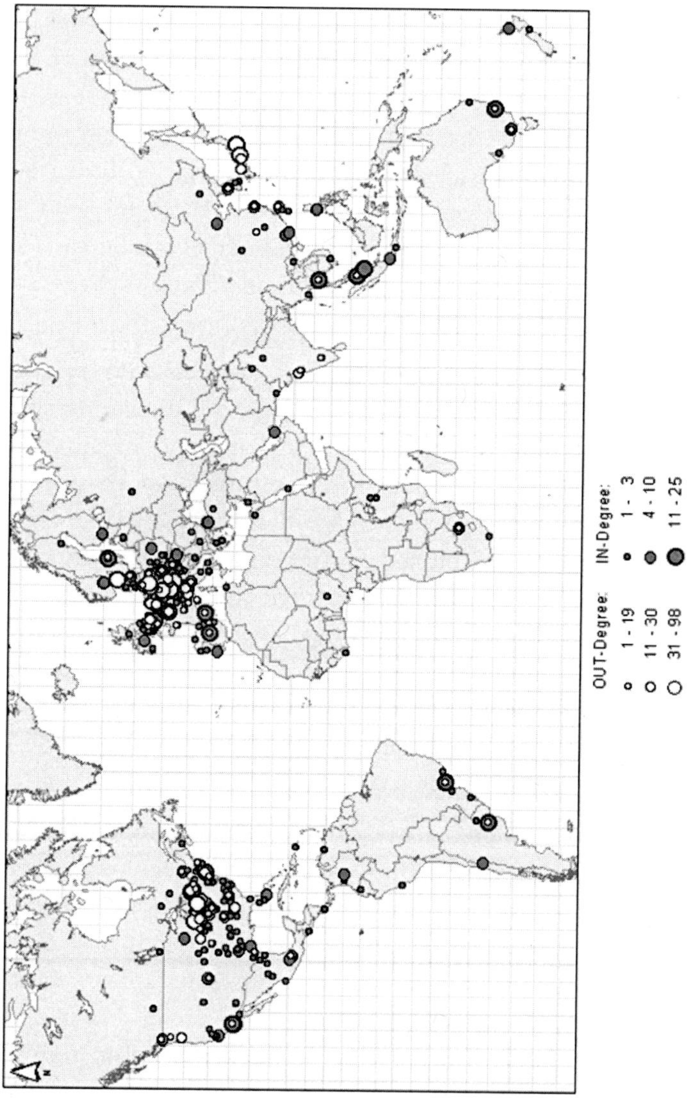

Figure 6.4

Central Nodes of Capital Flows in the Global Automotive Industry, 2010

(according to the Urban Region's Relational "Power" in terms of their Outdegree)

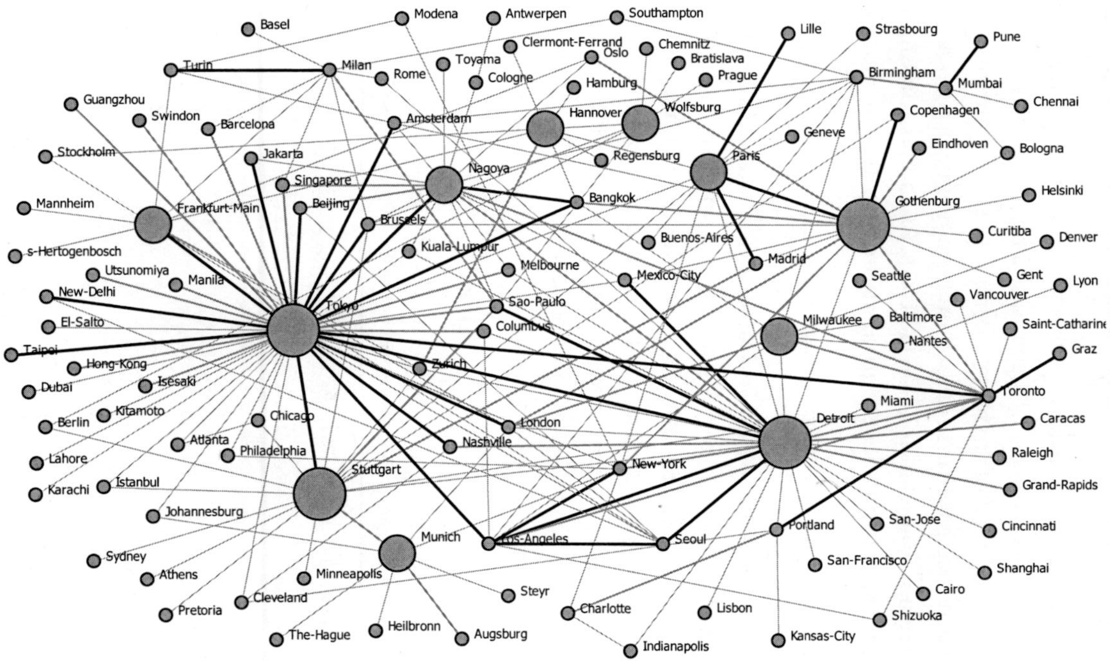

Selection of Urban Regions whose Connectivity exceeds a Degree of 1

Size of Nodes according to the Strength of Outdegree (Range 1 – 98)

Size of Lines according to the Strength of individual inter-city Linkages (Range 1 – 18)

Ranking of Cities according to their Role in the Automotive Industry's Global Networks

In the next step I'm going to present a more detailed account of my research findings in terms of a comparative 'ranking' of urban regions according to their 'relational power' and 'relational prestige' within the automotive industry's global networks. This ranking of cities doesn't refer to specific functions of individual corporate establishments or subsidiaries, or to the respective firms' output and employment figures in a particular urban region. The ranking solely refers to the positioning of individual cities in the capital-based production network of globally operating manufacturing firms.

The tabular representation of the city ranking (see Table 6.1) is sorted according to the included cities' out degree (outgoing links) and demonstrates the top 50 ranks of a total of 339 cities. The table distinguishes between out degrees' (outgoing links) and 'in degrees' (incoming links). Furthermore, for each city the difference between out degree and in degree is indicated. Urban regions with a strong 'surplus' of 'out degrees' (such as Tokyo) are primarily functioning as command and

Table 6.1

Urban Nodes of Global Networks in the Automotive Industry

(Based on the Organisational Networks of the Sector's 40 Largest Corporations, 2010)

No.	*Urban Region*	*Out Degree*	*In Degree*	*Difference Out-In*	*Betweenness*
1	Tokyo	98	15	83	16.098
2	Detroit	83	20	63	12.659
3	Stuttgart	57	4	53	4.736
4	Gothenburg	55	4	51	6.043
5	Milwaukee	49	3	46	5.279
6	Nagoya	46	2	44	2.380
7	Frankfurt-Main	38	19	19	5.022
8	Wolfsburg	37	1	36	3.789
9	Hanover	35	10	25	4.340
10	Munich	31	6	25	1.983
11	Paris	29	19	10	3.956
12	Milan	26	12	14	2.236

contd...

...contd...

No.	Urban Region	Out Degree	In Degree	Difference Out-In	Betweenness
13	Turin	24	5	19	1.723
14	Mumbai	22	2	20	2.565
15	Shizuoka	22	2	20	2.065
16	Atlanta	17	8	9	1.339
17	Portland	17	3	14	594
18	Hiroshima	16	0	16	442
19	New York	16	17	-1	1.776
20	Regensburg	16	2	14	1.895
21	Antwerpen	15	4	11	1.194
22	Amsterdam	14	8	6	1.260
23	Cambridge	13	2	11	1.135
24	Cleveland	13	5	8	577
25	Des-Moines	13	2	11	468
26	Mellansel	13	1	12	945
27	Osaka	13	3	10	71
28	Brussels	12	15	-3	1.367
29	Chicago	11	11	0	802
30	Toronto	11	25	-14	2.646
31	Clermont-Ferrand	10	1	9	251
32	London	10	25	-15	1.845
33	Ingolstadt	9	2	7	788
34	Seattle	9	2	7	792
35	Seoul	8	8	0	423
36	Shanghai	8	6	2	522
37	Stockholm	8	12	-4	839
38	Augsburg	7	1	6	44
39	Berlin	7	4	3	86
40	Charlotte	7	8	-1	269
41	Grand-Rapids	7	5	2	476
42	Los-Angeles	7	15	-8	565
43	Philadelphia	7	5	2	266
44	Sao Paulo	7	13	-6	1.067
45	Zurich	7	11	-4	228
46	Indianapolis	6	7	-1	560
47	Pune	6	2	4	54
48	Barcelona	4	13	-9	616
49	Prague	4	8	-4	695
50	Aalen	3	2	1	677

control centres of capital flows in the automotive industry. Urban regions with a strong 'surplus' of 'in degrees' (such as Toronto) are primarily functioning as 'platform'—locations for the supply of distinct market regions, the utilisation of local production capacities, or the access to specific knowledge resources and innovation capabilities. We might say that these cities possess of a significant 'relational prestige' in the automotive industry's global networks. Of course, there are also urban regions which show a rather 'balanced' relation of 'out degrees' and 'in degrees' (such as New York and Chicago), so that no definite 'primary' functional designation can be assigned to these cases.

'Out degree' and 'in degree' represent relevant measures of centrality in the network analysis context. However, the network analysis method offers a variety of more complex measures of centrality, such as the socalled 'betweenness-centrality', which is also reported in the tabular representation for each city included. The measure of 'betweenness-centrality' indicates to which extent an urban region is positioned as an intersectional node within the connecting links of all other cities included in the network, and thus has a 'mediating position' in the capital flows that run through the overall network structure. The highest betweenness-centrality is recorded for the urban regions of Tokyo and Detroit, which also corresponds to their outstanding position in terms of other (degree-based) measures of centrality. Comparatively high values of betweenness-centrality are also indicated for the urban regions of Gothenburg, Milwaukee, Frankfurt, Stuttgart and Hanover, which are all positioned on the upper-level ranks of 'out degrees'. However, the presentation of research findings will focus on the degree-based measures of centrality, which can be interpreted more easily.

The tabular representation of cities (Table 6.1) is sorted according to out degrees (outgoing links) which are interpreted as a measure of a city's 'relational power' within worldwide capital flows. With regard to the automotive industry, the urban regions of Tokyo and Detroit take on the first and second rank. On the subsequent ranks we find the urban regions of Stuttgart, Gothenburg, Milwaukee, Nagoya, Frankfurt, Wolfsburg, Hanover and Munich. Thus German cities are quite strongly represented amongst the top 50 ranks. The overall picture indicates the dominance of global firms from some European countries, the USA and Japan in the automotive industry. However, it is remarkable that several urban regions of the 'global South' appear on comparatively high rank positions: Two of these are cities of India, in particular Mumbai (rank 14), and Pune (rank 47). In China, the urban region of Shanghai (rank 36) has achieved a high rank, and in Brazil, the urban region of Sao-Paulo (rank 44) has joined the top 50 listing. This finding clearly indicates the increasing integration of the so-called 'emerging markets' in global production networks. Particularly Mumbai shows a comparatively strong 'surplus' of relational power, which reflects the fact that in recent times globally operating firms from India have entered the automotive industry's global production network.

As regards cities that are primarily functioning as 'platform'- locations and thus possess a strong 'relational prestige' within the automotive industry's global networks, which is measured according to a strong surplus of incoming links (in degrees), the urban regions of London, Toronto, Barcelona, Los Angeles and Sao-Paulo are to be highlighted.

It is also worth noting that in the group of 'outstanding' global cities such as London, New York, Tokyo and Los Angeles, which have been characterised as prime centres of the global financial industry and the advanced producer services, only Tokyo has a top position in terms of an outstanding surplus of 'relational power' within global networks of manufacturing, whereas the other global cities mentioned before take on comparatively low ranks. This corresponds to our preliminary thesis that there exist 'multiple globalisations' in the world city network, which means that globalising cities are characterised by differing profiles of globally connected economic functions.

As an addition to the representation of research findings, the results for the top 30 ranks of cities in the world region of Asia were extracted from the network analysis (see Table 6.2): Besides the number of high ranking cities of Japan which possess a comparatively strong 'relational power' in the automotive industry's global networks, the table demonstrates that six cities of India are registered in this 'league table', with Mumbai on rank number 3 and Pune on rank number 9 amongst the selection of cities in Asia. Furthermore, there are five cities of the People's Republic of China included in the list, with Shanghai on rank number 8 and the city of Wuhan on rank number 10. Altogether, these findings support the vision of an increasingly significant role of Indian and Chinese urban regions in the globalisation of manufacturing industries.

Table 6.2

Cities in Asia as Urban Nodes of Global Networks in the Automotive Industry

(Based on the Organisational Networks of the Sector's 40 Largest Corporations, 2010)

No.	*Urban Region*	*Out Degree*	*In Degree*	*Difference Out-In*	*Betweenness*
1	Tokyo	98	15	83	16.098
2	Nagoya	46	2	44	2.380
3	Mumbai	22	2	20	2.565
4	Shizuoka	22	2	20	2.065
5	Hiroshima	16	0	16	442
6	Osaka	13	3	10	71
7	Seoul	8	8	0	423
8	Shanghai	8	6	2	522
9	Pune	6	2	4	54
10	Wuhan	2	2	0	2
11	Bangkok	1	12	-11	260
12	Kuala Lumpur	1	11	-10	225
13	Taipei	1	4	-3	9
14	Bangalore	1	3	-2	29
15	Chennai	1	2	-1	366
16	Hamamatsu	1	2	-1	0
17	Jakarta	0	6	-6	17
18	Beijing	0	5	-5	93
19	Guangzhou	0	5	-5	48
20	Hong Kong	0	4	-4	9
21	Manila	0	4	-4	9
22	Hanoi	0	3	-3	0
23	Karachi	0	3	-3	3
24	New Delhi	0	3	-3	1
25	Taichung	0	3	-3	3
26	Lahore	0	2	-2	0
27	Akita	0	1	-1	0
28	Aurangabad	0	1	-1	0
29	Batangas	0	1	-1	0
30	Bogor	0	1	-1	0

Comparison of Outstanding Network Nodes of Global Services and Global Manufacturing

In order to prove our thesis that the contemporary world city network encloses 'multiple globalisations' particularly with regard to the differing sectoral profiles of globalising cities, we present a comparative ranking of the outstanding network nodes of global services and global manufacturing. The ranking of global service centres offered by the GaWC (Taylor, *et al.*, 2010) will be compared with the ranking of globally connected manufacturing centres that has been presented in the foregoing section. In the GaWC ranking, the individual cities' degree of connectivity is expressed as a fraction of the highest scoring city's connectivity (London = 1.00). The same expression of relative connectivity has been calculated for the cities' degree of connectivity in the manufacturing sector (as represented by the automotive industry). However, we have to note that the GaWC method of calculating degrees of connectivity (Taylor, 2004) differs from the procedure of the network analysis presented here: The GaWC operation of measuring inter-city connectivity by multiplying the 'service values' of firm units located in the respective cities assigns a particularly strong weight to global firms' headquarters and regional headquarters or divisions, whereas the network analysis procedure, which doesn't include this kind of weighting, offers the possibility to functionally differentiate between outgoing and incoming links. For the comparison, the ranks of the cities' connectivity in manufacturing were calculated according to the sum of 'out degrees' and 'in degrees' (without taking diagonal values, i.e., the 'internal' connectivity between a global firm's different establishments in a particular city, into account). Since globally connected manufacturing activity is represented here by a specific subsector (i.e., the automotive industry), we should be aware that the analysis would yield a more differentiated account, if more sub-sectors of manufacturing were included. We can expect, for example, that global firms of the high-technology manufacturing subsectors will show a stronger presence in prominent global city regions such as New York and London (as compared to the urban locational centres of the global automotive industry).

The comparison focuses on the difference between the cities' rank positions in global service and manufacturing activity. In the tabular representation of selected cities (see Table 6.3), the left section (cities No.

1-50) displays cities that possess a 'surplus rank' in manufacturing in terms of a positive rank difference. These cities are characterised by strong global connectivity in manufacturing activity, which considerably exceeds their rank position in the sphere of global services. The right upper section of Table 6.3 (cities No. 51-67) presents cities with a relatively balanced relation of global connectivity in both the service and manufacturing sector. Globalising cities such as Tokyo, Boston, Toronto, Bangalore, Sao-Paulo, Milan and Paris are functioning to nearly the same extent as globally connected centres of manufacturing firms than as global service centres. The right lower section of Table 6.3 (cities No. 68-98) contains cities with a *negative* rank difference, which means that these cities possess a 'surplus rank' in the finance and service sector. Here, we find well-known examples of leading global cities such as New York and London as well as a number of globalising cities in the Asian region, such as in particular the Chinese cities of Hong-Kong, Beijing and Shanghai. Cities that appear in this section of Table 6.3 are characterised by strong global connectivity in service sector activities, which exceeds the degree of global connectivity they have achieved in the sphere of manufacturing (as represented by the automotive industry). However, the point of delimitation between the three city groupings mentioned before is in some way 'fuzzy' and open to adjustment (see for example, the delimitation between city No. 67 and 68).

The main finding of our comparative ranking of the urban network nodes of global services and global manufacturing confirms our thesis that different profiles of globally connected economic activities can be detected in globalising cities all across the world. The world city network includes globalising cities focusing on advanced producer services and the financial sector in particular, as well as many cities with differing profiles of their globally connected activities. Thus there are possibly different pathways or sectoral trajectories of cities in globalisation, a perspective which might have significant implications for urban economic development strategies.

Table 6.3

Comparison of Cities' Global Connectivity Rankings with Regard to the Service Sector and the Manufacturing Sector (Automotive Industry)

No.	Urban Region	GaWC Rank	Manufacturing Rank	Rank Difference	No.	Urban Region	GaWC Rank	Manufacturing Rank	Rank Difference
1	Hannover	57	8	49					
2	Nagoya	55	7	48	51	Chennai	39	34	5
3	Milwaukee	53	6	47	52	Los Angeles	23	18	5
4	Detroit	46	2	44	53	Barcelona	26	22	4
5	Turin	57	14	43	54	Tokyo	5	1	4
6	Stuttgart	41	3	38	55	Berlin	29	27	2
7	Osaka	51	23	28	56	Stockholm	20	19	1
8	Cleveland	49	21	28	57	Boston	33	33	0
9	Birmingham	47	19	28	58	Dallas	33	33	0
10	Indianapolis	52	25	27	59	Hamburg	31	31	0
11	Charlotte	51	24	27	60	Toronto	11	11	0
12	Portland	45	19	26	61	Bangalore	32	33	-1
13	Cincinnati	57	32	25	62	Helsinki	29	30	-1
14	Antwerpen	45	20	25	63	Milan	7	9	-2
15	Nashville	54	30	24	64	Cairo	31	34	-3
16	Newcastle	54	30	24	65	Melbourne	24	28	-4
17	Pune	54	30	24	66	Sao-Paulo	15	19	-4
18	Nantes	57	34	23	67	Paris	3	7	-4
19	Puebla	56	33	23					

contd...

...contd...

No.	*Urban Region*	*GaWC Rank*	*Manufacturing Rank*	*Rank Difference*	*No.*	*Urban Region*	*GaWC Rank*	*Manufacturing Rank*	*Rank Difference*
20	Rochester	56	33	23	68	Dubai	28	33	-5
21	Raleigh	54	31	23	69	Chicago	13	18	-5
22	Cologne	53	30	23	70	Mumbai	12	17	-5
23	Munich	33	10	23	71	Zurich	15	21	-6
24	Bologna	52	30	22	72	New Delhi	27	34	-7
25	Utrecht	57	36	21	73	San Francisco	26	35	-9
26	Southampton	56	35	21	74	Bangkok	16	25	-9
27	Strasbourg	56	35	21	75	Auckland	23	33	-10
28	Salt Lake City	55	34	21	76	Lisbon	18	28	-10
29	Valencia	55	34	21	77	Budapest	21	32	-11
30	San Jose	53	32	21	78	London	1	12	-11
31	Kaohsiung	56	36	20	79	Caracas	22	34	-12
32	Winnipeg	56	36	20	80	Rome	17	29	-12
33	Curitiba	55	35	20	81	Seoul	11	23	-12
34	Leipzig	55	35	20	82	Madrid	9	21	-12
35	Liverpool	55	35	20	83	New York	1	13	-12
36	Ankara	55	36	19	84	Athens	21	34	-13
37	Dresden	55	36	19	85	Istanbul	17	30	-13
38	Penang	55	36	19	86	Mexico City	15	29	-14
39	Basel	54	35	19	87	Buenos Aires	12	26	-14
40	Philadelphia	45	26	19	88	Kuala Lumpur	12	26	-14
41	Porto Alegre	54	36	18	89	Dublin	16	33	-17

contd...

...contd...

No.	*Urban Region*	*GaWC Rank*	*Manufacturing Rank*	*Rank Difference*	*No.*	*Urban Region*	*GaWC Rank*	*Manufacturing Rank*	*Rank Difference*
42	Memphis	53	35	18	90	Taipei	16	33	-17
43	Baltimore	52	34	18	91	Jakarta	15	32	-17
44	Kansas City	51	33	18	92	Warsaw	14	32	-18
45	Bristol	52	36	16	93	Shanghai	7	25	-18
46	Saint Louis	52	36	16	94	Sydney	6	25	-19
47	Hanoi	50	34	16	95	Singapore	4	25	-21
48	Seattle	43	27	16	96	Moscow	10	35	-25
49	Leeds	51	36	15	97	Beijing	8	33	-25
50	Lyon	50	35	15	98	Hong Kong	2	33	-31

Conclusion

We are used to think global economy as a mosaic of national state territories that are the 'containers' of national economies. I have presented a different view, one which starts from a relational perspective and characterises the world economy as a globally extended network of cities and metropolitan regions. Urban development might be regarded as a process of networking that is unfolding on different but intertwined spatial scales, resulting in the interplay of local, regional and global networks that are constitutive forces in the production of urban space. Transnational and local actors are constitutive elements of these multiple relational networks. Global firms' activities (as well as international migrants) contribute to the formation of transnational urban spaces. Apparently, these do not cover a city's territory as a whole. Rather, we will find 'globalised' fragments of urban economic and social space. It is also worth noting that the interrelations between different fragments of urban space may come into conflict, for example in terms of transnational firms' activities crowding out local firms in the competition for skilled labour and other resources, labour market competition between 'home' and 'migrant' workers, extensive processes of residential gentrification in cities that are characterised by a strong presence of global players combined with growth of the group of highly skilled urban professionals who are running the urban economy's 'globalised' segments.

I have presented new empirical research on the formation of a world city network that functions as a backbone for channelling worldwide capital flows. My research confirms the thesis that globally operating manufacturing firms are connecting cities across the world and thus contribute to the emergence of 'multiple globalisations' in the world city network. The research detected different profiles of globally connected economic activities in globalising cities all across the world. Second, the 'ranking' of globally connected urban centres of manufacturing activity differs considerably from the well-known rankings of global service centres.

The inclusion of many cities in global value chains of the manufacturing sector also opens up a perspective on the variable 'positioning' of cities in a globalising economy. This concerns the question as to how the rather 'peripheral' cities could increase the economic returns from participating in global value chains. In this respect, the debate might concentrate on the prospects for 'upgrading' the position of 'peripheral' cities within global production networks. Today, such processes of 'upgrading' can be detected particularly in diverse countries of East and South Asia.

However, the unequal extent and different form of the cities' integration in global economic networks raises questions concerning the governance of urban economic and spatial development—for example, we might ask, in what ways might the urban government be able to actively influence the upgrading of a city's role in global economic networks, and in what ways it might deal with growing social and sociospatial inequality in globalising cities in order to spread the gains of 'globalised city fragments' in favour of the whole population of an urban area. In the sphere of urban governance, many cities are striving to take on global city functions in order to strengthen their reputation and position in a worldwide inter-urban competition. Very often, urban governance in the globalisation arena is geared towards restructuring the city's spatial fabric and built environment according to the presumed 'needs' of global finance and service firms, with the consequence of fostering sociospatial polarisation. We need more effort and initiative for developing strategies that are socially inclusive and might benefit urban residents beyond the upper strata of business elites in the finance and service sector. I have emphasised that there exist different pathways for cities in globalisation. A city's integration in the globalisation process might as well be taken as a resource for upgrading its industrial structure and employment standards and as a resource of urban policies in favour of the urban poor and the city's ordinary population.

References

Alderson, A.S. and J. Beckfield (2004). "Power and Position in the World City System", *American Journal of Sociology* 109: 811-51.

Beaverstock, J.V., R.G. Smith and P.J. Taylor (1999). "A Roster of World Cities", *Cities* 16 (6): 445–458.

Derudder, B. and F. Witlox (Eds.) (2010). *Commodity Chains and World Cities*. Oxford: Wiley-Blackwell.

Friedmann, J. (1986). "The World City Hypothesis", *Development and Change* 17 (1): 69–84.

Knoke, D. and J.H. Kuklinski (1982). *Network Analysis*. Sage University Papers No. 28. London: Sage.

Krätke, S. (2003). "Global Media Cities in a Worldwide Urban Network", *European Planning Studies* 11: 605-628.

Krätke, S. and P.J. Taylor (2004). "A World Geography of Global Media Cities", *European Planning Studies* 12(4): 459-77.

Krätke, S., K. Wildner and S. Lanz (Eds.) (2012). *Transnationalism and Urbanism*. New York, London: Routledge (forthcoming).

Sassen, S. (1991). *The Global City: New York, London, Tokyo*. Princeton: Princeton University Press.

Scott, A.J. (Ed.) (2001). *Global City-Regions. Trends, Theory, Policy*. Oxford: Oxford University Press.

Soja, E. (2000). *Postmetropolis. Critical Studies of Cities and Regions*. Oxford: Blackwell.

Taylor, P.J. (2004). *World City Network. A Global Urban Analysis*. New York, London: Routledge.

Taylor, P.J., P. Ni, B. Derudder, M. Hoyler, J. Huang and F. Witlox (2010). *Global Urban Analysis. A Survey of Cities in Globalization*. London: Earthscan.

Wall, R.S. and v.d. Knaap, G.A. (2011). "Sectoral Differentiation and Network Structure within Contemporary Worldwide Corporate Networks", *Economic Geography* 87(3): 267-308.

7 Meeting UK Government's 80% CO_2 Reduction Target in Local Authority Corporate Estate

Paul Kennedy

Introduction

The United Kingdom (UK) Government has set a strategic plan for change in energy and 'carbon' management, leading to a target reduction in CO_2 emissions of 80 per cent by 2050 (Great Britain, Climate Change Act 2008). UK Local Authorities (LAs) are expected to spearhead the drive in CO_2 emission reductions. Whilst energy management has been practised by UK LAs for over 35 years, 'carbon' management is still in its formative years. Despite the widespread recognition that 'greenhouse' gases are the cause of current and anticipated changes in climate and that government and LAs should take the lead in reducing emissions, there is limited research on whether this target is achievable (Kennedy, 2007) within a timescale and with a practical cost benefit within existing LA building assets. The full study looks into the practical application of carbon reduction measures to buildings, structures and services. The study identifies political inhibitors to progress, conformity in regulation and the application of appropriate management approaches to determine the preparedness of local authorities in energy/carbon reduction.

The study is supported by research carried out between 2000 and 2010, involving the network of professionals working in energy management within the London Boroughs (local authorities) and a separate case study. The research considered the extent to which LAs had identified the practicability's of 80 per cent CO_2 emission reductions in their operational buildings. The evidence from this research suggested that no

London Borough had undertaken a specific study looking at the full costs and practicalities to achieve an 80 per cent reduction target.

Whilst the broader research does not seek to define an all embracing solution to the issue, it does, through a separate case study, attempt to identify how significant CO_2 reductions might be achieved by the London Boroughs through an understanding of the theoretical forces at play and grounded on sound practical and organisational aspects.

Theoretical Perspectives and the Built Environment

For this study, theoretical perspectives are derived from the observation of LAs as organisations concerned with the management of carbon as a bi-product of energy usage. The subject matter is the reactionist behaviour of the organisations to a set of semi-imposed conditions to meet the government expectations on the reduction of CO_2 emissions through their own 'interpretation' of the legislation. LAs seek to comply due to corporate and social obligations which, in their view, necessitate such a reaction 'in the interests of good governance'.

Commenting on the philosophical approach to ethics and the built environment, as also the writings of others, Fox (2000) believes all 'players' or institutions possess a particular way of visualising the nature of environmental problem, which is reflected in differing commitments and approaches 'viewing green buildings as a social representation of differing commitments and design approaches...both time and space specific and shaped by a particular image and interpretation of nature'.

The issues in the view of Wapner, Kaplan and Cohen (1980) have to do with the way man experiences his/her environments, 'construe their worlds and undertake action on the basis of such experiences and construals'. In terms of paradigms they cite, Phenomenologists such as Husserl, Heidregger, Schutz, Gurwitsch who stressed the importance of the real and 'lived world' (German: *Lebenswelt*) of ordinary people from that of the objective and scientific world.

Wapner *et al.* (1980) believe that the phenomena which have been central to instigating the bulk of research related to interactionist behaviour between man/the built environment and 'the environment' (in general) is that of the large world threatening phenomena "dealing with phenomena at such a level of complexity would seem to demand forms of conceptualisation and methods of analysis in which individual experience and behaviour have no place."

The process of learning is central to dealing with BANJO or "wicked" issues (Kenny, 2006). Senge (1990) characterised three forms of organisational learning: adaptive learning, generative learning and incremental learning. A generative learning culture is one committed to genuine renewal and research; an adaptive learning culture aims to develop and adapt existing practices and ways of thinking; an incremental learning culture focuses on improvement and efficiency within the existing organisational framework (Kenny, 2006). These three forms of organisational learning connect with Chaffee's (1985) three models of strategy: interpretive, adaptive and linear (Kenny, 2006). They are effective provided a relatively 'stable' rational and predictable working environment exists, whereby decisions made at the highest level are (simply) transposable into working practice throughout the organisation.

Chaffee (1985), however, identified a more dynamic and chameleonic learning organisation based on an ecological paradigm where organisations adapt in a way that living organisms respond to their environments based on 'collection of social agreements' within an organisation. Action and experiential learning was identified by Mintzberg (1994) where 'staff are seen as co-strategists' forming and implementing radical strategic change.

Kenny (2006) summarised the two principle schools of learning theorists as the behaviourists (positivists) such as Skinner and Gagné (1977) and the constructivists (Jaramillo, 1996; Knight, 2002; Quay, 2003; Swain, 2003). In Kenny's view, Skinner and Gagné (1977) as behaviourists would opine that there is 'ultimate truth' which the learner can be taught using appropriately designed and planned learning activities (Swain, 2003). Constructivist approaches to learning are more dynamic and based on 'learn by doing' principle. Action research and action learning are examples of learning approaches based on this view.

For new organisational challenges the constructivist approach is appropriate for learning, because the solution is unclear, uncertain and potentially unique to each organisation. Many of the change processes in the literature advocate learning, which is clearly constructivist in nature

(Mintzberg, 1994; Senge, 1990). Crotty (1998) writing on the ideas of anthropologist Clifford Geertz, suggests 'we depend on culture to direct our behaviour and organise our experience', not only on macro or philosophical levels, but also at a working, thinking, organisational and behavioural level.

Kenny (2006) summarised the strategic organisational learning as presented in Figure 7.1. In the initial stage, since uncertainty is high, interpretive strategic approach would be appropriate with the learning model being generative. As understanding improves, a strategic solution can be found. As the organisation seeks to implement the strategic solution an adaptive strategic process becomes appropriate and, as the strategy becomes more embedded a rational strategic approach becomes appropriate.

Figure 7.1

The Maturity Model for Strategy Formation and Development

Interpretive	Adaptive	Rational (Linear)
Third Order Learning Generative/Critical	Second Order Learning Adaptive/Practical	First Order Learning Incremental/Technical
High Uncertainty (Poorly understood) → Time	Decision to implement	Low Uncertainty (Well understood)
Initiation	Implementation (Establishment)	Implementation (Consolidation)

Source: Kenny, 2006.

Heron and Reason (1997) believe that a constructivist approach is insufficient due to the exclusion of experience resultant knowledge. Heron and Reason suggest that a 'participatory approach' is more appropriate due to 'objective-subjective' ontology and affirms the roles of practical knowledge in human advancement. The participatory (worldview) approach lays a greater emphasis "on the person as an embodied experiencing subject" amongst other subjects.

The implications of recent UK policy decisions such as the UK's Carbon Reduction Commitment (Energy Efficiency) Scheme, is that carbon management is no longer 'optional'. As a strategic approach, a LA needs to establish how to reach, (from a current carbon base) 80 per cent reduction from 1990 baseline, i.e., C-80 in Figure 7.2. Let us assume that LAs are at position 1. Applying the best good housekeeping measures, LAs may attain 10 per cent reduction in CO_2 emissions relatively easily. With further (improvement in) building services systems' control adjustment and the best practice in housekeeping LAs may reach further reductions of 15 per cent. With rigorous and aggressive application of state of the art low and zero carbon technical and managerial measures, a further 20-30 per cent reduction might be achieved (C-40 in Figure 7.2). These are theoretical aspiration targets. In addition, one could apply piecemeal project specific initiatives. What hasn't been investigated or determined are the long

Figure 7.2

Radicalisation of Carbon Management: Reduction Pathway

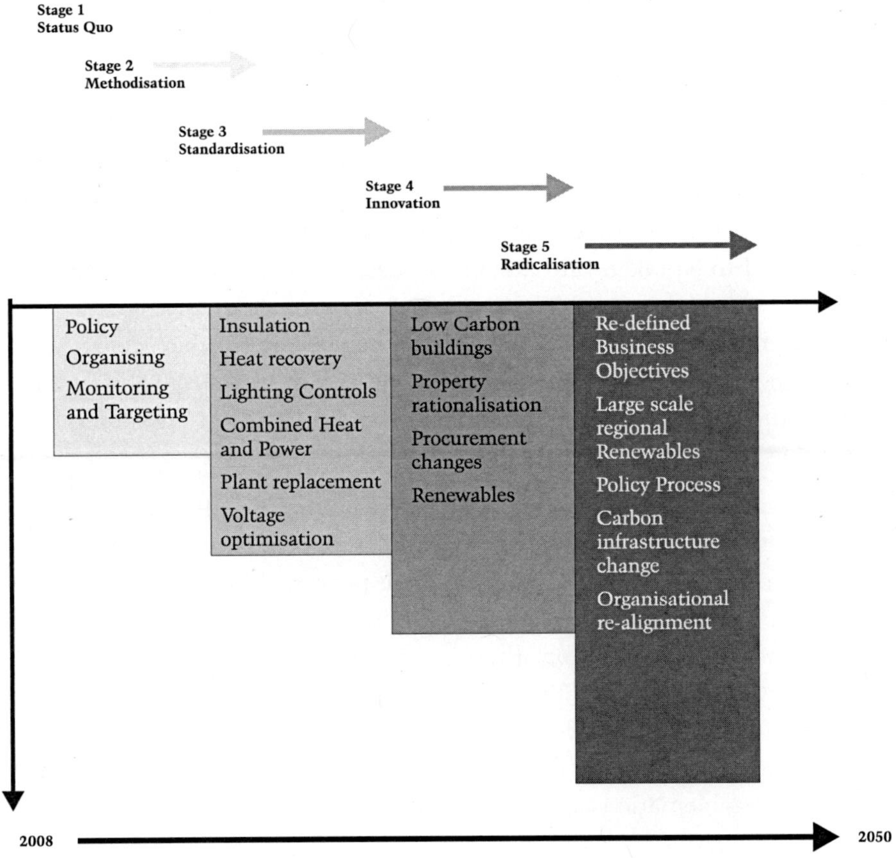

term and strategic costs involved in moving beyond methodisation and standardisation methods (stages 2 and 3 respectively in Figure 7.2) towards innovative and radical measures aimed at carbon emission reduction and applies to existing LA building stock (stages 4 and 5 in Figure 7.2). This raises questions of preparedness, strategy, policy and cost.

Understanding the full implications of the scale of 'carbon reduction' that is expected of LAs is a real challenge for LAs and the one that goes way beyond the Energy Manager's independent remit. An over-simplification of 'greening' the estate is not uncommon. Guy and Farmer's (2000) work focussed on new-build and 'greening' in architecture, which has been broadened and interpreted here at a built environment level. The technical performance approach to understanding green buildings that is now being capitalised on (for example through energy certificates of the European Performance of Building Directive) has bought benefits but, as suggested by Guy and Farmer, this approach may tend to detract from a contextualised and social understanding of the environmental problem.

The 'greening' of buildings cannot happen through an individualist approach. Whilst the Architect, the Energy Manager or perhaps the Chairman of the local authorities Policy committee may wish a building to be 'green', a number of factors (such as technology, finance, people, policy) need to be taken into account to determine the holistic investment case and financial aspect. There requires a rationale change in the long term determination of policy direction by 'embedding carbon capacity' in buildings, management and policy. Individualism or the narrow minded view of the subjectivist would not hold sway in the open and democratic arena that is the local government.

Guy also draws on the work of John Hannigan (1995) in suggesting that society's willingness to recognise and solve environmental problems depends more on the way these claims are presented by a limited number of people, rather than the severity of the threats the problems pose. The concept of a 'green building' therefore becomes a social construct. Guy identified five discourses (Table 7.1) that dominate the perception of the 'ecological dilemma' (Hajer, 1995). Each of the five discourses highlight the way the green building debate is framed differently depending upon the particular "emblematic issue" (Hajer, 1995).

Table 7.1

Five Competing Discourses of Green Buildings

Discourse	*Ecological*	*Smart*	*Aesthetic*	*Comfort*	*Community*
Emblematic Issue	Sustainability	Flexibility	New millennium	Sick buildings	Democracy
Building Image	Polluter	Asset	Symbol	Healthy	Home
Risk	Planetary survival	Market survival	Cultural life	Individual	Alienation
Life cycle	Inter-generational	Business cycle	Design fashion	Daily	Generational
Rhetoric	Ethical	Commercial	Architectural	Medical/ scientific	Societal
Design strategy	Reduce footprint	Max. efficiency	Express nature	Living building	Create identity
Urban scale	De-centralised	Urbanised	Contextualised	Localized	Centralised
Mobility	Ban cars	Virtual travel	Hide car parking	Lessen car-use	Minimise trips
Networks	Autonomous	Integrated	Reveal networks	Diminish intensity	Locally managed
Technology	Local, renewable	Hi-tech, BMS	Organic, recycled	Selective/ nontoxic	Appropriate
Evaluation	Holistic	Cost-benefit	Truth to nature	Productivity	Social cohesion

Note: BMS – Building Management Systems.

Source: Guy, 1997.

With respect to the operation and management of existing buildings, the first two discourses are the most appropriate, whilst the last three/ four more relate to architectural and sustainability in built environment. Buildings as ecological polluters are arguably the main discourse that would be popularly associated with the image of 'green' buildings. The overall aim of the ecological approach is to reduce the ecological footprint of the building. Hence, buildings must be made more environmentally friendly not just for the current generation of occupiers and local inhabitants but for future generations. This is a deeply ethical argument. All the same, the eco-centric discourse is fundamentally flawed, as without doubt planetary survival is well and truly assured.

In contrast, Guys 'smart' discourse believes in techno and fiscal centric solutions. Science and technology can provide the solutions to environmental problems and the concerns are wrapped up within wider organisational innovations. The techno/fiscal-centricity of the "smart" discourse is most familiar in the world of commercial and property development. Commercial organisations are increasingly concerned with reducing overheads and increasing value additions in a highly competitive market. Operating a building's services in the most efficient manner reduces overheads. Increasingly, they are becoming corporate eco-identities, symbolising an organisation's eco-credentials, besides corporate and socially responsible attitudes.

Guy (1997) believes techno-centrics recognise the existence of environmental problems and want to solve them through the management of the environment through a commercially oriented business case (fiscal-centric). Effective environmental solution can proceed without upsetting sensitive development equations and investment criteria, thereby allowing commercial development actors to make "new kinds of decisions about design, management and the environmental standards of their workplaces." (Duffy *et al.*, 1993). The competing issues around 'greening' buildings are issues of building/space/energy efficiency, concerns for global environmental problems, climate change, resource depletion and ethical responsibility.

Guy (1997) suggests that a social constructivist approach to understanding green buildings could help in defining both a wider and fuller interpretation of the nature of the green design problem and may also contribute to developing contextual and socially based methods of ethical analysis. Building ethics can then be viewed as concepts that we test, qualify and reconstruct through the ongoing dynamics in the creative design process. Further, a social accounting of moral positions may help to make ethical analysis more practically significant and ... "would more closely coincide with the context of real life building types" (Guy, 1997).

Energy and carbon management professionals struggle to persuade 'those to be persuaded' of the long term, true life and ethical issues of 'greening' and sustainable management of buildings and the built environment. Guy and Farmer (2000) suggest that the real benefit of social constructivist analysis may lie in it's ability to demonstrate "how the power relations amongst competing interests are revealed to be the primary context for decision making," suggesting this as an important future direction in research. This research could then help to identify those actions with "most influence over decision-making and enable various professional actors to recognise their own positions and role in the provision of more sustainable lifestyles." In doing so, the research must identify the complex competing nature of organisational management of single issues amongst competing priorities.

The Initial Research Results

The primary investigation into carbon management practices was conducted in 2000 by requesting professionals working in energy management in the 33 London Boroughs to fill out a self assessment questionnaire. The questionnaire was in two parts, a self-assessment matrix system to score the strategic approach a local authority has for the management of energy, and 10 open ended questions. The primary assessment matrix (Appendix A-7.1) focused on energy reduction and was based on the UK Government published Good Practice Guide (GPG) 167: 'Organising energy management'. The scores (1=poor; 5=excellent) are awarded on the basis of the comprehensiveness of energy policy, it's organisational management and conformity and associated data management in relation to both energy, estate assets and investments. Twenty four out of 33 London Boroughs responded to the questionnaire.

The results from the self-assessment matrix indicated the following:

- there was great disparity among the responses from the 24 local authorities questioned;
- there is a tendency to score more highly on target setting and policy than data management and investment; and
- the 'mean' score tends to mask the disparate nature of a London Boroughs individual scoring and prioritising.

In addition to the matrix exercise, the participating London Boroughs were also asked to answer and/or comment on the following 10 secondary questions:

1. What is the approximate cost of your LA's Energy Bill? (£Millions)
2. What is the cost of your LA's Water Bill?

3. In which Department is the Energy Team Located?
4. How many full-time equivalent employees work in Energy Management?
5. Does the Energy Manager work for the whole LA or certain Departments?
6. Which Departments (if any) carry out their own Energy Management?
7. Who does the Energy Manager report to?
8. How are Capital Investments funded?
9. Does the Energy Manager report directly to a Member (elected) level committee?
10. Which of the following functions do you undertake or are responsible for directly: monitoring and targeting; provision of advice to the general public; utility and account verification; purchasing; strategic policy advice; design advice; advice on 'good housekeeping'?

In summary, the overall results from the questionnaire identified the following issues:

- London Boroughs with a dedicated energy professional (team) scored more highly whilst London Boroughs with no dedicated professional scored poorly;
- London Boroughs with 'outsourced' energy management services scored poorly;
- the departmental positioning of the energy team played no part in the overall effectiveness score;
- high scoring London Boroughs may employ an energy manager from either a technical or non-technical background;
- the average number of energy staff per £million energy spent for the top six scoring LAs was 0.67 (Year 2000 energy prices);
- four of the top six LAs have a specific fund for energy efficiency or positive discrimination for 'green schemes'.

Whilst many LAs have recognised proper management of energy and carbon as issues of fiscal and social conscience, they have not addressed the issue with any degree of longevity or strategic pose. Where they have and a 'strategy' has been informed, this has tended to be more of an exercise in aspirational targeting, such as, 'we will reduce carbon emissions by 25 per cent', 'we will be carbon-neutral by 2025'. The research results from the case study suggest that the strategy for achievement of these targets is not based on the necessary engineering, building stock characteristics, organisational and facility operations.

In 2010, investigations into current carbon management practices led to the development of a modified matrix (Appendix A-7.2) based on the original GPG 167, by requesting completion of a self-assessment questionnaire by professionals working in energy management in the 33 London Boroughs. Thirteen London Boroughs responded to the questionnaire. Comparing the results from the initial survey it is apparent that although the scores on carbon policy matters have increased compared to the energy policy, the scores relating to practicalities and investments remain low. This would imply a widening of the differential between rhetoric and practice.

Building on the theoretical analysis presented and the findings from the case study, a conceptual framework has been devised that integrates organisational learning and performance with day-to-day practice involving people, technology and procedure (Figure 7.3). The three primary areas are defined as building 'Performance', organisational 'Reform' and legal 'Conformity'. They reflect the inter-relationships between compliance with political directive and legislations, strategic organisational management and the practical engineering and thermodynamic performance of buildings. Improving building performance will necessitate a more positive approach whilst determining whether a local authority is accepting a change in its management principles, requires far greater alignment to interpretivist techniques. Conformity will likely be achieved through interpretation of the two. However, as implementing strategic changes is difficult without high level staff engagement and on-going adaptation to both processes and technologies, (Chaffee, 1985; Mintzberg, 1994), building 'performance', organisational 'reform' and legal 'conformity' must be integrated with further factors: people or the players within and associated with the organisation, the role of written procedures and policies and the role and application of technology (futurity), which together may in the long term embed organisationally coherent strategic direction.

Figure 7.3

Conceptual Framework Model

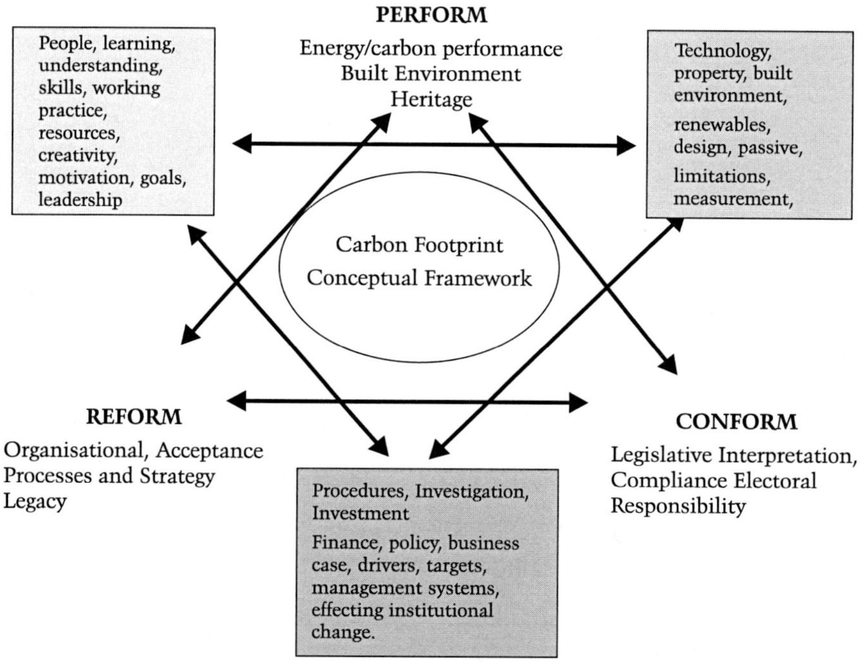

This is a 3-phase (organisation change) process of direction and guidance, leadership and organisational maturity through learning and understanding. Through the identification of key organisation playmakers and, finally, by embedding conceptual priorities with order and logic within the organisation, local authorities, can define the way they manage. Kenny's constructivist view (2006) that the process of learning was central to dealing with difficult or 'wicked' issue, strikes a chord with the challenges faced. How an organisation will learn and adapt are issues of: organisational learning, strategic planning, strategy formation, strategy implementation and change management. Senge (1990) characterised three forms of learning to survive strategic change management with generative learning that enhances our capacity to create as being the most appropriate.

'Learning' leadership and understanding by taking note of the natural organisational components 'people' within an organisation is also important as Chaffee (1985) stressed, bringing organisations to a collection of social agreements or, as Mintzberg described 'staff as co-strategists'. Heron and Reason's (1997) theoretical view is at contrast to Kenny's (2006) constructivist stance, concluding that a constructivist approach is insufficient due to the exclusion of experience resultant knowledge. Guy and Farmer (2000) consider buildings in a broader social context. Hannigan (1995) considers greening buildings as a social construct.

Guy (1997) considered the five competing discourses of green buildings at various ends of the discourse scale with ecologically driven discourse of making buildings more environmentally friendly being a deeply ethical argument. By contrast, the techno/fiscal-centric view is more familiar with the commercial and business focussed commercial and property market.

UK LAs have a duty and obligation to prepare themselves and the communities they serve to face the challenge of a low carbon society, the research evidence suggests that LAs are not properly prepared and that significant and appropriate carbon reduction management would therefore remain patchy and piecemeal.

Conclusions

The UK government is preparing the 'UK towards a low carbon' economy with an expectation to reduce national carbon dioxide emissions by 80 per cent. This paper provides the evidence that more comprehensive studies need to be carried out to determine the cost and practicalities of the impact of this expectation with regards UK LAs.

LAs have no legal obligation to reduce their energy and carbon emissions. However there is significant political and moral obligation and 'duty of care' on LAs to prepare themselves and the communities they serve to face the challenge of a low carbon society. Various powers place an obligation on LAs to improve the social economic and environmental well-being of the area and properties they maintain.

Whilst many LAs have identified the proper management of energy and carbon as issues of fiscal and social conscience, the challenge is to address the issue with a degree of longevity and strategic pose. Where this has been addressed and a 'strategy' has been informed, this has tended to be in the form of an aspirational target 'we will reduce carbon emissions by 25 per cent'; 'we will be carbon-neutral by 2025' (Kennedy, 2007).

By reviewing the theoretical perspectives of ethics and the built environment, it is apparent that there remains a gulf between the desire to protect nature and LAs' ecological impact and the disconnection of practical choice when it comes to decision making. The social construct that influences our determination in decision making and eco, fiscal and techno centric influence of players leads us to stall.

The study highlights the shortfall in strategic planning and preparedness of UK LAs (for the reductions envisaged) using evidence from the London Boroughs. Whilst this study may be local in scope, the results will have national relevance. The results of the study will help LAs determine whether further property management strategic decisions with respect to energy/carbon reductions need to be taken.

References

Amaratunga, D., B. Baldry, M. Sarshar and R. Newton (2001). *Quantitative and Qualitative Research in the Built Environment: Application of "mixed" Research Approach*. 1st International Postgraduate Conference. School of Construction and Property Management, University of Salford.

Chaffee, E.E. (1985). "Three Models of Strategy", *The Academy of Management Review* 10(1): 89-98.

Collis and Hussey (2003). *Business Research, A Practical Guide for Undergraduate and Postgraduate Students* (2nd edition). Palgrave Publishing.

Cook and Golton (1994). *Sustainable Development Concepts and Practice in the Built Environment: A UK Perspective*. Sustainable Construction. Chartered Institute Building, Task Group 16. Nov. 6-9th, pp.677-85.

Crotty, M. (1998). *The Foundations of Social Research, Meaning and Perspective in the Research Process*. Sage Publications.

Duffy, F., A. Laing and V. Crisp (1993). *The Redesign of Work and Offices: The Responsible Work Place*. Butterworth Architecture (London).

Fleming, P.D. (2004). *Local and Regional Greenhouse Gas Management*. Elsevier.

Fox, W. (2000). "Ethics and the Built Environment", in S. Guy and G. Farmer (eds.), *Contested Constructions: The Competing Logics of Green Buildings and Ethics*. pp. 74-75. Routledge.

Guy, S. (1997). *Alternative Developments: The Social Construction of Green Buildings*. Royal Institution of Chartered Surveyors Cutting Edge, University of Newcastle.

Great Britain Climate Change Act 2008 (2008). *Elizabeth II*. Chapter 27. London: The Stationery Office.

Hajer, M. (1995). *The Politics of Environmental Disclosure: Ecological Modernisation and the Policy Process*. Oxford University Press.

Hannigan, J. (1995). *Environmental Sociology: A Social Constructivist Perspective*. Routledge.

Heron, J. and P. Reason (1997). "A Participatory Inquiry Paradigm", *Qualitative Inquiry* 274 (21), Academic One File. Gale Publishing.

Kennedy, P. (2007). "The Management of Energy at the City of London Corporation: The Energy Manager's Perspective", *Paper 1 ARU*. April.

———. (2008). "Meeting the Government's 60% CO_2 Reduction Target in Local Authority Operational Buildings", *Paper 2 ARU*. August.

Kenny, J. (2006). "Strategy and the Learning Organisation: A Maturity Model for the Formation of Strategy", *The Learning Organisation* 13(4): 353-68. Emerald Publishing.

Kuntz, P.G. (1968). *The Concept of Order*. Seattle University Press, University of Washington Press.

Mintzberg, H., Quinn, James B. (1994). *The Strategy Process, Concepts, Context and Cases*. 3rd Edition. Prentice Hall.

Murray, J. (2008). *Evaluating the Scope for Energy-efficiency Improvements in the Public Sector: Benchmarking National Health Service Scotland's Smaller Health Buildings*. Elsevier.

Senge, Peter M. (1990). *The Fifth Discipline*. Century Business Publishers.

UNEP (2007). *Buildings and Climate Change: Status, Challenges and Opportunities*. pp. 4-7. Available from: *http://www.unep.org/sbci/pdfs/BuildingsandClimateChange.pdf*

UK (former) Department of Environment (2000). *Good Practice Guide 167, Organisational Aspects of Energy Management: A Self Assessment Manual for Managers*.

———. (former) Department of Environment (1997). *General Information Report 47*. Energy Efficiency Best Practice Programme. The Stationery Office.

———. (former) Department of Environment (1996). *Good Practice Guide 200*. Energy Efficiency Best Practice Programme.

Urge-Vorsatz, D. (2007). *Appraisal of Policy Instruments for Reducing Buildings' CO_2 Emissions*. London: E & FN Spon Publishers, an imprint of Chapman Hall.

———. (2008). *Potentials and Costs of Carbon Dioxide Mitigation in the World's Buildings*. Elsevier.

Wapner, S., B. Kaplan and S.B. Cohen (1980). "An Organismic-developmental Perspective for Understanding Transactions of Men and Environments", in G. Broadbent, R. Bunt and T. LLorens (Eds.) (1980). *Meaning and Behaviour in the Built Environment*. pp. 223-24. Chichester: Wiley Publisher.

Yin, K. (1994). *Case Study Research: Design and Methods*. Newbury Park, California, USA: Sage Publication.

Appendix A-7.1

Original Energy Self Assessment (Scoring) Matrix from Good Practice Guide 167: Organisation Energy Management Criteria

Score	*Energy Policy*	*Organising*	*Motivation*	*Information Systems*	*Marketing*	*Investment*
5	An energy policy, action plan and regular review with commitment of top management all as part of an environmental strategy?	Energy management fully integrated in management structure with clear delegation of responsibility for energy consumption?	Formal and informal channels of communication regularly exploited by energy manager and energy staff at all levels?	Comprehensive system sets targets, monitors consumption, identifies faults, quantifies savings and provides budget tracking?	Marketing of both the value of energy efficiency and the performance of energy management within the organisation and outside it?	Positive discrimination in favour of 'green' scheme with detailed investment appraisal of all new-build and refurbishment opportunities?
4	A formal energy policy, but no active commitment from top management?	An energy manager accountable to energy committee representing all users, chaired by a member of the council?	Contact through an energy committee which is used as the main channel, together with direct contact with major users?	M&T reports for individual premises based on sub-metering but savings not reported effectively to users?	Programme of staff awareness and regular publicity campaigns?	Same pay back criteria employed as for all other investment?
3	An unadopted energy policy set by an energy manager or senior manager?	An energy manager in post, reporting to adhoc committee, but with unclear line management and authority?	Contact with major users through ad hoc committee chaired by senior departmental manager?	Monitoring and targeting reports based on supply meter data.	Some ad hoc staff awareness training?	Investment using short-term pay back criteria only?
2	An unwritten set of guidelines?	Energy management as a part-time responsibility of someone with only limited authority or influence?	Informal contacts between technical staff and a few users?	Cost reporting based on invoice data with technical staff compiling reports for internal use within technical department?	Informal contacts used to promote energy efficiency? No Promotion of energy efficiency?	Only low cost measures undertaken?
1	No explicit policy?	No energy management or any formal delegation of responsibility for energy consumption?	No policy?	No information system and no accountability for energy consumption?		No investment in energy efficiency in premises?

Appendix A-7.2

Suggested 'Carbon Reduction Preparedness' Survey (Scoring) Matrix for Local Authorities Based on the Original Energy Self Assessment Matrix from Good Practice Guide 167: Organisation Energy Management Criteria

Score	*CO_2 Policy*	*Organisation*	*Conformity*	*Data Management*	*Practicalities*	*Investment Cost*
5	A formulated carbon policy and action plan supported at Member level.	Integrated carbon management action plan with clear lines of responsibility at senior level.	The organisation has pre-planned and costed Carbon Reduction Commitment (CRC) and is preparing for internal/external trading.	Smart meter installed for all meters, remote downloading and monthly reporting of energy, cost and carbon loads.	Full property database, asset management, property review metering and carbon data, fully evaluated opportunities for carbon reduction of 60 per cent.	Strategic review of all carbon investments carried out for all operational properties for 60 per cent carbon reduction
4	Formal carbon policy but no Member endorsement.	Carbon manager in post with clear lines of responsibility and recognition of strategic importance of carbon management.	The organisation is preparing for Display Energy Certificate (DEC) 2, revised Energy Performance Building Directive, CRC and planning for carbon management.	Centralised data gathering using half hourly and smart meters. Data available but not managed.	Full property database, asset management and corporate property review, matched with energy meters data.	Whole life costs taken into account for investment on additional installed equipment excluding fabric improvements.
3	A target set by a dedicated professional energy/carbon manager	Energy Manager in post with responsibility for carbon reduction plans	The organisation is familiar with DECs, has carried some out and is aware of CRC	Central data recording of 90 per cent + via direct and local reads with invoice reconciliation	Corporate property review undertaken, listing property details, age, built form, structure etc.	Investment using strict payback period -5 years approach
2	An aspirational target set by central policy unit	Energy/carbon management is part time responsibility or integrated with broader sustainability activities.	The organisation is aware of some pending legislation.	Data recording based on invoice data only	Asset list of all energy consuming properties.	Low cost measure undertaken opportunistically
1	No explicit target	No energy or carbon management whether in-house or delegated.	The organisation is unaware of any requirement to 'manage' carbon	No data records or accountability for energy/carbon consumption.	Uncertain of extent of property portfolio.	No investment in carbon reduction

8 Energy Transition Policies in Europe and their Social Impact

Ulrich Schachtschneider

Introduction

Urbanisation has led to an increasing demand for energy, particularly for traffic, heating, cooling and electricity. As people in cities do not produce their own energy, but obtain it from energy suppliers, they are often not aware of the negative effects on their environment of their ever rising energy consumption.

Aiming to check the uncontrolled consumption, European countries have, over the past 20 years, changed their policies on sustainable energy. The main policy goals are reduction in the dependence on fossil fuels and the reduction of CO_2 emission to 20 per cent of the present quantum. The maximum permissible emission needs to be brought down to 2 tonne CO_2 per capita per year. At present in Germany it stands at 11 tonnes. The emission is somewhat lower in the cities (9.8 tonne CO_2 per capita and year), but the emission generated outside the cities has to be added. The emission from private households in Germany is about 2.3 tonne CO_2 per capita, which is about double the emission in Delhi (1.1 tonne CO_2 per capita per year) and also includes emission from industry, trade and traffic.

The energy transition activities are being carried out with three goals—consistency, efficiency and sufficiency—based on the strategies decided upon during the discourse on sustainability at the UN conference in Rio de Janeiro in 1992.

The first goal is the shift to renewable energy, which would result in greater consistency. Ideally speaking, this would mean a massive decrease in anthropogenic emissions that disturb the natural cycles, such as the carbon cycle. The second goal is greater efficiency in the transfer from the production point to the user, resulting in an overall improvement in the use of energy. The energy can come from sustainable sources, but this is not necessarily the case. The third goal is to save energy by changing the behaviour pattern of the consumer, such as switching off the lights when not needed and keeping the room temperature low. This is called self-sufficiency.

The goals having been discussed, the methods used to achieve them in the cities in Germany and Europe (as well as the results obtained) are discussed in the following section. The focus is on private households. Studies reveal that the CO_2 emission has been reduced only slightly despite the efforts. A thesis is thus presented that an attempt at any greater change to achieve sustainable energy goals may lead to social frictions which the present green government or green market policies would fail to contain. Finally, some alternative approaches are reviewed critically.

Energy Transition Policy in German and European Cities

Many cities and towns in Germany and at least all the bigger cities in Europe have implemented energy policies based on the three goals mentioned earlier. The following are a few of the many examples:

- The application of solar energy (for hot water and electricity) is supported financially or is regulated. Awareness programmes are carried out to demonstrate the use of solar energy in public buildings. Energy awareness is stimulated through competitions, awards, advice as well as by specifying the constraints in new residential areas.
- The same holds for energy efficiency. Subsidies are given to insulate housings, replace old electrical equipment, etc. Moreover, awareness campaigns are launched. Strict rules are applied for the construction of new buildings. The cities set ambitious goals for their buildings and for the equipment, enforcing stricter rules. The energy consumption of the buildings is monitored.
- These activities are not limited to technical aspects, but also include information campaigns, neighbourhood assemblies and brochures to stimulate the citizen's consciousness about their own energy consumption. The aim is to get the society more and more involved in the activities.

Energy Transition Policy and Economic Performance

How successful have the European cities been? A team of scientists formulated the "European Green City Index" (EGCI) to assess the sustainability of about 30 major European cities on a scale from 0 to 100. The following indicators of this index are of relevance:

- CO_2 emission per capita per year, CO_2 emission per GDP, a measure of the ambition of their CO_2 reduction strategy.
- Energy consumption per capita per year, energy consumption per GDP, share of renewable energy, the quality of the programmes to stimulate the use of renewable energy and energy efficiency.
- Energy consumption of buildings per m^2, the number and extent of regulations, the quality of the support measures.
- Number of ecomobility[1] participants, length of bicycle paths and of the public transport network, measures to stimulate ecomobility, quality of the measures to reduce traffic jams.

In sum, the authors reached the conclusion that environmental performance increases with the increase in economic performance (Figure 8.1). This is at least clear for the 30 European cities. For the German cities the picture is somewhat different (Figure 8.2). The environmental performance is essentially the same, regardless of economic performance. One reason for this is that all German cities have an extensive environmental policy as a result of the environmental awareness of their administrations. The other reason is that the national energy policy in Germany affects all cities equally. This result seems to be in agreement with the theory behind the Environmental Kuznets Curve: initially, environmental problems increase with the increase in economic performance, but after a certain level of wealth has been accumulated, the problems are abated.

---

1. Ecomobility is an environmentally friendly and socially inclusive way of transportation, including cycling, wheeling, walking and the use of public transportation.

Figure 8.1

European Cities: Wealth and Environmental Policy Performance

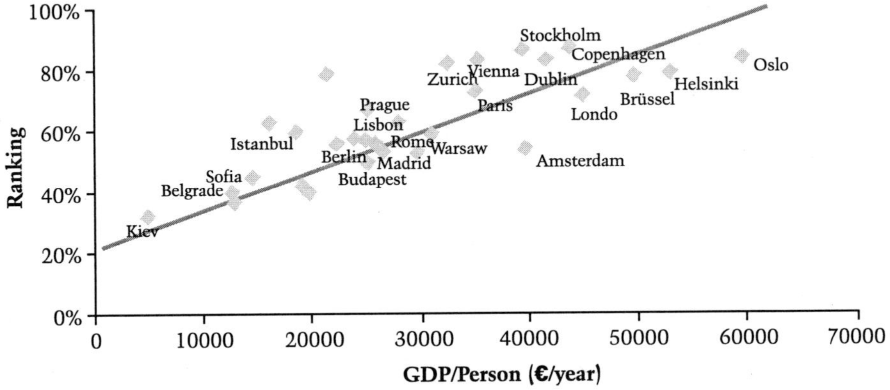

Source: *Economist Intelligence Unit 2011: European Green City Index.*

Figure 8.2

German Cities: Wealth and Energy Transition Policy Performance

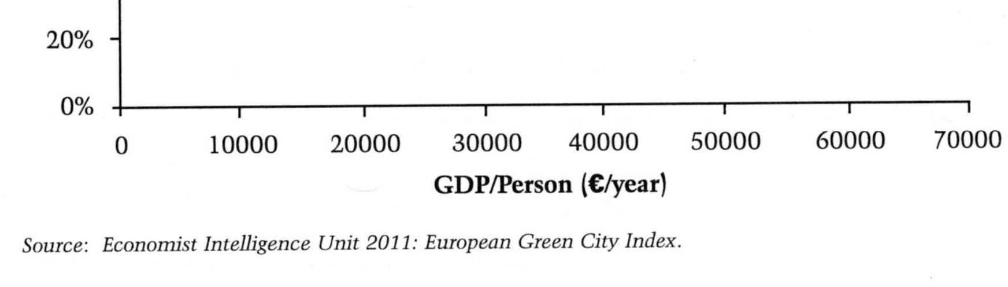

Source: *Economist Intelligence Unit 2011: European Green City Index.*

CO_2 Emission and Economic Performance

The result is quite different when we look at the relationship between CO_2 emission and economic performance. One would expect that the emission decreases with GDP, but going by the same EGCI data, one finds that the opposite is the case (Fig. 8.3)! The reason for this is not entirely clear. There are a few outliers such as Oslo or Stockholm, which have

Figure 8.3

European Cities: Wealth and CO_2 Emissions

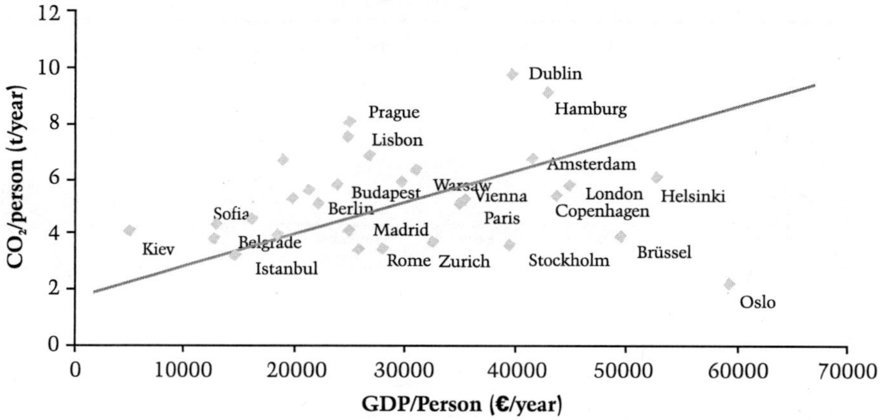

Source: *Economist Intelligence Unit 2011: European Green City Index.*

different and ambitious energy policies. Their low CO_2 emission can, however, be explained by other factors. Stockholm has almost no heavy industry and the city can afford to expand its district heating network, as it mainly uses biomass. Oslo's total energy consumption (heat and electricity) is—as is the tradition in that country—64 per cent covered by hydro power, which is a very high percentage for a European nation. For all German cities we find the same CO_2 emission-GDP ratio (Figure 8.4), except in the case of Bremen. This city is relatively small, but 48 per cent of its energy consumption is caused by a big steelwork. Minus the steelwork's consumption, the emission-GDP ratio would be equal to the average of other cities.

When the environmental performance with GDP and CO_2 emission with GDP are compared, one can conclude the following: the environmental performance increases with GDP, but this does not result in successfully reducing the CO_2 emission. From all appearances the GDP's effect on CO_2 emission is the major deciding factor (This is, of course, a snapshot conclusion). In the analysis of the "German Green City Index" (GGCI) this is mentioned indirectly at one point: "Environmental regulation contributes decisively to the good results of the German cities." Further down it says:

"German cities show weaknesses with regard to the actual consumption and infrastructures."[2]

Figure 8.4

German Cities: Wealth and CO_2 Emissions

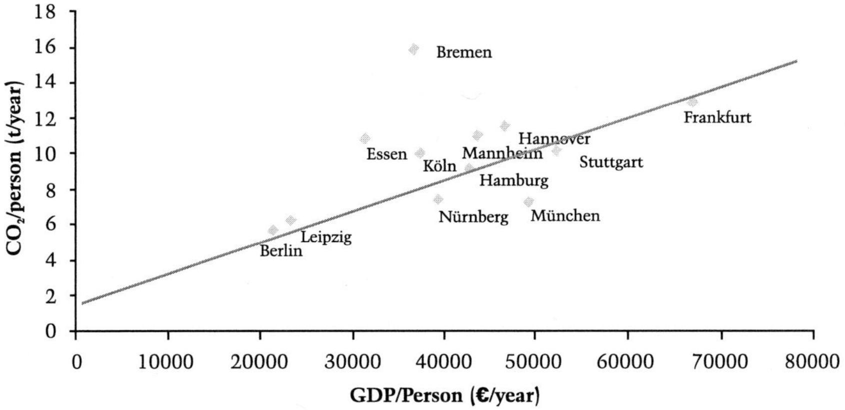

Source: *Economist Intelligence Unit 2011: European Green City Index.*

Tendency in the Past 15 Years

The current situation in Europe does not augur well for the future of energy transition, despite its well-conceived environment policy. Has there been any worthwhile progress during the past years? Let us have a look at the data from Germany.[3] The energy consumption per capita per year in all sectors (i.e., industry, services, transport and private households) has, truth be told, stagnated, while the total CO_2 emission per capita per year has declined by 10 per cent (Figure 8.5). In the following sections, information is given on the situation for private households. The heat consumption per m^2 per year has decreased, but not the heat consumption rate (Figure 8.6). This means that the efficiency has increased, but this positive effect has been undone by an increase in the per capita living area. In economic terms, there has been a rebound effect. The picture for electricity consumption is no different (Figure 8.7): it has even increased slightly, but less hot water

2. *Economist Intelligence Unit 2011: German Green City Index*, p.13.

3. *Federal Environmental Authority (ed.) 2011: Energy Efficiency in Figures*. (In German: *Umweltbundesamt (Hrsg.) 2011: Energieeffizienz in Daten*).

Figure 8.5

Germany: Overall CO_2 Impact and Energy Use per Person in Private Households

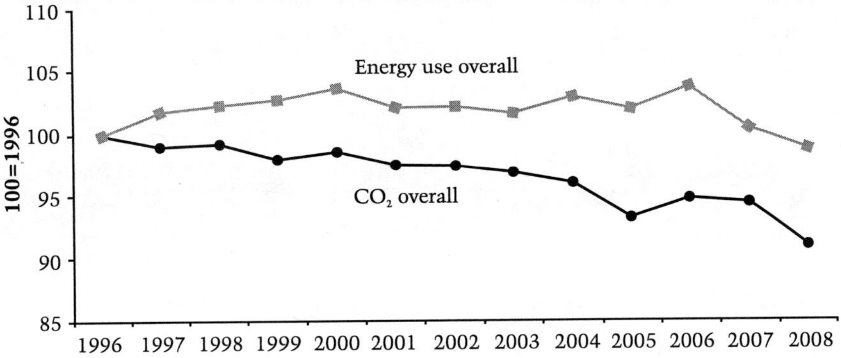

Source: *UBA (Hg.) 2011*: Energy efficiency in figures.

Figure 8.6

Germany: Energy Use for Space Heating in Private Households

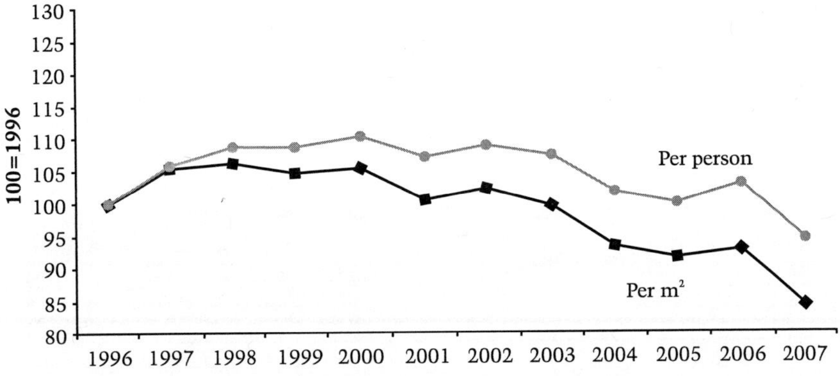

Source: *UBA (Hg.) 2011*: Energy efficiency in figures.

has been used. The CO_2 emission caused by electrical equipment has increased (Figure 8.8). No doubt the new equipment is more efficient and a larger ratio of the electricity is generated by renewable energy, but the CO_2 emission has increased nevertheless due to an increased use of equipment. A slight decrease in CO_2 emission per capita per year caused by heat consumption was recorded. In this case, the increase in efficiency

Figure 8.7

Germany: Energy Use per Person in Private Households

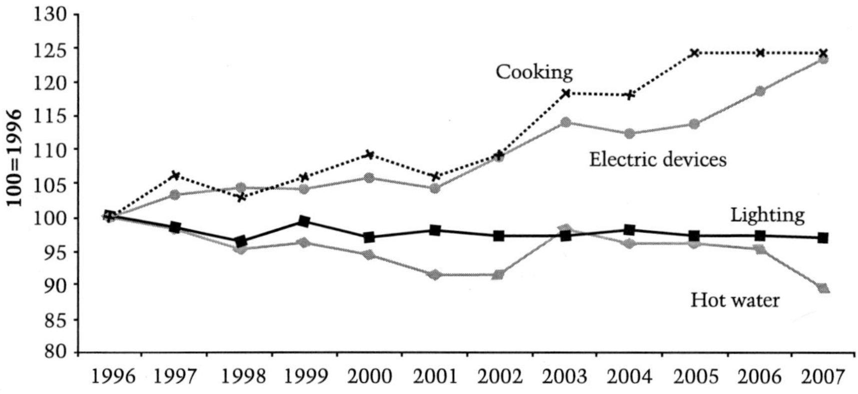

Source: *UBA (Hg.) 2011*: Energy efficiency in figures.

Figure 8.8

Germany: CO_2 Impact per Person in Private Households

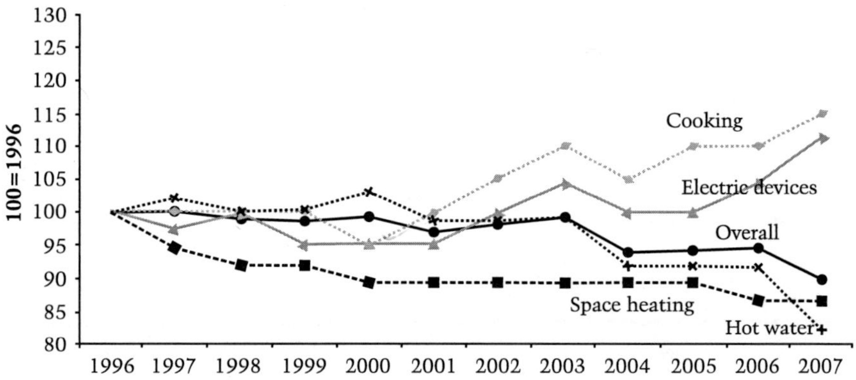

Source: *UBA (Hg.) 2011*: Energy efficiency in figures.

due to insulation and new heating equipment is larger than the increase in living area per capita, thus resulting in a 10 per cent reduction in the CO_2 emission rate. As about five times more energy is used for heating than for electrical equipment, the overall effect (heating and electrical equipment) is a slight decrease in CO_2 emission.

Interim Conclusion

In so far as the numbers are concerned, the following interim conclusion can be drawn. Although Germany has tried to move towards greater energy transition during the past 15 years, only limited results have been obtained. The current reduction of approximately 10 per cent is caused by two purely technical strategies: switching to renewable sources and increasing the energy efficiency. There is yet no result seen from the strategy to change consumer behaviour.

Thesis

My thesis is: any attempt at a definitive energy transition is likely to lead to serious social problems as it promotes socio-economic inequality. The present policy (a majority formulation) will find very poor response. This is because a basic mechanism to regulate capitalistic societies is no longer acceptable or possible. It was cheap energy and cheap resources that made unequal distribution in the so called developed countries of the North bearable.

Social Problems at the Beginning of Energy Transition

Already, with just a CO_2 emission reduction of 10 per cent the social problems are visible. This is shown by the price trend in private households: The price for electricity has increased by 50 per cent during the past 10 years, and the price of natural gas used for heating has increased by as much as 100 per cent in the same period. Natural gas price hike has been caused by the increase in the world market prices. The tax itself (27%) is not very important. The percentage of tax is higher for electricity (47%). The tax consists of sales tax, license tax, levy for renewable energy and eco-taxes, which was introduced about 10 years ago. Actually, all these taxes work in the same way as eco-taxes as they depend on the amount of energy consumed. Politicians are afraid to increase these taxes to accelerate the energy transition as it would lead to mass protests.

Taking the social issue into account, to what extent can the sustainable energy policy move forward in Germany and in Europe? This question will be answered taking into account two drivers on the energy transition track—the green market and the green state. The social consequences of their actions, especially on income distribution, will be assessed using some examples.

Green Market

The green market method consists of steering the change to renewable energy technology through positive and negative economical incentives. These methods can be used by businesses and consumers alike. Here are a few examples:

The first example is the "EEG[4]", the Renewable Energy Law in Germany. It guarantees the operator of a facility which creates electricity from renewable sources, a specific reimbursement from the energy company which operates the network. This reimbursement is set above the market price for producing electricity. In Germany it is about 5 euro cents per kwh. However, the difference of the market price is not paid by the energy producers but by all consumers. The energy supplier's added costs are reimbursed through a fund created by setting an additional charge to the end cost, the EEG levy. With the development of renewable energy this additional charge has been rising. In 2011, it was 3.5 euro cents per kwh, or 15 per cent of the price for electricity. At the moment, 18 per cent of the electricity in Germany is from renewable sources. The industry is to a large part freed of these costs. The more renewable energy is invested, the higher will be the shared costs. In practical terms, every private consumer, from infants to the aged, poor to rich, will finance these guaranteed profits of private investors in renewable energy. This method of green market has spread to many European countries. There are similar laws in other countries.

The second example is the energy tax. A tax is paid by the consumer for the use of electricity, gas, heating oil and gasoline/diesel, which is about 5-10 per cent of the price. This also applies to companies who receive certainly generous exceptions. Approximately 90 per cent of the revenue (about 20 billion Euros per year) goes into the public pension fund. In Germany, employers and employees pay the same amount into the government pension fund. Through this tax, both pay a monthly amount

4. The German Renewable Energy Act [In German: *Erneuerbare-Energien-Gesetz (EEG)*].

of about 10 per cent into the pension fund. Even those who have no employment have to pay into the public pension fund. Everyone—part-time workers, students, the unemployed and those receiving public assistance—are required to pay up as long as they are consumers, even if they receive no benefits.

The third example is the market incentive programme—'Renewable Energy'. Whoever installs a thermal solar system, a heat pump or a biomass heating, etc., receives a government investment subsidy, which comes from the tax revenue. Subsidies are also available for renovating housing space. The owner receives a favourable credit or direct subsidy up to 17.5 per cent of the investment sum in accordance to the energy efficiency of the renovation. Therefore, the rate of modernisation of houses and apartments rises. Normally the rate of modernisation is 1 per cent per year, but the government expects a rate of 2.5 per cent through this programme. Through this energy mode modernisation the rent is raised. Calculations have proven this. The landlords have the right to raise the rent up to 11 per cent of their investment costs. But the tenants will get back at maximum half the rent risen by decreasing energy costs. This means a big raise in the rent, which causes many problems and protests, such as those witnessed in Berlin. Because of this, poorer occupants in older city areas which are to be modernised are forced to move. In city research this is called 'gentrification'.

Green State

The green state method consists of laws, rules and regulations for the use of energy. As opposed to green marketing, here energy savings is made mandatory, not just encouraged. The regulations are enforced and followed up by inspections. The first example is the EnEV[5] (energy saving ordinance). It sets maximum limits for the use of primary energy for the heating of dwellings. For the construction of new buildings there are relatively strict regulations. Depending on the shape of the building, they can use at the most 60-100 kwh per square metre, which is a third of the average energy use of older buildings (about 200 kwh per year).

5. In German: *Energieeinsparverordnung (EnEV)*.

How the building owners arrive at these values is left up to them. There are, however, some obligations: 15 per cent of the heating must come from renewable energy sources, such as solar heating, heat pumps, or combined heat and power generation. However, better insulation can help to keep the consumption below 15 per cent. For older buildings there are few regulations. For example, only the ceiling of the upper floor must be insulated. This is relatively easy, since it is easily accessible. Measures which require a higher investment, for example insulating outer walls or replacing windows, are not required for older buildings.

Another example is the BImSchV[6] (the governmental emission protection ordinance). This ordinance allows a heating loss of 9-11 per cent from the boiler, depending on the size of the building. Otherwise, it has to be replaced. These poor values are generally for boilers that are over 20 years; the regulation mandates their replacement. The case is similar for the older "night storage heaters" which use a large amount of primary energy. They too have to be replaced, but only when they are 30 years old and only after 2019! Regulations for the renovation of buildings take into account the house owners' and renters' position. They are not forced to make expensive and uneconomical renovations.

The third example is the ban on light bulbs based on the EU-eco-design guideline. Bulbs above 60 watts are no longer in the market. A ban on lower wattage bulbs will follow, but such direct bans are not common.

The manufacturers of large appliances (for example, refrigerators) are required to state the energy usage for the information of the consumer. These labels are often confusing, since the calculations are based on 25 year old averages. 98 per cent of refrigerators today are given the label "A". An appliance with an above average energy consumption is therefore given the label A+ (the better ones A+++). The manufacturers have successfully managed to avoid exact labelling.

The further implementation of the EU-eco-design guideline is so planned that manufacturers must document the measures they are taking to improve product efficiency. A ban on certain devices with too high energy consumption is very rare. Here also the influence of the manufacturer is obvious. They don't want too many restrictions.

---

6. In German: *Bundesimmissionsschutzverordnung (BImSchV).*

Green New Deal with Dilemma

Green market and green state are features of the political strategy of the 'Green New Deal', not only for the political party—the Greens, but also for UN institutions and NGOs, and is being propagated by a growing number of economists and environmental researchers.[7] The Green New Deal aspires toward answering the economical and ecological crises in an integrated way. The main idea consists of a governmentally-supported innovation and investment impetus to bring green technology to the field of green marketing. The idea is that economic growth should go hand in hand with ecological wellbeing, specially since new technology is expected to help keep environment out of harm's way.

The reference to the historical model of the New Deal lends the Green New Deal the spirit of intelligent transformation and feasibility within the capitalistic system.

The New Deal, which was begun by President Roosevelt in the 1930s and developed further after World War II, also consisted of governmentally-supported investments in infrastructure which was, at that time, railroads and education. In retrospect, we find that through these initiatives the capitalistic system was finally able to free itself of the structural problems of capital assessment, expressed through the deep depression of the 30s.

Both of the main strategies of the Green New Deal, Green Market and Green State, however, find themselves in a dilemma. If the taxes and cost sharing are too low, they have little effect on ecological management. If they are too high, they are considered antisocial. The same is true for the regulations: if they are too lax, they have little effect. If they are too high, they force the poorer population to make expensive renovations. The Green New Deal requires massive mandatory investments in energy transition, which must sooner or later be paid for by the majority of the population. These additional costs will need to be compensated for by new jobs and higher income. Two questions arise. Will it result in more jobs and higher income? Will such a growth strategy prove to be ecologically advantageous in the long term?

---

7. For example, New Economics Foundation (2008). *A Green New Deal*. London.

Alternatives

There are a few suggestions as to how an increase in social inequality through rising energy prices can be moderated or avoided.

The first step would be to introduce social tariffs. The person whose income is below a certain margin receives a basic amount of electricity or heating at no charge. Some energy providers exemplarily do this already for a limited number of customers. In certain cities 'social tickets' are handed out to the economically less privileged for a rebate in travel costs. Implementing the principal of cheaper social tariffs, raises certain problems. First, the question of funding has not been solved. Until now social tariffs were offered to a limited extent. If this principle is to be introduced everywhere, it has to be resolved who will pay—the other consumers, the indebted communities, or should there be a rise in taxes, etc.? Second, it means a higher administrative expenditure for the communities, for those entitled and for the providers of energy services. Evidence of income must be examined, etc. Third, application of low-income tariff means a social stigmatisation. This means many people will not accept their benefits out of a sense of shame. Fourth, there is a problem of fair play in demarcation. Up to a certain income level, one is entitled to a price advantage or free delivery, but anyone who earns even one euro more does not receive this advantage.

A similar idea is holding energy consultation with lower income people. This is being carried out in certain areas. Recipients of public assistance receive a visit at home by an energy consultant free of charge and informed of energy-saving possibilities. This consultation is mainly directed towards encouraging frugality among the users. Other strategies, such as investing in renewable energy or the purchase of more efficient appliances are not affordable for the poor. The problem with this is that a certain change in attitude is expected from the poorer segment of the society. Such expectations could lead to lesser allowance being meted out as public assistance rates. Energy consultation, especially for the poor, also leads to stigmatisation.

Another idea is the green common. The basic idea consists of creating self-determined production attitudes. This can take place in the framework of a cooperative. This could also mean returning the control of energy services to the communities and cities by the private sector. Such a movement to a re-communalisation is found, for example, in Germany. The participating members or citizens will, hopefully, conduct themselves respectfully towards nature, by carefully generating their energy from locally available renewable sources such as wind, sun, biomass, and, eventually, hydropower. Their strategy of energy production will be planned in a participative, democratic process, independent of profit goals. They will therefore carry out the distribution and sale of energy in a socially just way. But the problem of the rising cost of energy is not solved even with a joint production and distribution. Indeed, the pressure of making a profit does not exist. But even cooperatives need to invest in expensive, efficient techniques and renewable energy, which affects the price of energy. Some of the best examples in Germany show that the energy prices of cooperatives and municipal utilities are not lower than that of businesses. Even non-profit cooperatives are confronted with the problem of the intensification of social inequality through their energy-transition policies. Perhaps they have a greater motivation to find a solution to this problem.

A third solution is the "basically-progressive" tariff. A basic amount of energy is free for every citizen. Consumption beyond the basic use, in other words 'luxury consumption', becomes more expensive. With this revenue the basic free amount is financed. The price per energy unit rises thereby and investment in efficiency and change in behaviour becomes more profitable. Preliminary calculations have shown that poorer families and those with many children profit from these tariff structures: they receive more in return in the form of the basic free amount than they need to pay in the form of a price rise for 'luxury use'. A concrete example of this idea already exists: the city of Basel levies, a so-called 'guidance-fee electricity' pays via the energy bill, the income to all citizens equally, which is about 60€ per person per year. It functions free of the red tape of bureaucracy.

The charm of this model lies in the fact that it connects redistribution and ecological supervision without discrimination, without a problematic demarcation of entitled persons, besides being free of red tape. Furthermore, it is a solution without more governmental regulations for correct consumption. It is left up to the individual as to how much he wants to use, but receives tougher limits in the form of monetary restrictions. This principle is similar to the combination of green market, green state, and green common. An ecology tax becomes associated with redistribution from the green social state. The element of the green common is at least partially introduced with the basic free use of energy.

This model is also described as 'ecology-bonus' or 'ecological basic income' in discussions.[8] However, in politics and science, it is rather marginal. The principal of per-person payout of eco taxes does not only suit for the use of energy supply of cities, but could also be excellently used in international climate politics.[9] Poorer countries in the south would profit financially because of their lower consumption and higher population. The model of the eco bonus with its social compensation could bring the stalled global climate diplomacy as well as energy transition in European cities back into action again.

References

Barnes, Peter (2008). *Capitalism 3.0: A Guide to Reclaiming the Commons*. San Francisco: Berret-Koehler.

Ekardt, Felix (2010). *Soziale Gerechtigkeit in der Klimapolitik*. Düsseldorf.

---

8. Peter Barnes (2008) introduced this in the form of the idea of a '*Sky Trust*'.
9. This is proposed for example by Felix Ekardt (2010) with his conception for social justice in climate policy.

9 Addressing the Ultimate Urban Exclusion: Slums

Raymond J. Struyk

Introduction

Urban exclusion refers to processes in cities and towns through which individuals and entire communities of people are systematically blocked from rights, opportunities, and resources normally available to members of the society. Such exclusion takes many forms, but the obvious outcome is that the individual's standard of living is visibly lowered. Ruthlessly discriminatory action is one of the tools of this exclusionary process. But, surprisingly, discriminatory methods are more often subtle, such as when a minority community member seeking to rent an apartment is told that a two-bedroom unit is available but not the one-bedroom, even though both are available. 'Audits' are systematic methods to identify such discriminations. They involve both majority and minority group applicants seeking the same apartment, job or service. Audits have identified pervasive discriminatory behaviour in the United States against minority home seekers, for both rental and owned dwellings, against those in marginal neighbourhoods and minorities trying to buy property, rent a house, or get a job or insurance.[1] Audit results are now accepted by US courts and are routinely used to prosecute discriminators.

Exclusion on the basis of race, ethnicity, or economic resources is another form. Gated communities offer an example. Typically, to reside in most such communities a household must have the economic assets to purchase or rent a unit and to pay the taxes or other fees that support the provision of high quality services. Some communities and real estate

1. Fix and Struyk (1992) give an overview on the methods and findings in several sectors. More recent findings on labour market discrimination are in Pager *et al.* (2009), which also reviews major other studies.

agents selling properties in them make it abundantly clear that 'outsiders' are not welcome. In municipalities where public provision of basic services is problematic, gated communities with their money power can arrange everything for themselves starting from regular water and power supply to police services. These self-sufficient communities are common urban phenomena in a number of developed and developing nations.

One can argue that gated communities represent an extension of Charles Tiebout's basic theory: jurisdictions offering varying combinations of services permits citizens to better match their public service demands (and their tax payments) with service packages on offer, thereby increasing their utility (Nelson, 2005). These efficiency gains may, however, be offset by negative consequences. First, social segregation often results in public service disparities inconsistent with the 'separate but equal' rule which can create life-long disadvantage for the excluded community. Second, there is every likelihood of both the included and excluded parties falsely maligning each other, which can heighten social tension and foster discrimination in the workplace and elsewhere. While one must avoid oversimplification, gated communities do raise serious issues (e.g., Durington, 2006).

Slums, probably the most pervasive and pernicious manifestation of social exclusion, result from a combination of poor public policy performance and inadequate household incomes of the residents. The list of policy failures is lengthy and includes:

- unnecessarily high standards for sub-divisions and residential construction that drive the cost of 'formal' housing beyond the reach of many families;
- utility companies' failure to provide services, (or services consistent with slum residents' ability to pay) to areas failing sub-division standards, even where providing services may be allowed by local standards; such areas are given lower priority than 'formal' neighbourhoods;
- costly and complex procedures for plot owners to acquire official confirmation of land rights, thereby making it more costly or impossible to accelerate housing development through borrowing funds;

- ineffective urban planning that in cases isolates slums from jobs;
- inefficient within city passenger transport that pressures low income workers to live in unsafe areas near the city centre where jobs are concentrated; and
- insufficient allocation by national government to local governments of financial resources (either taxing authority or intergovernmental transfers for infrastructure investment that can be flexibly used). Dire need for decision-making authority and responsible urban development body.

This paper focuses on the ways of mitigating the problems and improving the conditions in current informal areas in developing countries' cities. It begins in the next section with a selective overview of the problems and human costs, such areas entail and the attendant isolation of impoverished households. Owing to space constraints not all issues are discussed. In the third section some of the numerous examples of projects that have successfully addressed most of these problems are highlighted. The fourth section reviews the formidable impediments to moving beyond projects to national programmes. The final section concludes.

Informal Settlements

Although some informal settlements and urban slums are dynamic centres of microenterprises and social interaction, they are nonetheless beset with a host of problems which constrain the aspirations of their residents to achieve a better life and to contribute more to the economic, civic and social development of their neighbourhoods and the greater urban areas.

In the public's mind slums or informal settlements (the terms are used interchangeably here) where the residences of the poor are concentrated, are the most distinctive image of developing countries' cities. The UN uses five shelter deficits to measure slums: lack of access to treated water, lack of access to sanitation, non-durable housing, insufficient living area, and insecurity of tenure (UN-HABITAT, 2008: 90).

Slums result from a toxic combination of weak governance, underinvestment in basic infrastructure, poor planning to accommodate growth, unrealistically high standards for residential neighbourhoods and infrastructure standards that are unaffordable to the poor, insufficient public transportation that limits employment access and, of course, significant poverty. To understand slums, one must first understand the economic make-up of urban residents.

The latest estimates are that one-third of urban residents in low and middle-income countries live in poverty; this is about one-fourth of all the poor in these countries (World Bank definitions, Ibid.: 51). While in most regions, the poor are relatively concentrated in rural areas, Latin America is the exception with two-third of the poor huddled in cities. Overall, an increasing share of the poor is urban located.

The percentage of poor persons in urban population differs dramatically among regions, as illustrated in Table 9.1. The highest rates by a very large margin are in South Asia (76% of urban residents are poor) and Sub-Saharan Africa (68%). In South Asia, 80 per cent are in Indian cities.

Table 9.1

Urban Poverty Estimates, 2002

Region (World Bank Definition)	*Per cent Urban Population Below Poverty ($2 per day[a])*	*Per cent of All Poor in Urban Areas*
East Asia-Pacific	18	15
Europe-Central Asia	11	10
Latin America	28	66
Middle East-North Africa	12	29
South Asia	76	25
Sub-Saharan Africa	68	31
Total	34	26

Note: [a] : $2 cut-off adjusted for urban-rural differences in prices.

Source: Ravallion *et al.* (2007).

The migration of families from the countryside to cities has been an important factor in poverty reduction—both through the opportunities for migrants and indirect benefits to those staying back. From 1993 to 2002 the poverty rate in developing countries fell by 8.7 percentage points, of which 4.8 is assigned to rural poverty reduction, 2.3 to urban poverty reduction, and the balance (1.6%) to the population shift effect.

While not all the urban poor live in slums, most do; nor are all people living in slums poor—some find the economic advantages outweighing the hardships. Estimates are that about 1 billion people live in slums in developing countries—i.e., one-third of the population. The share of urban households living in slums in 2001 varied sharply region wise with African cities having by far the highest incidence: Sub-Saharan Africa (72%); Asia Pacific, including South Asia (43%); Latin America and Caribbean (32%); Middle East—North Africa (30%) (Tannerfeldt and Ljung, 2006). But in no region is the incidence below 30 per cent. Little wonder that the UN Millennium Development Goals call for a significant improvement in the lives of at least 100 million slum dwellers by the year 2020.

In a large share of slums most dwellings are owner-occupied. Owners, who believe they are safe from eviction, incrementally upgrade over time to have walls, roofs and floors of durable materials and make other improvements. But in a significant share of slums, including Kibera in Nairobi, for example, occupants rent from landlords who often have legal claims on the land. Some landlords own hundreds of badly maintained dwellings and have little incentive to invest on them. For the tenants, making improvements is risky because of the lack of formal leases or other tenure security rules (Gulyani and Talukdar, 2008).

It is hard to describe slum conditions with sufficient vividness. The data in Table 9.2 on the incidence of children's diseases of various locations in Kenya underscore the consequences of dirty water, non-existent or primitive sanitation, as also flimsy and crowded housing. Nairobi's informal settlements, especially the two largest and worst slums, have incidence rates much higher than those for rural areas. The under 5 mortality rate is a staggering 25 per cent in the Embakasi settlement, compared with 11 per cent in rural areas and 6 per cent in Nairobi overall.

Residents of most slums live in extremely crowded housing conditions—typical slum families inhabit one room structures of less than 300 sq. ft., often partitioned only by curtains. Indoor toilet facilities and individual house water connections are rare. In such close quarters, diseases spread very quickly. The lack of privacy also means that children are exposed to sexual relations of family members at a very young age, contributing to the early onset of sexual activity found in many slum communities. This is reinforced by high levels of prostitution resulting from lack of economic opportunities for many young slum girls leading to the high levels of unwanted pregnancies and sexually transmitted diseases (STDs), including HIV/AIDS (Zulu *et al.*, 2000).

Table 9.2

Infant Mortality Rates and Diarrhoea Prevalence in Kenya by Location

Location	*Infant Mortality Rate*	*Under Five Mortality Rate*[a]	*Prevalence of Diarrhoea in Children under 3*[b] *(%)*
Kenya	74	112	3
Rural Kenya	76	113	3
Urban Kenya, excl. Nairobi	57	84	2
Nairobi—all areas	39	62	3
- Informal settlements	91	151	11
-- Kibera settlement	106	187	10
-- Embakasi settlement	164	254	9

Notes: [a]: per 1,000 births; [b]: In the two weeks prior to the interview.

Source: Tannerfeldt and Ljung (2006).

Slum families, particularly in Sub-Saharan Africa, often cook with solid fuels such as bio-mass and coal. This causes indoor air pollution, leading to high levels of respiratory diseases, particularly in children. It is estimated that indoor air pollution is responsible for between 2.7 and 2.8 million deaths worldwide annually, mostly in developing countries (UN-HABITAT, 2008: 125). UN-HABITAT cites a recent study showing that multiple housing deprivations can lead to a 25 per cent greater risk of disability or severe ill health across a life span, especially if poor housing is exposed during childhood (UN-HABITAT, 2003: 75).

Slum communities are frequently located on land unsuitable for residential purposes—occupying low lying terrain or precipitous slopes, adjacent to environmentally hazardous land uses such as polluting industry, railroad tracks and landfills. Without adequate storm drainage during the rainy season in low-lying areas, streets, pathways and residences are subject to frequent flooding, and communities on slopes are subject to landslides and erosion of makeshift barriers. A case in point—almost every other year the 55,000 slum dwellers living in Asuncion's river flood plain are driven out of their homes (Ibid: 69).

The stresses caused by the harsh living conditions in urban areas, particularly the slums, lead to higher levels of bad habits such as, high and increasing incidence of alcohol and drug use, and domestic abuse, as also ailments such as cardiovascular disease, diabetes, depression (World Bank, 2003: 134). The WHO estimates that by 2030, the proportion of the disease burden represented by non-communicable diseases will increase from 44 to 54 per cent in low and middle income countries and that the poor in urban slums will suffer the most (Barbiero, 2007: 197).

Understanding slums' location is necessary for the discussion later about urban transport services. They are either in the city centre, close to employment opportunities, or in peri-urban areas where land is more readily available but where settlements tend to be isolated. As noted above, those in the centre often occupy land unsuitable for other purposes, such as zones subject to flooding or parts of large railroad yards. While this is the general pattern, there are African cities where the interweaving of informal and formal areas is quite intense. Regardless of location, informal settlement residents usually have only undependable rights to the land they occupy. Tenant rights in such areas are severely restricted. Such uncertainty discourages residents from improving their housing.[2]

Water and Sanitation

Access to a clean and adequate supply of water is a fundamental human necessity. Yet in 2004, almost 1.07 billion people in the world almost all in developing countries—lacked access to 'improved' sources of drinking water. Millennium Development Goal (MDG) Target 7c challenges the world to reduce the number of people lacking sustainable access to safe drinking water to half by 2015. Despite serious efforts to address the problem, between 1990 and 2004, the number of people without such access decreased by less than 120 million. About 85 per cent of people (900 million) without access to improved sources of drinking water live in rural areas while 15 per cent (170 million) live in urban areas. Given the existing trends, by 2015 the number of people in rural areas without such access will decrease to 679 million while the number of people in urban areas will

2. On weak tenant rights see Gulyani and Talukdar (2008), Tannerfeldt and Ljung (2006); evidence on the effects of tenure insecurity effects on investment is presented in Field (2005).

actually increase to 240 million (UNICEF and WHO, 2006: 12). Almost all of this increase will be in developing countries.[3]

Many municipal systems in developing countries suffer from enormous water losses caused by broken pipes and water piracy and the result is that water may only be available for short periods at certain times in a day.[4] Broken pipes also lead to much higher levels of microbial contamination and hazardous levels of chemicals such as arsenic and fluoride.

It is the poor who suffer disproportionately from poor quality and limited availability of clean water. Around 70 per cent of households in developing country cities have access to clean water as opposed to just 40 per cent in informal settlements (UN-HABITAT, 2003: 113). Most residents of urban slums do not enjoy water connections at the household level. Because of the quality and availability issues, many urban slum residents are forced to purchase water from itinerant vendors at severely inflated prices. The median water price in informal settlements is almost five times the average price from the municipal system. As a result, slum dwellers tend to use less than half of the amount of water as used by the average user in the same cities (Ibid.: 114). This exacerbates poor hygienic practices.

The situation regarding sanitation is even more daunting. In 2004, in Sub-Saharan Africa, just 53 per cent of urban residents were covered by improved sanitation services; in southern Asia, 63 per cent; and in Latin America and the Caribbean, 86 per cent. Coverage is generally substantially

---

3. What the official figures mask, however, is that the measure of 'reasonable access' (a source within one km.) is much more appropriate to rural areas than to urban. Given much higher urban densities, if urban residents have to travel one km. for water, either the queues will be exceeding long (because of the large catchment area) or they will pay high prices to private source vendors who are located nearer. This leads to the conclusion that urban coverage statistics for 'reasonable' access to water are seriously over-estimated (McGranahan, 2007: 95).

4. The World Bank's *2004 World Development Report* (p.160) notes that in Karachi, water is available only for 3-4 hours per day, in Delhi just 4 hours, in Phnom Penh 12 hours, in Dhaka and Manila 17 hours. In Jakarta and Nairobi, over 50 per cent of the water is unaccounted for, in Phnom Penh over 60 per cent and in Karachi 30 per cent. Some areas of Accra have a water supply for one or two days a week and others do not get flow for several weeks (McGranahan *et al.*, 2006). A study carried out in Mombasa, Kenya in the late 1990s showed that very few neighbourhoods had an average of only three hours of water a day and some have seen no water in their pipes for several years (USAID, 2004).

lower in informal settlements than in urban areas (Table 9.3). For example, in Sub-Saharan Africa, where conditions are the worst, only 19 per cent of households have water connections and a mere 7 per cent have sewerage services.

Table 9.3

Water and Sewerage in Informal Settlements, 1998

(in per cent)

Region	*Water Connection*	*Sewerage Service*	*Access to Water*
Sub-Saharan Africa	19.1	7.4	40.0
North Africa/Middle East	35.7	21.5	42.7
Asia/Pacific	38.3	7.4	89.1
Latin America and Caribbean	57.9	30.3	66.8
All Developing Regions	37.2	19.8	57.6

Source: UN-HABITAT (2003).

The global statistics for sanitation are misleading. Coverage is almost certainly over-reported in urban areas, as it is for water. Moreover, the standards for adequate levels of service should be higher in urban areas. Whereas sharing a simple pit latrine may suffice in rural areas because of much higher densities, especially in the slums; it is generally inadequate in urban areas.

Lack of toilet facilities is often more of a concern for slum dwellers than housing conditions or clean water, particularly for girls and women. Most housing in informal settlements does not have indoor sanitary facilities. Instead, slum residents must rely on public toilets. These are often insufficient for the number of households served, forcing people to queue up at certain times of the day and if not properly maintained they can easily overflow and contaminate the surrounding environment.[5] Impatience or disgust with the public toilets leads to people defecating in the open or in a plastic bag and in worst cases using it as weapons of intimidation. The absence of sufficient toilets is particularly devastating for women who suffer indignities, jeopardise their health and risk their safety as they have to wait until dark to defecate.

5. In Accra, 70 per cent of people in lowest income quintile and in Jakarta, 30 per cent, share toilets with 10 or more households (World Bank, 2003: 161).

The storm and sanitary sewer systems of cities in many developing countries, particularly in informal settlements, have insufficient capacity or function so poorly that much of the industrial, commercial and household wastewater and storm water run-off is not captured (to say nothing of waste-water treatment capacity), especially during rainy seasons. Poor drainage leads to frequent flooding and pools of stagnant polluted water that function as vectors for water borne diseases such as malaria and cholera.

Needless to say, the negative consequences of the health of urban residents, especially for children, due to contaminated or insufficient drinking water, the lack of adequate sanitation facilities, poor hygiene practices and poor drainage are dire (UN-HABITAT, 2003: 113).

Transportation

Anyone who has visited Bangkok, Cairo, Lagos or Mexico City—or has traversed a mid-size city in India or Pakistan—has seen first the results of underinvestment in road and mass transit infrastructure and poor traffic management. The scale of transport problems, in terms of adverse effects on mobility, economic efficiency and the environment, are greatest in the mega-cities. But medium size cities suffer as well. Overall, transportation problems are worst where population growth surges ahead of economic growth—all of Sub-Saharan Africa and many Latin American countries (Mitric, 2008: 8). In many major cities, slums occupy central lands of low commercial value but high job access, such as flood plains, which permits the poor to be self-sufficient in commuting.

Transportation problems fall into three types: service deficiencies due to congestion, non-congestion deficiencies and inequitable transportation services that systematically disadvantage definable citizen groups (Ibid: 85-6). We focus on the last category.

Urban transport systems systematically discriminate against the poor in two ways, with the form of discrimination depending on where they live. In very high density central cities, walking or biking to work is common for the poor and non-poor. In Mumbai, 66 per cent of poor and 45 per cent of all households commute this way (Baker *et al.*, 2004). In Chennai, 59 per cent of pavement dwellers walk to work in less than a half hour.

Chinese commuters across the economic spectrum have traditionally relied on bicycles. But pedestrians and bikers now struggle to find a place on the crowded streets; separate lanes for them are very rare. They are both in physical danger and contribute to congestion.[6]

On the other hand, the poor living in peri-urban areas suffer from poor access to job opportunities because of limited-to-no service from public companies and because congestion makes commuting by a van or bus time consuming. The average distance of black townships from the central business districts of South Africa's seven largest cities is 28 kilometres. The same pattern holds for many Latin American Cities (World Bank, 2002: 26). Against this, one can pose the affirmative discrimination in favour of urban roads investment (as opposed to mass transit) for the 20 per cent of households who commute by car.[7]

What Works?

In many metropolises the problems are so great and growing so rapidly that the task of achieving significant improvement in the urban fabric is truly daunting. Is there sufficient accumulated experience with successful programmes to make one confident that more resources can be effectively employed? The answer is a strong 'absolutely yes', as the following cases illustrate.

Slum Upgrading and Prevention

An essential first step in developing an approach to the proliferation of slums is simply raising the awareness of a country's and a city's political leadership of the issue through accurate information. National and city governments often turn a 'blind eye' to the concerns of slum dwellers until social stability appears threatened or a health problem begins to spread throughout the general populace. A good example of such heightened awareness is Egypt, where in the early 1990s the government became

6. To quote the World Bank (2002: 65), "Nearly 0.5 million people die and up to 18 million people are injured in urban road accidents in developing countries each year... A majority of victims are poor pedestrians and bicyclists. Fears for personal safety and security significantly deter the use of non-motorised transport."
7. Figure for selected Latin American cities. Car users have incomes 2 to 3.7 times higher than incomes of non-car users (World Bank, 2002: 33).

convinced that the slum problem was becoming a national emergency and created a special budget for slum upgrading. Since then, the country has reduced the proportion of slum dwellers by over 22 per cent. Similarly, Sri Lanka has reduced slum prevalence from 25 per cent to less than 11 per cent over the past 18 years after adopting a series of national level pro-poor reforms (UN-HABITAT, 2008).

There is now overwhelming consensus that citizen engagement with government in decisions on programme design, prioritisation of interventions, financing methods and on management and maintenance of facilities and infrastructure are critical to the task of slum upgrading. Citizen engagement instils a sense of community ownership of the improvements essential to their maintenance. Although slum dwellers and community leaders know better than everyone else, what challenges they face, they may not have the requisite skills or knowledge to make informed decisions on designing sustainable upgrading programmes. UN-HABITAT (2003: 31) suggests an "enabling approach" whereby local governments "empower" the residents by helping them acquire needed training, financial and management support. This leads to a more equal partnership between the government and the slum dwellers.

Despite the complexity of the challenge, there are a number of successful slum upgrading examples and approaches that can be drawn on as best practices.

- The World Bank supported Indonesia's Kampung Improvement Program (KIP) over a 14 year period from 1974-1988. For a cost averaging from $23 per person in smaller cities to $118 in Jakarta, almost 4.3 million *Kampung* residents in 11 cities benefited from improved footpaths, roads and drainage, garbage bins and collection vehicles, safe drinking water through public taps, public washing and toilet facilities, neighbourhood health clinics and primary school buildings. There was noticeable improvement in the living conditions of the *Kampongs* and the investments yielded an economic return at the rate of 12 per cent, even over a useful life of five years (World Bank, 1995). In addition, as a result of the programme, the *Kampong* residents became better educated, household size declined and employment rates increased (World

Bank, 2000). Unfortunately, the infrastructure has deteriorated over time due to a lack of maintenance and mismanagement of government-run monopolies in water, sanitation and power.

- Based on some 25 years of experience in addressing a growing problem of slums and informal settlements, in 2004 the Government of Morocco initiated its "Cities without Slums" programme with a goal of eliminating or transforming slums housing over 280,000 families in over 80 cities by 2010. The national programme has strong political support. It uses a combination of *in situ* upgrading and demolition of substandard housing with the provision of replacement/resettlement housing, the creation of new subsidised serviced housing sites on public land, the establishment of a guarantee fund for "social" housing and tax incentives for builders to create low cost apartments. Although a national programme, the interventions are carried out by local authorities in close consultation with neighbourhood residents. Through 2008, 140,000 households had benefited from the programme (Belhaj, 2008).
- The Mexican government has a large-scale effort, *PisoFirmo*, underway to replace dirt with cement floors in slum dwellings—by 2007, 300,000 floors had been replaced out of a total initial stock of 3 million units with dirt floors. The cost is about $150 per unit. To be eligible, occupants must prove unit ownership, and possibility of receiving the benefits is an inducement to obtaining essential documentation. A careful impact evaluation documents striking results on young children's health: a 78 per cent reduction in parasitic infestations, 49 per cent reduction in diarrhoea, 81 per cent reduction in anaemia, and a 36-96 per cent improvement in cognitive development. Adult welfare also increased, as measured by increased satisfaction with their housing and quality of life, as well as significantly lower rates of depression and perceived stress (Cattaneo *et al.*, 2009).
- An impact evaluation of the effect of Peru's nation-wide programme distributing titles to urban squatters on public land found that investment in housing renovations and improvements

associated with land titling increased 68 per cent in the four years followed by receiving a title, compared with those not receiving a title (Field, 2005).

Slum prevention is at least as important as upgrading. Planning for the inevitable growth of the urban population is a key factor in the pre-emptive process.

- The municipality of Bishkek reacted quickly and effectively to channel post Soviet Union rural-to-urban migrants into laid out subdivisions that initially lacked public services but were ready to receive them (Struyk and Roy, 2006).
- Cities in El Salvador have largely been able to prevent the formation of new slums through good planning and timely investments in transportation providing decent access to peri-urban locations (Olinger, 2006).
- In Indonesia, private developers laying out sub-divisions with un-serviced plots for sale to low-income families is fairly common, with dwellings being constructed and consolidated over time incrementally (Struyk *et al.*, 1992).

Access to secure land plots—provided by municipalities or private developers—is the key to encouraging the incremental housing construction by which the majority of the urban poor attain decent housing. The process is accelerated by access to micro finance that permits the use of higher quality materials in making each improvement than would otherwise be possible.

Water and Sanitation

The high densities in urban areas are a blessing as well as a curse because innovative solutions can reach far more people than they can in rural areas and municipal services can be provided much more cost effectively. Examples of successful programmes demonstrate that over time, with increased and well-directed investment and policy improvements, regulation (including community oversight) as well as utility operations and management, the trend of increasing numbers of urban dwellers lacking adequate water and sanitation can be reversed.

Of note are several examples of effective interventions.

- Beginning in 1988, an alliance of three Indian NGOs, the Society for the Promotion of Area Resource Centres (SPARC), the National Slum Dwellers Federation (NSDF) and Mahila Milan ("Women Together") supported urban community organisations that over a 12-year period designed, built and now manage toilet blocks that serve over half a million low income urban dwellers in eight cities. The community toilets typically cost less than $80 per seat. The design and construction of the toilet blocks by neighbourhood associations has not only provided a much needed service to the slum residents but the process has also demonstrated to municipal authorities, the capacity and competence of urban poor organisations and changed the nature of the relationship with municipal authorities from one of clientism to one of partnership. The success of the programme has also resulted in the national government providing a 50 per cent subsidy for the creation of community toilets (Burra *et al.*, 2003: 11-25).
- The nine year (1995-2004) World Bank (IDA) supported Senegal Water Project which increased access to water services for 1.6 million people, expanding coverage from 74-81 per cent of the urban population in 1996 to about 98 per cent in 2004, with household connections reaching 76 per cent, the highest rate in sub-Saharan Africa. Through an innovative public-private partnership, water losses, mostly from leakages, decreased from 32 per cent to less than 20 per cent over the project life. It is estimated that through improved water management and sanitation, malaria in urban areas will fall by 20 per cent (IDA, 2008: 5, 18).
- The International Development Association (IDA) financed a water and sanitation project in 11 small towns in Uganda, drastically reducing the average price of water (from 100 to 25 shillings for a 20 litre Jerri can). It significantly reduced the time and distance required to fetch water, increased average consumption and expanded urban coverage notably. The overall Economic Internal Rate of Return (EIRR) of the project was 9.80 per cent (IDA, 2008: 5, 18).

Transportation

Two complementary policy sets can work effectively to improve urban transport: (a) traffic-cum road-focused regulation, management, enforcement and institutional development; and (b) improving public transportation, broadly defined to include related land use and transportation planning (Mitric, 2008: 63-4). We focus on the second here.

There are concrete examples of effective infrastructure investment planning projects that break down the isolation of peri-urban informal settlements. Some of the more impressive projects developed bus rapid transit systems (BRT) that are now fairly common in major Latin American cities, but have also been implemented in Jakarta and Chinese cities. BRT involves reserved lanes for buses and bus depots (instead of traditional bus stops) where passengers purchase tickets before boarding and where multiple buses can load and unload simultaneously.

One of the better documented BRTs is Bogota's, which began service in 2000. It employs a flat fare system (for single ticket for BRT and feeder bus rides) that favours the poor, who live further from the city centre. The combination of the bus depots, large articulated buses, and high ridership resulted in high productivity, with nearly 2,000 passengers per bus per day in 2001. Fatalities from traffic accidents involving buses were sharply cut, and users' travel times reduced by 32 per cent (Gilbert, 2008).

The experience of Curitiba, Brazil, a city of 1.6 million, is noteworthy because its BRT was part of a coherent, integrated, and consistently implemented master plan that has made the city quite liveable and efficient. Industry is located in designated areas away from main settlement areas. Particularly noteworthy is that the transport system provides good access to poor families living in peri-urban settlements, thereby increasing their employment opportunities in the city centre (MacLeod, 2002).

Common Threads

Many of the interventions just described share three common characteristics. First, strong and deep citizen involvement is an essential success ingredient. Second, new forms of subsidies reward certain behaviours that work better than the previous ones, i.e., stronger targeting and greater cost effectiveness. In the cases cited above, the examples include the Mumbai toilet programme and *PisoFirmo* in Mexico. Third, coping with developing minimally adequate shelter, including transport access and infrastructure services, is an ubiquitous challenge, which suggests that it deserves prominence in urban planning generally.

The above section has provided positive examples from all investment areas. This is consistent with the World Bank's finding that urban development projects have higher success rates than other project types (at 88% over the 1992-2004 period), despite the more complex implementation environment (Buckley and Kalarickal, 2006: Table 2.2). We know how to execute projects and programmes, but systemic policy challenges remain.

Accelerating Progress

The examples just reviewed give confidence that discrete projects and programmes across a range of sectors can be successfully executed in municipalities. The reality, however, is that these projects and programmes often succeed in spite of the broad policy environment in which they are implemented, rather than being facilitated by it. Donors circumvent these problems by demanding special operational arrangements for their projects. For its slum upgrading projects, the Inter-American Development Bank (IDB) requires national government to transfer project funds to the municipality; procurements must be done by the municipality following IDB regulations; a qualified technical staff has to be in place for the project; and a single decision point be established for all project aspects (water, land, etc.), which is usually the municipal planning department. Not surprisingly, a continuing challenge for municipalities is in "scaling up" demonstration projects in the absence of special provisions to activity levels that significantly mitigate the problems addressed, such as slum upgrading or prevention (Hartmann and Linn, 2008).

This section briefly addresses four policy blocs whose shortcomings often inhibit local governments from achieving more. Sometimes municipalities control these policies but often the constraints are imposed by national legislation. Working with municipalities and national governments to design and implement better policies is the single most productive action the donor community can take to enhance the impact and sustainability of interventions.

Insufficient Decentralisation

The World Bank distinguishes among broad policy packages according to the degree of urbanisation of the sites, although each needs adjustments to local circumstances.

- Where urbanisation is incipient, i.e., if the place is largely rural, one needs to ensure that key services, which benefit everyone is regardless of location are in place, this means a 'spatially blind' policy-package regulations regarding land, labour and social services, such as education, health, water and sanitation.
- For intermediate urbanisation cases, add [punctual] transportation, water and sanitation, and communications infrastructure that enhances access within cities and binds hinterlands to them.
- Where urbanisation is advanced, beyond enhanced transportation and communications infrastructure investments, add targeted interventions to address slums that may have developed. The Bank's view is that the other policies and investments will not be sufficient by themselves to tackle existing slums (World Bank, 2009: 22-8).

This is sensible guidance, but African cities with little growth will need to explicit slum mitigation and infrastructure development programmes if the countries are to reach an advanced stage of urbanisation.

The Bank's expert consensus is that effective policy coordination among national, state, and local governments is essential for implementing the policies outlined. Is it realistic to expect such coordination?

Municipal governments in developing countries are typically allocated limited core set of service delivery responsibilities in areas like fire fighting, refuse collection, parks, traffic management, local transit service, primary and secondary education and public health (Shah and Shah, 2006). Even for these core services they are reliant on higher levels of Government for capital expenditures.

National ministries for water, transportation and other types of infrastructure control the allocation of funds among local governments for new capital investment projects and often control their designs. Most countries lack a Ministry for Urban Development but even where one exists, the key infrastructure agencies are not subordinate to it. In reality the Ministry of Finance or Ministry of Planning is the key player in deciding on the type of urban investments to be funded. Typically, these ministries lack expertise or sufficient staff to develop such programmes—which probably creates a bias against comparatively complex transportation, slum upgrading and other major infrastructure projects in the largest cities.[8] The result is extreme fragmentation in municipal-national government relationships—relationships that are typically made even more complex by regional governments also having an active role to play (Tannerfeldt and Ljung, 2006: 68, 152).

Local governments' efforts at comprehensive planning within such a fragmented framework are extremely complex and time consuming, owing to the number of players involved and cities' limited powers. They often result in partially developed plans. The situation also creates the distinct possibility of a series of uncoordinated investments working against each other in determining a city's future development. A clear policy improvement would streamline these intergovernmental relationships with municipalities leading a comprehensive planning process that includes all relevant government agencies.

The local planning and implementation process itself often requires improvement along two dimensions. First, most cities' boundaries include only a limited part of the metropolitan area, and planning must be at the metropolitan level for investments in areas like transportation services, water supply and pollution control that fundamentally effect the location of economic activity in space. Either through creation of metropolitan governments (by the national legislature) or by more sector-specific ad hoc solutions, design of metropolitan-wide solutions for areas like transportation is essential for effective interventions (UN-HABITAT, 2008). Second, strengthening the capacity of local government agencies to plan

8. Some donor staff interviewed reported that for transportation projects, staff tended to develop rural projects that were much simpler than their urban counterparts. It follows that when countries have the chance to develop their own program choices—such as those funded under Millennium Challenge Corporation compacts—the lack of expertise, the press to complete proposals quickly, and the five year maximum compact life, strongly favours comparatively simple rural programs.

and implement investment programmes is very badly needed. Moreover, distinct agencies must break out of their silos and work more closely together for effective plans to take shape.[9]

Care is needed not to devolve responsibility, before cities are ready to take on this role. Readiness requires both technical competence and a viable political agreement among city, regional, and national governments. Donors can play a key capacity building role and are beginning to do so. But quicker action can be taken to simplify investment funds allocation (see below) and make them more dependable and to simplify the investment decision process.

The rewards for good planning can be huge. Chinese cities' aggressive infrastructure investments and facilitation of private housing construction largely prevented the creation of squatter communities. Curitiba, Brazil has largely avoided new informal colonies through good planning and timely investments in transport to provide effective access to sites comparatively distant from jobs (MacLeod, 2002).

Resource Devolution

Municipalities' planning environment is difficult at best. The structure of government finances generally makes it worse. A common situation is that municipalities have little authority to raise revenue themselves and are forced to rely on grants from and direct service provision by higher government levels. Figure 9.1 illustrates that sub-national governments in most countries collect well under 20 or even 10 per cent of total revenues and spend about the same amount. India and China with their federal systems are exceptions—although local governments in India spend under 5 per cent of the total because of the dominance of state governments (Shah and Shah, 2006).

9. On the need for capacity development in municipal planning and project administration, see UN-HABITAT, 2008: 207; Peirce and Johnson, 2008: 184. Tannerfelt and Ljung (2006: 153) list the following areas as those where strengthening is required: aspects of good governance, public administration, utility reforms, municipal financing, environmental management, local development planning, land and tenure, and building and planning regulation.

Figure 9.1

Sub-national Governments' Share of Total Government Revenues and Expenditures

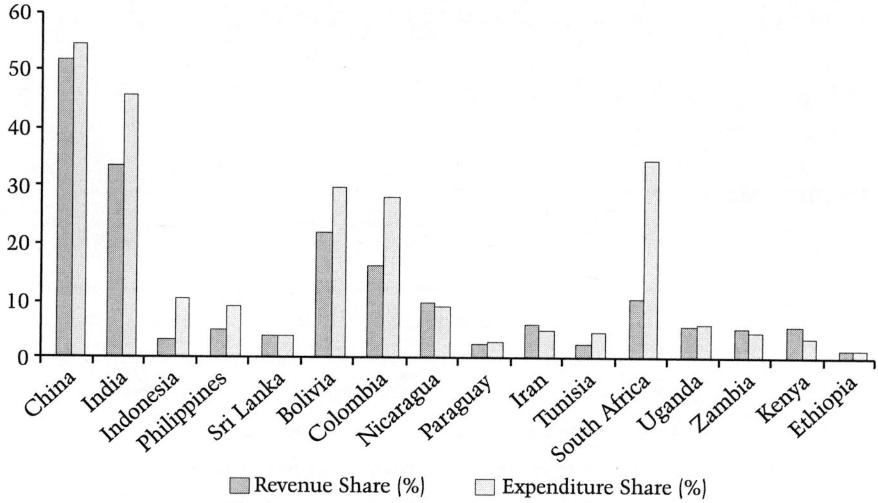

Note: Based on IMF data; figures for late 1990s.
Source: Tannerfelt and Ljung (2006): Table A.11.

Multiple problems stem from the current constructions. One is the uncertainty of local government revenues. This is particularly severe for investment funds, but can be problematic even for basic operations. Such dependency makes it impossible for local officials to be held accountable for service shortfalls because they can always put the blame on the scarcity of funds from higher government authorities (to be fair, not all local governments take full advantage of the tax bases they control, the property tax being the clearest case in point).

The solution is to permanently assign more revenue to local governments—either by granting them the rights both to levy taxes on a specific base, as also to set the tax rate, or by allocating them a share of the national sales or income tax. With the resources comes responsibility for financing certain services and investments. Inequities arising from differences in localities' tax bases can be compensated through equalisation grants from the national government. Critically important is for capacity building to accompany the reassignments. Decentralisation of this type is under way in some countries, but progress is slow. Again, capacity building before the devolution is essential.

Cities will need large amounts of capital to fund the necessary investments. These can come from several sources: tapping capital markets, national government, donor loans and grants. Access to long-term funding is of high value because the resultant infrastructure would serve multiple generations.

Urban Citizens

We know from the successful project examples cited earlier that citizen involvement is a key component for most urban initiatives. Such participation results in projects consistent with users' needs and therefore are more efficient and effective than top-down project development. Community-based organisations (CBOs) are a full participant in the preparation of City Development Strategies in the Cities Alliance process, which have served successfully as the foundation for practical plans for city development in Yemen and other countries. As laudable as these and other cases are, such broad consultative process is not common.[10]

More broadly, there are additional constructive roles for CBOs. First, monitoring by citizens of local government spending and revenue collection has been highly successful in increasing government accountability. Second, mature CBOs under proper conditions can effectively deliver services themselves. The Mumbai toilet campaign cited earlier is a shining example. There are an increasing number of cases where CBOs are operating at scale to help the poor; a well-known example is BRAC (Bangladesh Rural Advancement Committee) that now excels the national government in assisting the poor. In Africa where local governments hardly function in smaller towns and cities, NGOs are the dominant provider of services in some sectors. Strengthening the capacity of both NGOs and governments is likely to result in accelerated and sustained improvements in part because NGOs' close work with CBOs results in broad dissemination of better practices and maintenance of infrastructure investments.[11]

---

10. Several examples are listed and presented in summary boxes in Garau *et al.* (2005), chapters 3 and 4.
11. See Werlin (1999) on degradation of upgraded slum areas.

Often the approval of an elected city council is viewed by city governments as sufficient citizen input into the decision-making process. In practice, of course, its members are not seriously involved in developing plans for major projects, not to mention those at the neighbourhood level. They also tend to be members of the city's elite. Inclusion of NGOs, CBOs, civil society, and other stakeholder groups representing the whole community should be standard practice in municipal planning and project development.

Land Rights Management and Regulation

Getting land policies 'right' is frequently cited as the single most important contributor to a balanced and equitable urban development for all elements of the population. Several different policy elements are present. Secure land tenure is the most often discussed. Confidence in land rights has been shown to promote investments in the premises of poor households both by the dwellers and informal businessmen. Though this point is widely recognised, progress in granting and registering secure land rights is slow in informal settlements and even in upscale areas in some countries. As an example, only 10 per cent of urban properties are registered in Egypt. In part, this is because the required standard applied for acquiring a conventional land title to demonstrate ownership is too expensive and complicated for most informal settlement residents. There is general recognition that a range of less costly intermediate instruments can serve well, and they have been successfully implemented in countries as diverse as Kenya and Bolivia.[12]

Equally important is land management and regulation. One component is a system of land use zoning that operates flexibly to accommodate necessary changes in land use in central areas as the city develops. Striking are the increased housing densities over time in the same

12. Buckley and Kalarickal (2006, fn.6, p.94) list the following examples: declarations of possession and future use rights in Colombia; housing permits in francophone Sub-Saharan Africa; certificates of comfort in Trinidad and Tobago; credit contracts in Bolivia; certificates of rights in Botswana; concession to the real right to use in Brazil; community land trusts in Kenya; temporary occupation licenses in India and Kenya; communal ownership in South Africa; and, land rentals in Thailand. The authors also note that formal titles are probably more appropriate in densely populated megacities where the value of land put to different uses is high. Options are further discussed in Payne (2001).

formal neighbourhoods as access to the centre becomes more valuable. As an illustration, Amman has undergone such transformations over the past 50 years. Efficient development of housing for the poor requires realistic standards for rights-of-ways, pavement standards, plot sizes, building and utility services, so that dwellings conforming to the rules will be affordable to most families (Buckley and Kalarickal, 2006: Chp.3, esp. Box 3.4).

Finally, low fees for registration and other real estate transactions are key to get widespread adoption of property registration and the reporting of accurate sales prices (if fees are computed as a percentage of the price and the rates are high, the strong incentive is to underreport values). Some of these policies, e.g., zoning rules, are generally under local control. In contrast, in many countries property registration requirements and fees are set at the national level, making it difficult for municipal governments to improve policies. But national governments are increasingly beginning to recognise the impediments caused by high fees: Egypt cut its registration fees dramatically in 2006 and Rwanda in 2008.[13]

Conclusions

The costs of the combination of poor policies and very low household purchasing power extracts a high cost to those living in slums and to the cities in which they live in terms of resultant waste of human resources. The positive news is that the scope and cost of this form of social exclusion has attracted the attention of governments and some members of the donor community. Lessons from successful interventions are being absorbed.

The challenge ahead is to make cities work closely with their citizens, who are after all, the central player in improving their operations in all areas. Slum upgrading needs to be considered in a much broader context of city improvement. The costs to businesses of frequent brown outs and massive daily traffic jams are enormous and undermine the cities'

13. Fees in Egypt a few years before were as high as 12 per cent of the property value. After a series of reductions over the years, in summer 2006 they were set at a minimum of LE 500 (about US$ 87 at the then current exchange) rate for a unit of 100 sq.m. or less (Struyk, 2007). In Rwanda, two major fees associated with home purchase with a mortgage were sharply cut in the context of adjusting the law on local government revenues: (1) the transfer fee (formerly 6 per cent of appraised value) and (2) the mortgage lien recordation fee (formerly 1.2 per cent of the recorded amount). Each is now a flat fee of RFr 20,000, or about US$ 40 (Struyk *et al.*, 2008).

international competitiveness. More efficient cities are essential. Access to jobs is at least as important as better housing. A result of improving living environments of the poor, ranging from better water service to upgraded access to jobs to better health facilities will promote greater integration of neighbourhoods and society, as well as increased living standards. Exclusion will decline.

Happily, scholars (e.g., Gulyani and Bassett, 2007) have indicated that there were signs of this approach being adopted. The World Bank's evolving urban and local government strategy appears to embrace it (World Bank, 2009a). Governments and donors are beginning to accept it. A World Bank municipal project just being implemented in Kenya is squarely along these lines. That said, one cannot underestimate the challenge of shifting the control of significant resources from national governments to cities and of strengthening cities' capacity to employ them effectively, including integrating citizens into the process at many levels.

References

Baker, J.L., R. Basu, M. Cropper, S. Lall, A. Takeuchi (2004). *Urban Poverty and the Case of Mumbai.* Washington, DC: World Bank. Working paper, Draft.

Barbiero, V. (2007). "Urban Health: An Inevitable International Imperative", in B. Ruble, A. Garland and M. Massoumi (eds.), *Global Urban Poverty: Setting the Agenda*, Washington, D.C.: Woodrow Wilson International Center for Scholars. pp.189-203.

Belhaj, A.F. (2008). "Upgrading Slums: A Brief Assessment of the Moroccan Experience", in CHF International (ed.), *Back to the Future: Deconstructing Urban Change, Five Case Studies Prepared for the World Urban Forum IV.* Silver Spring, MD: CHF International.

Buckley, R.M. and J. Kalarickal (eds.) (2006). *Thirty Years of World Bank Shelter Lending: What Have We Learned*? Washington, DC: World Bank.

Buckely, R.M., M. Singh, and J. Kalarickal (2007). "Strategizing Slum Improvement in India: A Method to Monitor and Refocus Slum Development Programs", *Global Urban Development* 3(1): 1-24.

Burra, S., S. Patel and T. Kerr (2003). "Community-Designed, Built and Managed Toilet Blocks in Indian Cities", *Environment and Urbanization* 15(2): 11-32.

Cattaneo, M.S., S. Galiani, P. Gertler, S. Martinez, and R. Titunik (2009). "Housing, Health and Happiness", *American Economic Journal: Economic Policy* 1(1): pp.75-105.

Durington, M. (2006). "Race, Space and Place in Durban: An Ethnographic Assessment of Gated Community Environments and Residents", *GeoJournal* 66: 147-60.

Field, E. (2005). "Property Rights and Investment in Urban Slums", *Journal of the European Economic Association* 3(2-3): 279-90.

Fix, M. and R. Struyk (eds.) (1992). *Clear and Convincing Evidence: Measurement of Discrimination in America.* Washington, DC: Urban Institute Press.

Garau, P., E.D. Sclar, and G.Y. Carolini (2005). *A Home in the City.* London: Earthscan for the UN Millennium Project Task Force on Improving the Lives of Slum Dwellers.

Gilbert, A. (2008). "Bus Rapid Transit: Is *Transmilenio* a Miracle Cure?", *Transport Reviews* 28(4): 439-67.

Gulyani, S., and E.M. Bassett (2007). "Retrieving the Baby from the Bathwater: Slum Upgrading in Sub-Saharan Africa", *Government and Planning C: Government and Policy* 25: 486-515.

Gulyani, S. and D. Talukdar (2008). "Slum Real Estate: The Low-Quality High-price Puzzle in Nairobi's Slum Rental Market and its Implications for Theory and Practice", *World Development* 36(10): 1916-37.

Hartmann, A. and J.F. Linn (2008). *Scaling Up: A Framework and Lessons for Development Effectiveness from Literature and Practice.*Washington, DC: Brookings Institution, Wolfensohn Center for Development.

International Development Association (IDA) (2008). *Sanitation and Water Supply: Improving Services for the Poor.* Washington, DC: World Bank.

MacLeod, K. (2002). "Orienting Urban Planning to Sustainability in Curitiba, Brazil". Toronto: ICELI-Canada. Available from: *http://www3.iclei.org/localstrategies/summary/curitiba2.html*

McGranahan, G. (2007). "Improving Water and Sanitation Services in Deprived Urban Neighborhoods: Avoiding Global Distractions and Pursuing Local Priorities", in B. Ruble, A. Garland and M. Massoumi (eds.) *Global Urban Poverty: Setting the Agenda,* Washington, D.C., Woodrow Wilson International Center for Scholars. pp.89-116.

McGranahan, G., C. Njiru, M. Albu *et al.* (2006). *How Small Water Enterprises (SWEs) can Contribute to the Millennium Development Goals: Evidence from Accra, Dares Salaam, Khartoum and Nairobi,* Loughborough, U.K: WEDC, Loughborough University.

Mitric, S. (2008). *Urban Transport for Development: Towards an Operationally-Oriented Strategy.* Washington, DC: World Bank, Transport Paper TP-22.

Nelson, R.H. (2005). *Private Neighborhoods and the Transformation of Local Government.* Washington, DC: Urban Institute Press.

Oates, W.E. (1999). "An Essay on Fiscal Federalism," *Journal of Economic Literature* 37.

Olinger, D. (2006). *The Role of the Private Sector in Delivering Low Income Housing in Developed and Developing Countries.* Washington, DC: International Housing Coalition, Prepared for the World Urban Forum III.

Pager, D., B. Western and B. Bonikowski (2009). "Discrimination in a Low-Wage Labor Market: A Field Experiment", *American Sociological Review* 74(5): 777-99. October.

Payne, G. (2001). "Urban Land Tenure Policy Options: Titles or Rights", *Habitat International* 25(3): 415-29.

Peirce, N.R. and C.W. Johnson (2008). *Century of the City: No Time to Lose.* New York: Rockefeller Foundation.

Ravallion, M., S. Chen and P. Sangraula (2007). "New Evidence on the Urbanization of Global Poverty", *Policy Research Working Paper* 4199. Washington, DC: World Bank.

Shah, A. and S. Shah (2006). "The New Vision of Local Governance and the Evolving Role of Local Governments", in A. Shah (ed.) *Local Governance in Developing Countries.* Washington, DC: World Bank.

Struyk, R., S. Butler, P. Hedstrom (2008). *Rwanda Mortgage Liquidity Facility: Work Plan.* Washington, DC: NORC report to the Ministry of Finance, Government of Rwanda, processed.

Struyk, R. (2007). "Egyptian Consumers' Knowledge of Mortgage Finance and Property Registration", *Housing Finance International* 31-44, December.

Struyk. R. and F. Roy (2006). "Kyrgyzstan's 'Squatter Communities' and the Potential of Housing Micro Finance to Support Upgrading", *Housing Finance International* 21(1): 22-28.

Struyk, R., M. Hoffman and H. Katsura (1992). *The Market for Housing in Urban Indonesia.* Washington, DC: Urban Institute Press.

Tannerfeldt, G., and P. Ljung (2006). *More Urban Less Poor.* London: Earthscan.

Tiebout, C.M. (1956). "A Pure Theory of Local Expenditures", *Journal of Political Economy* 64.

UN-HABITAT (2003). *The Challenge of Slums: Global Report on Human Settlements,* Sterling Virginia and London: Earthscan Publications.

———. (2003). *Global Report on Human Settlements: The Challenge of Slums.* Table 6.9. London and Sterling, Virginia: Earthscan.

———. (2008). *State of the World's Cities 2008/2009.* London: Earthscan.

UNICEF and WHO (2006). *Meeting the MDG Drinking Water and Sanitation Target: The Urban and Rural Challenge of the Decade.* Geneva: author.

USAID (2004). *Urban Profile of USAID Obligations: Agency Summary.* Washington, DC.

Werlin, H. (1999). "The Slum Upgrading Myth", *Urban Studies* 36(9): 1523-34.

World Bank (2009). *World Development Report: Reshaping Economic Geography.* Washington, DC: World Bank.

———. (2009a). *World Bank Urban and Local Government Strategy: Concept and Issues Note.* Washington, DC: World Bank, Finance, Economics, and Urban Department, Sustainable Development Network.

———. (2008). *Status of Projects in Execution in FY08, Nigeria.* World Bank: Operations Policy and Country Services Division.

———. (2003) *World Development Report 2004: Making Services Work for Poor People.* Washington, D.C.: World Bank and the Oxford University Press.

———. (2002). *Cities on the Move: World Bank Urban Transportation Strategy Review.* Washington, DC: World Bank.

———. (2000). "Interview with Chris Banes, Municipal Engineer, World Bank", *The Kampung Improvement Program.* Web Discussion of the Urban Services to the Poor Thematic Group. Washington, D.C.

———. (1995). *Indonesia: Impact Evaluation Report: Enhancing the Quality of Life in Urban Indonesia, The Legacy of Kampung Improvement Program.* Washington, DC: Operations Evaluation Department, Report no. 14747-IND.

Zulu, Eliya, A. Ezeh and F. Dodoo (2000). "Slum Residence and Sexual Outcomes: Early Findings of Causal Linkages in Nairobi, *Kenya", Working Paper* No 17. Nairobi: African Population and Health Research Center.

10 India's Rapid Urbanisation and Exclusion of the Poor

Jayshree Sengupta

Introduction

The UN-Habitat observations in respect of slum settlements are:

> The urban poor are trapped in an informal and illegal world in slums that are not reflected on maps, where waste is not collected, where taxes are not paid and where public services are not provided. Officially they do not exist. In the majority of cases, slum dwellers exist outside of the law where they live and work. They are not able to access most of the formal institutions of society and lacking a legal address they are often unable to access social services.

In this paper, I shall discuss social and economic exclusion of the poor in big cities and towns in terms of the problems they face in getting jobs, medical facilities, good and reliable schooling, access to potable water inside their homes, sanitation and toilet facilities and affordable housing. They are also facing financial exclusion in urban areas in their access to credit. They are not, in many cases, able to practice their trade like pulling rickshaws and vending food items in residential areas or on street corners. I shall also emphasise the need for participation of the low income groups in city administration and in general, in making cities sustainable.

Urban Characteristics and Nature of Exclusion

The problems of exclusion have manifested themselves in many ways and the poor are being shifted physically to peripheral areas of cities from where they have to undertake increasingly expensive and long commutes to get to their place of work. They have no social safety net as they are forced to join the informal sector after migrating from villages. They have to forgo their earnings when they fall sick and their work entail no maternity benefits, compensation in case of accident or allowance for children's education.

The newly arrived migrant workers' dwelling space is often in unauthorised slums which are hotbed of crime; drug dealing and alcoholism is rampant. Children are made to fend for themselves and frequently absent themselves from school due to illness, lack of money for small tuition fee or uniforms, or not being able to complete homework or sheer parental neglect, after which they drop out. They are forced to take to begging or do small jobs and frequently run away from home and are inducted into criminal gangs or forced to work as child labour. Increasingly, the trend in all big cities has been a segregation of residential colonies from industrial and commercial areas, also separating slums from the residential areas. People seem to prefer this segregation, even though it means uncertainty of service providers from coming on time.

Over the last two decades all big cities have put in place a policy of moving small and medium industries to the city outskirts and the valuable vacated space has been taken over by real estate developers for urban middle class housing. In their pattern of development and layout of cities, Indian metro cities are becoming global, where the poor are pushed to the brink and are becoming more and more invisible. Slums have been relocated or demolished through court orders (Dupont, 2008).

Contrary to expectations, urban India is growing and the 2011 census has revealed an increase in urbanisation with urban residents increasing from 27.8 per cent of total population in 2001 to 31.16 per cent in 2011, an increase of only 3.35 percentage points over a decade. This is not a huge increase. Just one third of the population live in urban areas, which is significantly less than in many other developing countries.

But for the first time since Independence, the decadal increase in the size of the urban population (90.99 million people over 2000-2011) was greater than that of the rural population (90.47 million). The trend in urbanisation has been strongest in south India. All states except Andhra Pradesh have more than 35 per cent of their population in urban areas. Southern states also saw the fastest economic growth in the last decade, drawing migrants from other states. In some of the larger states like Tamil Nadu and Kerala, the proportion of urban to the total population is already approaching nearly 50 per cent and Maharashtra and Gujarat are not too far behind.

High economic growth, especially from 2005-2009 has spurred this urbanisation process. Sex ratios—the number of females per 1000 males—improved faster in urban India to 926 from 900. In rural India it increased to 947 from 946. Lower sex ratio in urban areas is due to access to medical facilities for sex determination. Literacy rate also grew faster in urban areas. In 2011, the literacy proportions for rural and urban areas stood at 68.91 per cent and 84.98 per cent respectively. The number of urban *Lok Sabha* (The House of the People) seats also rose from 70 to 100.

Due to the many hardships faced by the poor migrant labour in cities, many experts believed that urbanisation would slow down (Kundu, A., 2009). The 2011 results have proved that migration is going on at a rapid pace especially from villages to small towns, but much of the increase in rural-urban migration, it seems, has been due to the definition of cities which include small towns. The change in classification has been instrumental in showing a big increase in migration from 42 per cent to 56 per cent between 1991-2001 and 2001-2011. There has been a huge increase in the number of new towns and this has contributed to the migration. Otherwise, there has been a significant decline in growth rate of migration in big cities.

Take any of the big cities of India, housing needs have grown exponentially in the past few decades due to the huge population increase. Land acquisition for urban housing has been carried out at a frenetic pace in all big cities like Delhi, Kolkata and Mumbai. Land acquisition for other requirements of urban life is also taking place. The major impetus to urbanisation in modern times has been a shift in livelihood from primary to secondary and tertiary occupations.

The price of urban land has been skyrocketing and more and more outlying areas are being developed for middle class housing. Satellite towns are coming up near all big cities with multi-storey housing complexes. The beautification and gentrification drives have been carried out in all big cities, leading to the removal/demolition of slums from residential areas (Banerjee-Guha, 2011).

Indian cities are becoming 'global cities' with the same features as those of big cities across the world—shopping malls, high rise office buildings in down town areas, banks, hotels, restaurants, clubs, golf courses and super-specialty hospitals and clinics alongside posh residential colonies.

Increasingly, the small corner shops and restaurants (*dhabas*) are moving out of city centres and are giving way to branded retail outlets of multinational companies as well as franchised international fast food outlets. Supermarkets are replacing the small grocery stores and shops selling other household items. Over the years, the number of the self employed—the lowest earning and least secure of workers—have increased and the number of regular employees has gone down. Even wage-paid casual work opportunity has declined (Hashim, 2009).

Restructuring and dismantling of large factory industries in cities has also contributed to the casualisation of work. Workers have had to take jobs in the informal sector as self employed workers.

Cities on the other hand do not have space for informal economic activities and often they have to be carried out clandestinely in which the informal sector workers have to pay bribes in order to stay in business. It is not easy for vendors to enter gated communities. Home-based and self employed workers are most vulnerable to lose their sources of livelihood because they have to work from the streets where they are harassed, or live in dwellings that are not permanent.

The high and middle income localities have welcomed the policy of segregation by constructing entry barriers to the general public, especially vendors. Residents welfare associations (RWAs) are asking the residents for police verification of servants and most of urban India is buying washing machine type technologies that reduce the need for casual part time labour and domestic help. People engaged in white collar jobs do not seem to want to have an overlap of space with the poor, nor do they want to have any interaction with them (Kundu, 2009).

RWAs have filed public interest litigations (PILs) for the eviction and relocation of the poor as they are seen as polluting the immediate urban neighbourhood. As a result, there is an increase in segmentation of the city. Increasingly, the RWAs have been involved in infrastructure projects, planning and participatory budgeting and maintenance of neighbourhood security. All this has resulted in sanitisation of the cities and policing of public space within their jurisdiction. Some of these societies have received unprecedented importance in cities where they have been empowered by the master plan to determine the land use of colonies.

Nevertheless, migrations to small towns are rising because of lack of work in the villages. People are constantly moving into urban areas in search for better wages and job opportunities. One of the prime reasons is that urban wages are higher. Many migrants are temporary migrants and the migration may be circular in nature, with migrants going back to their villages after some time. By working in cities and towns, migrant workers are able to send money to the villages thus enhancing the incomes of families back home. With the money earned in towns, important expenditures like building a house, buying farm animals or helping in the marriage of a sibling or daughter, can be undertaken.

Big cities have been able to attract migrants from near and far away villages in the past and some of these migrants never returned home on a permanent basis. They have permanent homes in the city's ghettos and slums. According to the National Sample Survey Organisation (NSSO) data, 55 per cent of slum dwellers have been living in them for over 15 years and another 12 per cent between 10 and 15 years, establishing the fact that slums are an integral part of the phenomenon of urbanisation and are contributing significantly to the economy of cities. By being a source of affordable labour supply for production in both the formal and informal sectors, slums are a reflection of the exclusionary socioeconomic policies and planning of the city.[1]

Some Facts about Slums

About 49,000 slums were estimated to be in existence in urban India in 2008-09, with 24 per cent of them located along *nallahs* and drains and 12 per cent along railway lines. About 57 per cent of slums are in public land owned by local bodies, state governments, etc. In 64 per cent of

---

1. According to the Government of India, "a slum is defined as a compact settlement with a collection of poorly built tenements, mostly of temporary nature, crowded together usually with inadequate sanitary and drinking water facilities in unhygienic conditions."

notified slums (NSSO, 2009), a majority of the dwellings were *pucca*, the corresponding percentage for non-notified ones being 50 per cent.[2]

The urban poor often live in unimaginable poverty and squalor, totally neglected by the city authorities. Many do not even possess a ration card and they have to buy their food from the open market. They are victims to various types of petty corruption and police harassment within the city. Urban poor constitute a large proportion of the urban population in many big cities. In Mumbai, 62 per cent of the population lives in slums, in Delhi 20 per cent, Kolkata 33 per cent, Bangalore 20 per cent and Chennai 18 per cent.

Around 75 per cent of slum households have not received any benefits from any of the government programmes designed to alleviate poverty, 15.7 per cent of households have received land-related benefits and the balance received other miscellaneous benefits (Mathur, 2009). Slum population differs from city to city, the maximum numbers being located in Mumbai. Many seek domestic jobs or work in miserable conditions in small enterprises or are self employed vendors and all but a few join the informal sector economy. They form the core of the city's service sector which serves the urban middle class households throughout the year. They are mostly in domestic service—watchmen, drivers, handymen, petty traders, cleaners, mechanics, plumbers, electricians, itinerant tradesmen, street food sellers—who constitute the transient/floating service population living in slums and ghettos. Many urban poor also manufacture small items like in Dharavi slum locality of Mumbai, there is a flourishing leather goods business sustained by the workers residing within the slum.

Some permanent slums have better facilities than the temporary ones. Most slums have electricity and water supply though not always inside their small living spaces. During monsoons however, most slums are badly affected. Around 48 per cent of the slums are usually affected by water-logging during monsoon—with 32 per cent of the slums experiencing water-logging inside the slum as well the approach road to the slum. There is no health system structure and there is an urgent need to reform the

---

2. A non-notified slum is a slum with at least 20 households which are non-notified by any authority, and a notified slum is one which is 'notified' by municipalities, corporations, local bodies and development authorities.

delivery mechanisms for education so as to ensure the urban poor and disadvantaged children of their relevance. Basically, they have to ensure that enrolment does not fall and there is gender and marginalised people parity. Sanitary conditions in the slums in terms of latrine facility during 2008-09 showed considerable improvement since 2002. Latrines with septic tanks or similar facility were available in 68 per cent notified and 47 per cent non-notified slums. At the other extreme, 10 per cent of notified and 20 per cent non-notified slums did not have any latrine facility at all. About 10 per cent notified and 23 per cent non-notified slums did not have any drainage facility. Underground drainage systems or drainage systems constructed of *pucca* materials existed in about 39 per cent notified slums and 24 per cent non-notified slums. Underground sewerage existed in about 33 per cent notified slums and 19 per cent non-notified slums. Government agencies were collecting garbage from 75 per cent of the notified slums and 55 per cent of the non-notified slums. Among such slums, garbage was collected at least once in seven days in 93 per cent notified and 92 per cent non-notified slums. About 10 per cent notified and 23 per cent non-notified slums did not have any regular mechanism for garbage disposal (NSSO, 2009).

Future Infrastructure Constraints in Big Cities and Implications for the Poor

In the future, big cities and towns will face huge problems as pressure on the infrastructural facilities will mount tremendously. The poor will be the worst hit as they will not be able to afford the user charges that are likely to be imposed in the future for basic amenities and services. Most cities will go for user charges and more privatisation for housing and basic services, as it is already being worked out under the Jawaharlal Nehru National Urban Renewal Mission (JNNURM). Basic amenities that would come under user charges would include housing, water supply, toilets, power, roads and garbage collection. About 75 million households in India (35% of all urban households) cannot afford housing at market prices. About 17 million households live in slums. India has not been able to plan to build affordable housing systematically and the government has built less than 200,000 units a year whereas the minimum that India needs is 2 million housing units annually.

According to the McKinsey report, urban India will face serious constraints not only in urban infrastructure in terms of water scarcity, solid waste disposal, sewerage, but will also face human development deprivation by 2030. Today every 8th urban child in India in the age group of 0 to 6 years lives in the slums. About 7.6 million children are living in slums in India, which constitute 13.1 per cent of total child population of the urban areas of 26 States/Union Territories. McKinsey predict that by 2030, double the number of the current 17 million households will be living in slums. Already, access to clean drinking water, though it has increased in the past few years, is not adequate and many households do not have taps inside their dwellings. The McKinsey report predicts that there will be a huge problem of disposal of solid waste in the cities in the future. There will be 377 million tons of solid waste generated by 2030 and only 295 million tons will be collected if inadequate facilities continue. There will be a big problem of treatment of sewage also. Only 366 million people had improved access to sanitation facilities in 2008—less than the number of mobile phones in India. Today around 60 per cent of sewage goes untreated and flows directly into the rivers. This problem will be magnified in the future. India will need to increase sewage treatment capacity by 11 times and total length of its sewage piping by 2.4 times; otherwise 70 per cent to 80 per cent of sewage will go untreated (McKinsey, 2010).

The cities and towns of India are increasingly emulating the global model with business districts that have banks, insurance companies, liaison offices and offices that arrange for services including hospitality and medical services, sewage disposal and garbage disposal. These services will become privatised. The new satellite towns will have their own generation of power and water which will be brought privately for the residents. Only the adjoining poorer areas will depend on municipal corporations for such services.

The modern Indian cities are aspiring to become global business centres with the same facilities for business as in London, New York and Hong Kong. Global cities are going to be hubs of financial and other commercial services and everything to facilitate this process is going to be adopted. They are becoming white collared enclaves in which IT and knowledge based services flourish. But they will also need cleaners, plumbers, electricians, washers, guards, load carriers, gardeners, construction workers and domestic servants. They will have to come from among the urban poor and unless they are well integrated into the city system, it will contribute to social tension despite the high level of business activity and income generation. It is in the four big cities in which India's 69 known dollar billionaires and 120,000 dollar millionaires live. They will need services from the poor which is going to be increasingly difficult to get.

Financial Exclusion

Financial exclusion of the poor in urban areas is also a serious problem. Self Help Groups that flourish in villages somehow have not taken off in cities and towns. The poor have to therefore depend on non-institutional sources and loan sharks. The reach of commercial banks in urban sector is still very low, standing at 3.2 per cent. This is because the low income low asset holding segment of urban poor has been largely bypassed by the overall expansion in financial intermediation. Microfinance intermediaries too choose not to work among urban population, given the peculiar dynamics of community formation in urban centres and towns, particularly in poorest settlements that predominantly house immigrant labour. Lack of permanent address of loan takers and group risk takers also act as an impediment to micro credit access.

Ever since the liberalisation policies that were first initiated in 1991, Indians who possessed wealth, property, and skills could manage to earn huge amounts and also not pay taxes. A parallel black economy has resulted and the city rich are getting richer, demanding more and more goods and services. Tax revenue collections are not adequate to provide facilities for the slums and the poor.

In many cities, foreign direct investment (FDI) has flowed into special economic zones (SEZs) for industrial collaboration. The low income groups and the poor can find work in these special zones and industrial parks that have been set up to encourage foreign and domestic investment. Lack of skills acts as a barrier to the poor from getting jobs except in the lowest type of menial jobs. Often the creation of such special economic zones has meant encroaching on the space meant for the poor.

The big cities are providing more and more services for multinational firms and have huge office spaces that are rented by multinational firms for establishing their production and sale delivery chains in India. They hire educated, English speaking youth in these offices, which become basically outsourcing centres for the parent organisation located in more developed countries. High salaries are paid to the staff and in the same offices where the menial workers are paid a paltry sum. While the young executives are buying flats in the newly established satellite towns, the poor are being pushed further away to the slums.

The construction of these high rise glass fronted buildings is going on everywhere in big cities. These are not always the most energy efficient structures and use power to lift water and people to top floors continuously. These modern buildings are being constructed by migrant workers who live in small tents pitched around the sites that serve as their temporary homes with children running around. They have no kitchen, toilet, nor education and healthcare facilities for their families. They work from morning till night but are given no basic amenities, while the construction work is going on.

The Jawaharlal Nehru National Urban Renewal Mission

JNNURM was started on December 3, 2005 with an investment of ₹ 50,000 crore in the mission period of seven years beginning from 2005-2006. The Mission is the single largest initiative of the government of India for planned urban development that integrates the two pressing needs of urban India—massive investments required for infrastructure development and reforms that are required to sustain investments. JNNURM aims at eliminating those statutory provisions and procedures that have constrained the functioning of the land and housing market, this being the single most important reason for the proliferation of slums in Indian cities and towns; and secondly, conferment of property rights; thirdly, it aims putting in place governance structures that are sensitive to the needs of the urban poor and civil society. JNNURM has provided substantial central assistance to cities and towns for infrastructural development, as also for housing the poor and has been effective in renewing the country's focus on the urban sector. But it has had a big city bias especially for cities that are located in relatively more developed states. Less than 50 per cent (45.5%) of the total allocations have actually been released under JNNURM so far (Kundu, 2011).

The ongoing Swarna Jayanti Shahari Rozgar Yojna and recently launched Rajiv Awas Yojana are other initiatives that aim at urban poverty reduction. The former aims at encouraging the unemployed and the underemployed urban poor to set up self employment ventures, while the latter focuses on accelerating the process of construction of housing for the urban poor.

The Constitution (74th) Amendment Act, 1992 and the JNNURM constitute a major departure from the way urban poverty has been conceptualised and addressed in the country, advancing an altogether different framework for its alleviation. Both these initiatives rest on sustainable reduction in urban poverty requiring emphasis on urban local bodies (ULBs), where they can play a vital role in urban poverty reduction, slum improvement and up gradation and urban planning. An inter-governmental fiscal system has been put in place that would ensure adequate flow of funds for poverty reduction.

Under the scheme, state governments and ULBs have placed emphasis on the recovery of full cost of operation and maintenance of all services provided by levying proper user charges and to ensure that each service, sale or use of municipal goods or resources provided to the general public is self sustaining. Further, it also allows for the participation and competition from the private sector in supplying comparative or better services, resources or goods. Under such a policy, the ULBs are supposed to charge for water supply, sewerage, solid waste management, public transport and other services. For many ULBs the last category would include street lighting, toll roads, municipal library, primary health/dispensary services, parks and education. Also included would be hiring of municipal assets like community halls, water tankers and cesspool cleaners, etc. But the lack of affordability to pay for water tankers or street lights would result in pricing out the urban poor from these services. Further, under the user charge policy, ULBs are encouraged to reduce non-revenue water supply. This policy if implemented would again have adverse effects on the poor. Also, adding the tag of user charge to health and education services would negate the social concerns of the state.

The primary objective of JNNURM has been to create economically productive, efficient, equitable and responsive cities. To achieve this objective, it focuses on integrated development of infrastructure services, receiving linkages between asset creation and maintenance for long run project sustainability, accelerating the flow of investment into urban infrastructure services, planned urban development, renewal of inner city areas and universalisation of urban services to ensure a balanced urban development. Under the section 'provision of household level basic services' reforms in the JNNURM, housing for the poor does figure. In this scheme private agencies are being encouraged to take up slum redevelopment where existing slums are being rebuilt as multistorey structures. However, the substantial land thus acquired in the name of housing for the poor is being regularly earmarked for community and residential uses for the non-poor. The subsidies directed to the poor are thus cornered by the private agencies either for themselves or for the section of the population who can afford market prices at prime locations in cities.

The increased participation sought from the private sector in providing municipal services by making it mandatory to frame state-level regulatory and policy initiatives for the purpose, is another reform that calls for attention. If municipal services are provided and managed by the private sector and determined by the market, there would be chances of the poor being priced out. Also, no standardised criteria have been worked out across states for identifying the beneficiaries under the BSUP (Basic Services for Urban Poor) programme.

In many states, however there has been no change in the functional domain of the ULBs following the 74th Constitution Amendment. Many attribute the status quo to the reluctance on the part of state governments to transfer any powers or functions to the ULBs. Thus, JNNURM is partially successful so far and is under the scanner for being able to provide inclusive growth of cities in the one year that is left for its completion.

Conclusion: Suggestions for Achieving Sustainable Urban Growth

Urbanisation can be sustained without creating social tension by promoting security of livelihood for the poor. If the poor have jobs, there can be peaceful coexistence between the poor and the middle-income and the high-income groups. There will have to be more participatory development of cities, which is possible only if the low-income groups have a voice and stake in the development of cities. There will have to be better quality basic education in slums, which will give all at least functional literacy. Similarly, training in marketable skills to unemployed youth and women will help them to get jobs.

Recycling waste can generate many jobs but humanising these jobs and making them safe and free from health hazards is important. The training in recovering of green construction materials from municipal and industrial waste for construction of buildings will also generate jobs.

Primary health care in slums, which is both preventive and curative, will be most important in ensuring that the poor do not spend their entire earnings on treatment of diseases. There will have to be health insurance for the poor and also one which covers accidents and maternity.

For energy conservation, tall buildings with glass fronts should be discouraged as they consume enormous amount of energy in lifting people and water to heights and also increases the cooling and heating costs. Conserving energy and water will be most important for sustainability of cities in the future.

Women have to be given crèche facilities and accessible medical care, which will enable them to participate in urban development and renewal. Many young women feel unsafe working in cities and need affordable accommodation in hostels. More women's hostels have to be built specially in SEZs in order to enable young women to work in them.

More mass rapid transport and cities with walkways will make cities environmentally sustainable and pollution free. Clogging of streets and traffic jams will make travelling inside cities a nightmare unless private vehicular traffic is reduced.

The government will have to undertake massive investment in upgrading the cities' infrastructure to cope with the increase in urbanisation in the future.

Appropriate partnership for local governance has to be evolved, involving citizen groups and local authorities that will provide effective means of conflict resolution. The 74th Amendment has opened up opportunities for the devolution of governance to the lowest political strata of society which must be utilised fully. Bureaucracy should be sensitised to simplify and streamline governmental procedures to minimise the mandatory citizen-bureaucrat interface. There should be decentralisation and devolution of environmental management. There should also be law enforcement but no excessive regulations, and lastly, the ULBs should be wholly and fully involved.

References

ADB (2011). *Asia 2050: Realising the Asian Century.*

Banerjee-Guha, Swapna (2011). *Contradictions of 'Development' in Contemporary India.* February 11. *http://www.opendemocracy.net/.*

Confederation of Indian Industry (2011). *Urban Infrastructure and JNNURM.*

Dupont, Veronique (2008). "Slum Demolition in Delhi since 1990s, An Appraisal", *Economic and Political Weekly*, July 12.

Hashim, S.R. (2009). *Economic Development and Urban Poverty in India: India Urban Poverty Report.*

Kundu, A. (2009). "Urbanisation in Asia: A Macro Overview", *Economic and Political Weekly,* November 28.

———. (2011). "Politics and Economics of Urban Growth", *Economic and Political Weekly*, May 14.

Kundu, Debolina (2009a). *Elite Capture and Marginalisation of the Poor in Participatory Urban Governance: A Case of RWAs in Metro Cities, in India Urban Poverty Report.*

———. (2011a). "Redefining the Inclusive Urban Agenda in India", *Economic and Political Weekly*, 29 January.

Mathur, O.P. (2009). *National Urban Poverty Reduction Strategy 2010-2020: Slum Free Cities: A New Deal for the Urban Poor.* National Institute of Public Finance and Policy.

McKinsey Global Institute (2010). *India's Urban Awakening—Building Inclusive Cities: Sustaining Economic Growth.*

Ministry of Finance (2011). *Economic Survey 2010-11.* Government of India.

Ministry of Housing and Urban Poverty Alleviation (2009). *India Urban Poverty Report.* Oxford University Press.

Mishra, Asit Ranjan and Liz Mathew (2011). "Fresh Thrust to Urbanisation", *Livemint*, July 11.

Nair, Tara S. (2009). "Urban Microfinance in the Context of Urban Poverty", in *India Urban Poverty Report.*

National Sample Survey Organisation (2009). *Some Characteristics of Urban Slums, 2008-09.*

Ramachandran, M. (2011). "JNNRUM: A Balance Sheet", *Economic Times*, 16 January.

11

Excluded Berlin: Housing at the Margins of Urban Citizenship

Andrej Holm

Berlin is internationally known as a tenants' city with only 14 per cent of the houses being used by the owners themselves and, for a long time, it was controlled by a relaxed housing market. Since around 2005, we observe a rise in the market prices of the rents in most of Berlin's neighbourhoods and a strongly market driven allocation of housing. This increase in competition for access to housing highlights structures of disadvantage beyond the ambit of economic sphere, that is social and ethnic discrimination.

This contribution will point out various forms of discriminations with examples of limited housing access to Roma-families with restricted residence permit status, and also Turkish house seekers and households depending on social transfer. The lack of residence authorisation, all kinds of racial discrimination and administrative restriction on housing will be interpreted as a different type of shortfall in urban citizenship regulations.

Housing in Berlin

As has been noted, the rents and living costs in Berlin are lower than those in other German and European cities. As a result of a large sector of public and social housing, the high construction activities in the 1990s and the vast availability of vacant spaces, Berlin's rents did not increase from those of the early 1990s right up to the year 2005. The city's average for rental housing cost in 2005 was around 4 euro per square metre per month and for condominiums, a buyer had to pay around 1,000 euro per square metre per month. This low level of housing costs afforded a low loan and income-level.

Especially for young academics, creative freelancers and sub-cultural peoples, the low-price economy provided space of experiments and self-fulfilment but it certainly did nothing to solve the economic crisis underlying Berlin's urban economy. Berlin has been losing this allure of cheap housing in the last five years because of the neoliberal shift to Berlin's Urban and Housing Policy. Nearly half of public housings were privatised, all housing subsidies were cut and a lot of administrative restrictions were placed in construction planning. Rent regulations on newly built constructions were abolished. In all the housing segments, we notice rising rent prices. On an average, the rent-levels have gone up by around 25 per cent since 2005. In inner city neighbourhoods it is higher and for new contracts the tenants have to pay twice the price that prevailed five years ago.

Housing at the Margins

The reduction of housing policies and emerging market dynamics are being interpreted as a common trend of Berlin's urban development in the last few years. We need to keep in mind that the rents are rising in almost all neighbourhoods. The gentrification-dynamics during the 1990s displacement is no longer restricted to single neighbourhoods and renewal areas. Gentrification had become the new urban vogue in Berlin. Its housing market is under pressure, as a consequence of the rising number of households, a low level of newly built constructions and liberalised rent-cum planning laws (Holm, 2011a).

The small number of newly built houses and investments (as also the physical upgrading of housing stocks) points to strategies being employed by real estate agents to capitalise on ground rents in the new contracts. The high level of the rent prices in the new contracts could be interpreted as being aimed at discouragement to further physical investment. Modernisation and the new constructions are not worth comparing to the profit rate of rising rents without investment. This kind of "rental gentrification" (Van Crieckingen, 2010) enforce exclusionary displacement (Marcuse, 1986) in many neighbourhoods. Beyond the 'classical' displacement of sitting tenants from the neighbourhoods, the question of access to the housing market promotes social and spatial exclusion in Berlin.

Most urban social phenomena like polarisation can be traced back to real estate market strategies of commodification and the hollowing out of social welfare politics. I don't dispute this general political-cum-economic interpretation of social urban realities, but I would like to go beyond this critique that is central to the issue, so as to highlight three particular forces of exclusion at the margins of urban citizenship.

Roma-Families

With the enlargement of the European Union, visa-restrictions on people from South-East European countries like Bulgaria and Romania were abolished. The new laws assuring freedom of movement opened the road for thousands of Roma families to escape from poverty, discrimination and harassment by violent antiziganistic forces. Berlin became one of the destinations of the Roma migrants. There are no current official records in Berlin regarding the number of Roma population. Unofficial estimates vary from 20,000 (Administration) to 200,000 (*Bund Deutscher Kriminalbeamter*, Federation of German Detectives) (Peters, 2010).

During the 1990s, most of the Roma families were coming to Berlin from former Yugoslavia and received the status of 'Civil-War-Refugees', which gave them residence permission, entitlement to accommodation (mostly in mass accommodations or refugee camps) and a supply of basic needs, but there was rigid restriction on their movement within the city under a regulation called 'residency obligation'. This mix of control and freedom was criticised by human right activists, left wing politicians and critical researchers who called it a form of state organised exclusion. In 1999, the German Aliens Authority reversed the residence status of the refugees and many of them were forced to leave Germany.

As different from the 1990s' legislations, Roma immigrants today are not subject to residence restriction and administrative control, but without a full work permit they are characterised as 'unregistered inhabitants with restricted employment permission' (Zacharakis, 2009; Senatsverwaltung für Integration, Arbeit und Soziales, 2011). This legal status constricts economic activities of the Romas to informal sectors, which means low and erratic incomes.

They therefore do not have the basic means to acquire rented housing. With all the doors closed on them, the Roma families are forced to stay in public places, such as parks or greens, or have had to accept contracts to live in miserable conditions at extortionate rents (Steger, 2011). A range of house owners (mainly in Neukölln locality of Berlin) exploited the plight of the Romas, forcing them to pay more than double the usual rent. Many Roma families try to compensate for the high costs by overcrowding—up to eight persons living in one small room. During the summer months, Roma families shift out to public (greens and streets) and semi-public spaces (courtyard and gardens) (Amaro Drom, 2011). Their public visibility and the use of the open spaces led to complaints and trouble as well as repression by police and the administrations, reinforcing media debates about "politics of stigmatisation" of the Romas.

Restricted employment and economic disadvantage (penury) are directly adding to the already severe constraints on access to housing and is generating the exclusion of Romas from this vital public good.

Turkish House Seekers

Since the 1960s, Berlin has been a witness to the rise in the population with Turkish roots. Waves of migration have created a large Turkish community in the city. Most of them have rights of residence and an increasing number have acquired German citizenship. As a result of earlier restriction to housing access and the establishment of a Turkish local economy-cum-infrastructure, the Turkish communities are concentrated in some inner-city neighbourhoods, namely Kreuzberg, Neukölln, Wedding (Greve and Cinar, 1997; Kleff and Seidel, 2009). Post 1990s, German citizens have been involved in heated debates on social segregation *versus* integration on the neighbourhood level (Häußermann and Kapphan, 2000; Dill, Jirjahn and Tsertsvadze, 2011). Dominating the political and public debates were the issues of spatial concentration of ethnic communities, as also segregation in schools. One strongly conservative apprehension expressed in this context is the so called 'formation of parallel societies'. It was assumed that the ethnic minorities did not have any interest in integration and were promoting segregation by creating their own residential concentrations.

A personal decision about the choice of place to stay aside, access to housing is an important factor in explaining ethnic spatial segregation. Emsal Kilic, sociologist and social worker, analysed the prospects—or the lack thereof—of people with Turkish names succeeding in getting houses in contested housing applications (Kilic, 2008). Based on hundreds of application letters sent by fictitious candidates (with similar socioeconomic backgrounds but different ethnic provenance), her study reveals a dramatic discrimination against 'Turkish' applicants in almost all boroughs, except for the neighbourhoods with a concentration of Turkish communities. Kilic observes that it was a blanket discrimination involving all types of owners (including housing cooperation and public housing associations).

In the context of the discussion on the relationship between citizenship and exclusion from housing, this case study points out that access to affordable public goods not only depends on the formal status of citizenship but also on informal discrimination shown by the self appointed 'gate keepers' of the housings markets.

Housing Restriction in Social Transfer Regulations

Around 350,000 households in Berlin are beneficiaries of the new social transfer law enacted in 2005, under which one of the functions of the administration is to deal with the absorption of housing costs. Presently the administrators are covering costs, but only till a local maximum rent price is fixed. Barring the expectations of households with special needs means households coming within the ambit of the social transfer rules suffer rigid limitations in access to housing. Household in existing rent contracts have to move out if they cannot afford an increase in rent crossing the limit of their ability to absorb the costs. In the context of general rent price dynamics in the previous years means that the person concerned had to search for an affordable accommodation in the neighbourhood. Mostly these are tenements in large real estates on the outskirts of Berlin. In the context of the emerging gentrification trends in the inner city, this regulation can best be characterised as administrative organised displacement, boosting the sociospatial polarisation in the city (Holm, 2011b).

Besides the above noted limitations, there is the requirement of permission from the administration for new rent contracts, which is an added handicap for the social transfer households. Administrative restriction for these households thereby exacerbates the economic inequality faced at housing markets.

Housing and Urban Citizenship

In sum, what has been highlighted by the above case studies is the fact that it is not just economic resources of the aspirant that determine his/her ability to gain access to housing facility and a right to urban public resources, but equally important is the negative role played by formal and informal restrictions and discrimination. It would be wrong to consider these cases of exclusion as being no more than an amplifier of real estate market workings, for what is involved here is the inviolable rights of citizenship that mandates equality for all before law, whatever is the market trend. Nevertheless, all kinds of urban citizenship issues are based on socioeconomic structures and particularly in the case of housing, it cannot be divided from the general questions of redistribution of wealth in our societies. But for those on the margins of urban societies undergoing social deprivation and ethnic discrimination, it is not just a question of lack of equality, but also of a deficit of equitability. Urban justice has therefore to be perforce, based on removing all the barriers of exclusion to housing access—and that too, not just to solve the problem of housing costs for the urban poor.

References

Amaro Drom (2011). *Zielgruppenspezifische Unterstützungsbedarfe der Roma-Communities im Flughafenkiez*. Studie im Auftrag des Quartiersmanagements Flughafenstraße. Berlin.

Dill, Verena, Uwe Jirjahn and Georgi Tsertsvadze (2011). "Residential Segregation and Immigrants' Satisfaction with the Neighbourhood in Germany", *SOEP (The German Socio-Economic Panel Study)*, 410/2011, Berlin: DIW.

Greve, Martin; Cinar, Tülay (1997). *Das Türkische Berlin*. Reihe: Miteinander leben in Berlin. die Ausländerbeauftragte des Senats. Berlin.

Häußermann, Hartmut; Kapphan, Andreas (2000). *Berlin: von der geteilten zur gespaltenen Stadt? Sozialräumlicher Wandel seit 1990*. Opladen: Leske+Budrich.

Holm, Andrej (2011a). *"Wohnungspolitik der rot-roten Regierungskoalition in Berlin"*, in Andrej Holm, Klaus Lederer and Matthias Naumann (Hrsg.), *Linke Metropolenpolitik. Erfahrungen und Perspektiven am Beispiel Berlin*. Münster: Westfälisches Dampfboot. pp.92-112.

———. (2011b). "*Kosten der Unterkunft als Segregationsmotor. Befunde aus Berlin und Oldenburg*", in *Informationen zur Raumbeobachtung, Heft* 9.2011, 557-566.

Kilic, Emsal (2008). *Diskriminierung von Migranten bei der Wohnungssuche – Eine Untersuchung in Berlin*. Unveröff. Diplomarbeit am Institut für Sozialwissenschaften der Humboldt-Universität zu Berlin.

Kleff, Sanem; Seidel, Eberhard (2009). *Stadt der Vielfalt, Das Entstehen des neuen Berlin durch Migration*. Berlin: Der Beauftragte für Integration und Migration.

Marcuse, Peter (1986). "Abandonment, gentrification, and displacement: The linkages in New York City", in Neil Smith/Peter Williams (eds.), *Gentrification of the City*. Boston: Allen & Unwin. pp.153-177.

Peters, Freia (2010). "Die Roma von Berlin-Neukölln", in *Die Welt*, 28.09.2010 (*http://www.welt.de/die-welt/politik/article9920445/Die-Roma-von-Berlin-Neukoelln.html*).

Senatsverwaltung für Integration, Arbeit und Soziales (2011). *Roma und europäische Wanderarbeitnehmerinnen und -arbeitnehmer: Rechtsgrundlagen zu Aufenthalt und Bildung sowie Kontaktstellen*. Informationsblatt für Mitarbeiterinnen und Mitarbeiter der Verwaltungen, August 2011. Berlin.

Steger, Lisa (2011). *Neue Heimat Hinterhof - Roma ziehen nach Berlin-Neukölln*. Radio-Feature Deutschlandradio Kultur, Länderreport vom 18.05.2011.

van Criekingen, Mathieu (2010). "Gentrifying the re-urbanisation debate', not vice versa: The uneven socio-spatial implications of changing transitions to adulthood in Brussels", *Population, Space and Place* 16(5): 381-94.

Zacharakis, Zacharias (2009). "*Roma in Berlin. Nomaden der Neuzeit*", in SpiegelOnline, 03.06.2009.

Bibliography of Urban Studies

3i Network (Infrastructure Development Finance Company Limited, Mumbai; Indian Institute of Technology, Kanpur and Indian Institute of Management, Ahmedabad) (2010). *India Infrastructure Report 2010: Infrastructure Development in a Sustainable Low Carbon Economy*. New Delhi: Oxford University Press.

Aijaz, Rumi (2012). *Democracy and Urban Governance in India*. New Delhi: Academic Foundation (in association with Observer Research Foundation).

Anbalagan, P. (2012). *Urban Development and Sustainable Transport*. New Delhi: Bookwell.

Anjaria, Jonathan Shapiro and Colin McFarlane (ed. 2011). *Urban Navigations: Politics, Space and the City in South Asia*. New York: Routledge.

Baud, I.S.A. and J. De Wit (ed.) (2009). *New Forms of Urban Governance in India: Shifts, Models, Networks and Contestations*. New Delhi: Sage Publications India Pvt. Ltd.

Beito, David T., Peter Gordon and Alexander Tabarrok (ed. 2006). *The Voluntary City: Market Communities and Urban Planning*. New Delhi: Academic Foundation (in association with Centre for Civil Society).

Bellush, Jewel and Murray Hausknecht (ed.) (1967). *Urban Renewal: People, Politics and Planning*. New York: Anchor Books.

Brenner, Neil, Peter Marcuse and Margit Mayer (ed.) (2012). *Cities for People, Not for Profit: Critical Urban Theory and the Right to the City*. New York: Routledge.

Bridge, Gary and Sophie Watson (ed.) (2011). *The New Blackwell Companion to the City*. West Sussex: Wiley-Blackwell.

Brooks, Nancy, Kieran Donaghy and Gerrit-Jan Knaap (ed.) (2012). *The Oxford Handbook of Urban Economics and Planning*. New York: Oxford University Press.

Brosius, Christiane (2010). *India's Middle Class: New Forms of Urban Leisure, Consumption and Prosperity*. New Delhi: Routledge.

Brugmann, Jeb (2009). *Welcome to the Urban Revolution: How Cities are Changing the World*. New York: Bloomsbury Press.

Campbell, Tim (2012). *Beyond Smart Cities: How Cities Network, Learn and Innovate*. New York: Earthscan.

Crawford, Adam (ed.) (2011). *International and Comparative Criminal Justice and Urban Governance: Convergence and Divergence in Global, National and Local Settings*. New York: Cambridge University Press.

Cross, Malcolm (1979). *Urbanization and Urban Growth in the Caribbean: An Essay on Social Change in Dependent Societies*. Cambridge: Cambridge University Press.

Davies, Jonathan S. and David L. Imbroscio (ed.) (2009). *Theories of Urban Politics*. Second Edition. London: Sage Publications Ltd.

Desai, Renu and Romola Sanyal (ed.) (2012). *Urbanizing Citizenship: Contested Spaces in Indian Cities*. New Delhi: Sage Publications.

Donald, Stephanie Hemelryk, Eleonore Kofman and Catherine Kevin (ed.) (2009). *Branding Cities: Cosmopolitanism, Parochialism and Social Change*. New York: Routledge.

Douglas, Ian, David Goode, Michael C. Houck and Rusong Wang (ed.) (2011). *The Routledge Handbook of Urban Ecology*. New York: Routledge.

Driessen, Paul (2005). *Eco-Imperialism: Green Power, Black Death*. New Delhi: Academic Foundation (in association with Liberty Institute).

Edensor, Tim and Mark Jayne (ed.) (2012). *Urban Theory Beyond the West: A World of Cities*. New York: Routledge.

England, Robert E., John P. Pelissero and David R. Morgan (2011). *Managing Urban America*. 7th Edition. Washington, DC: CQ Press.

Fainstein, Susan S. and Scott Campbell (ed.) (2011). *Readings in Urban Theory, 3rd Edition*. UK: Wiley-Blackwell.

Gaston, Kevin J. (ed. 2010). *Urban Ecology*. Cambridge: Cambridge University Press.

Geyh, Paula (2009). *Cities, Citizens, and Technologies: Urban Life and Postmodernity*. New York: Routledge.

Gopakumar, Govind (2012). *Transforming Urban Water Supplies in India: The Role of Reform and Partnerships in Globalization*. New York: Routledge.

Hall, Tim and Heather Barrett (2012). *Urban Geography*. 4th Edition. New York: Routledge.

Hamnett, Stephen and Dean Forbes (ed. 2011). *Planning Asian Cities: Risk and Resilience*. New York: Routledge.

Jagmohan (2005). *Soul and Structure of Governance*. New Delhi: Allied Publishers Pvt. Ltd.

Jain, A.K. (2010). *Inclusive Planning and Social Infrastructure*. New Delhi: Bookwell.

———. (2010). *Lutyens' Delhi*. New Delhi: Bookwell.

———. (2010). *Urban Planning and Governance: A New Paradigm*. New Delhi: Bookwell.

Jenks, Mike, Daniel Kozak and Pattaranan Takkanon (ed.) (2008). *World Cities and Urban Form: Fragmented, Polycentric, Sustainable*? London: Routledge.

Jenks, Mike and Nicola Dempsey (ed.) (2005). *Future Forms and Design for Sustainable Cities*. Oxford: Oxford University Press.

Jie, Wang (2007). *Cities in China*. Beijing: China Intercontinental Press.

Johnson, Chris (ed.) (2011). *Indian Cities: Managing Urban Growth*. Mumbai: Metropolis Publication in association with the National Institute of Urban Affairs.

Kaufmann, Vincent (2011). *Rethinking the City: Urban Dynamics and Motility*. New York: Routledge.

Kumar, Barun (2008). *Urban Economic Base of National Capital Region of India*. Ghaziabad: Globe Publishing House.

Kumar, Nagesh and Sachin Chaturvedi (ed. 2007). *Environmental Requirements and Market Access: Reflections from South Asia*. New Delhi: Academic Foundation.

Lehmann, Steffen and Robert Crocker (ed.) (2011). *Designing for Zero Waste: Consumption, Technologies and the Built Environment*. New York: Routledge.

Lipman, Pauline (2011). *The New Political Economy of Urban Education: Neoliberalism, Race, and the Right to the City*. Cambridge: Cambridge University Press.

Lorentzen, Anne and Bas van Heur (ed.) (2012). *Cultural Political Economy of Small Cities*. New York: Routledge.

Lorentzen, Anne and Carsten Jahn Hansen (ed.) (2012). *The City in the Experience Economy: Role and Transformation*. New York: Routledge.

Madanipour, Ali (2011). *Knowledge Economy and the City: Spaces of Knowledge*. New York: Routledge.

Mahadevia, Darshini (ed.) (2008). *Inside the Transforming Urban Asia: Process, Policies and Public Actions*. New Delhi: Concept Publishing Company.

Mahadevia, Darshini and Jeanne M. Wolfe (ed.) (2008). *Solid Waste Management in Indian Cities: Status and Emerging Practices*. New Delhi: Concept Publishing House.

Markandey, Kalpana and Geeta Reddy Anant (ed.) (2011). *Urban Growth Theories and Settlement Systems of India*. New Delhi: Concept Publishing Company Pvt. Ltd.

McGee, Terry, George C.S. Lin, Mark Wang, Andrew Marton and Jiaping Wu (2011). *China's Urban Space: Development under Market Socialism*. New York: Routledge.

Mckinsey Global Institute (2010). *India's Urban Awakening: Building Inclusive Cities, Sustaining Economic Growth*. London: Mckinsey Global Institute.

Mohanty, P.K., B.M. Misra, R. Goyal and P.D. Jeromi (2007). *Municipal Finance in India: An Assessment*. Mumbai: Department of Economic Analysis and Policy, Reserve Bank of India. Study No. 26.

Morgan, Bronwen (2011). *Water on Tap: Rights and Regulation in the Transnational Governance of Urban Water Services*. Cambridge: Cambridge University Press.

Nelson, Arthur C. and Robert E. Lang (2012). *Megapolitan America: A New Vision for Understanding America's Metropolitan Geography*. New York: Routledge.

Pani, Narendra, Sindhu Radhakrishna and Kishore G. Bhat (ed. 2010). *Bengaluru, Bangalore, Bengaluru: Imaginations and their Times*. Bangalore: Sage Publications India Pvt. Ltd.

Patel, Sujata and Kushal Deb (ed.) (2009). *Urban Studies*. New Delhi: Oxford University Press.

Peterson, George E. (2009). *Unlocking Land Values to Finance Urban Infrastructure*. Washington, DC: The World Bank.

Ramachandran, M. (2009). *Urban Renewal: Policy and Response*. New Delhi: Academic Foundation and Skoch Development Foundation.

Ramchandran, M. and Sameer Kochhar (2010). *Building from the Bottom: Infrastructure and Poverty Alleviation*. New Delhi: The Academic Foundation and SKOCH Development Foundation.

Ramesh, G., Vishnuprasad Nagadevara, Gopal Naik and Anil B. Suraj (ed.) (2010). *Urban Infrastructure and Governance*. New Delhi: Routledge.

Reddy, B. Sudhakara, Gaudenz B. Assenza, Dora Assenza and Franziska Hasselmann (2009). *Energy Efficiency and Climate Change: Conserving Power for a Sustainable Future*. New Delhi: Sage Publications India Pvt. Ltd.

Riemer, Svend (1952). *The Modern City: An Introduction to Urban Sociology*. New York: Prentice-Hall, Inc.

Roseland, Mark (2012). *Towards Sustainable Communities: Solutions for Citizens and their Governments*. 4th Edition. Canada: New Society Publishers.

Rosenzweig, Cynthia, William D. Solecki, Stephen A. Hammer and Shagun Mehrotra (ed.) (2011). *Climate Change and Cities: First Assessment Report of the Urban Climate Change Research Network*. Cambridge: Cambridge University Press.

Rossi, Ugo, and Alberto Vanolo (2011). *Urban Political Geographies: A Global Perspective*. London: Sage Publications Ltd.

Ruet, Joel and Stephanie Tawa Lama-Rewal (ed.) (2009). *Cities and the Urban Imperative: Governing India's Metropolises*. New Delhi: Routledge.

Sandhu, Ranvinder Singh, Jasmeet Sandhu and Balwinder Arora (2009). *Urban Poverty in Developing Countries: Issues and Strategies for Sustainable Cities*. New Delhi: Bookwell.

Sassen, Saskia (2011). *Cities in a World Economy*, 4th Edition (Sociology for a New Century). Canada: Sage Publicatons Inc.

Short, John Rennie (2011). *Globalization, Modernity and the City*. New York: Routledge.

Sivaramakrishnan, K.C. (2011). *Re-Visioning Indian Cities: The Urban Renewal Mission*. New Delhi: Sage Publications India Pvt. Ltd.

Smith, Andrew (2012). *Events and Urban Regeneration: The Strategic Use of Events to Revitalise Cities*. New York: Routledge.

Sridhar, Kala Seetharam and A. Venugopala Reddy (2009). *State of Urban Services in India's Cities*. New Delhi: Oxford University Press.

Stairs, Andrea J., Kelly A. Donnell, and Alyssa Hadley Dunn (2012). *Urban Teaching in America: Theory, Research, and Practice in K-12 Classrooms*. Canada: Sage Publications, Inc.

Stoyke, Godo (2009). *The Carbon Charter: Blueprint for a Carbon-Free Future*. Canada: New Society Publishers.

Tewari, Vinod K., Jay A. Weinstein, V.L.S. Prakasa Rao (ed.) (1986). *Indian Cities: Ecological Perspectives*. New Delhi: Concept Publishing Company.

The Energy and Resources Institute (2009). *An Exploration of Sustainability in the Provision of Basic Urban Services in Indian Cities*. New Delhi: TERI Press.

The World Bank (2010). *Eco² Cities: Ecological Cities as Economical Cities*. Washington: The World Bank.

————. (2011). *Guide to Climate Change Adaptation in Cities*. Washington: World Bank.

————. (2009). *Climate Resilient Cities: A Primer on Reducing Vulnerabilities to Disasters*. Washington DC: The World Bank.

Thirmurthy, A.M. (1992). *Environmental Facilities and Urban Development in India: A Systems Model for Developing Countries*. New Delhi: Academic Foundation.

UN-HABITAT (2011). *Building Urban Safety through Slum Upgrading*. Nairobi: UN-HABITAT.

————. (2011). *Cairo: A City in Transition*. Nairobi: UN-HABITAT.

————. (2010). *Informal Urban Development in Europe: Experiences from Albania and Greece*. Nairobi: UN-HABITAT.

————. (2010). *State of the World's Cities 2010/2011: Cities for All - Bridging the Urban Divide*. London: UN-HABITAT.

Urvashi, Dhamija (2006). *Sustainable Solid Waste Management: Issues, Policies and Structures*. New Delhi: Academic Foundation.

Vertovec, Steven (ed.) (2011). *Anthropology of Migration and Multiculturalism: New Directions*. London: Routledge.

Williams, Joanna (2011). *Zero Carbon Homes: A Road Map*. New York: Routledge.

Yudelson, Jerry (2010). *Dry Run: Preventing the Next Urban Water Crisis*. Canada: New Society Publishers.

Zusman Eric, Ancha Srinivasan and Shobhaker Dhakal (ed.) (2011). *Low Carbon Transport in Asia: Strategies for Optimizing Co-benefits*. New York: Routledge.